SUNY series in Women in Education
Margaret Grogan, editor

# TENURE IN THE SACRED GROVE

# TENURE IN THE SACRED GROVE

Issues and Strategies for
Women and Minority Faculty

*edited by*

JOANNE E. COOPER
DANNELLE D. STEVENS

STATE UNIVERSITY OF NEW YORK PRESS

From *Writing Down the Bones* by Natalie Goldberg, ©1986 by Natalie Goldberg. Reprinted by arrangements with Shambhala Publications, Inc., Boston, www.shambhala.com.

Selection from Ann Lamott, *Bird by Bird: Some Instructions on Writing and Life* (p. 17). New York: Pantheon, 1994.

Selection from Natalie Goldberg, *Wild Mind: Living the Writer's Life* (p. 73). New York: Bantam New Age, 1990.

Selection from "Meditation by the Stove," from *PM/AM: New and Selected Poems* by Linda Pastan. Copyright ©1982 by Linda Pastan. Used by permission of W. W. Norton & Company, Inc.

Selection from Anne Sigismund Huff, *Writing for Scholarly Publication* (p. 38). Thousand Oaks, CA: Sage, 1999.

Published by
State University of New York Press, Albany

© 2002  State University of New York

For information, address State University of New York Press, 90 State Street, Suite 700, Albany, NY 12207

Production by Susan Geraghty
Marketing by Jennifer Giovani

Library of Congress Cataloging-in-Publication Data

Tenure in the sacred grove : issues and strategies for women and minority faculty / edited by Joanne E. Cooper, Dannelle D. Stevens.
    p. cm. — (SUNY series in women in education)
    Includes bibliographical references and index.
    ISBN 0-7914-5301-4 (alk. paper) — ISBN 0-7914-5302-2 (pbk. : alk. paper)
    1. College teachers—Tenure—Handbooks, manuals, etc. 2. Women college teachers—Handbooks, manuals, etc. 3. Minority college teachers—Handbooks, manuals, etc. I. Cooper, Joanne E. II. Stevens, Dannelle D. III. Series.

LB2335.7 .T46 2002
378.1′21—dc21

                                                                                2001034381

10  9  8  7  6  5  4  3  2  1

# CONTENTS

*Foreword*                                                          *vii*

PART I    Surveying the Landscape of the Sacred Grove

1. The Journey Toward Tenure                                        3
     *Joanne E. Cooper and Dannelle D. Stevens*

2. Case Studies: Learning from Others                              17
     *Joanne E. Cooper and Jacqueline B. Temple*

3. Making the Persuasive Tenure Case:
   Pitfalls and Possibilities                                      31
     *Phyllis Bronstein and Judith A. Ramaley*

4. Tenure and Academic Freedom in the Academy:
   Historical Parameters and New Challenges                        57
     *William G. Tierney*

PART II    Faculty as Individual Learners: Sharing Personal Perspectives

5. Finding a Home in the Academy:
   Confronting Racism and Ageism                                   71
     *Joanne E. Cooper, Anna M. Ortiz,*
     *Maenette K. P. Benham, and Mary Woods Scherr*

6. Balancing Work and Family                                       89
     *Michelle Collay*

7. Coping with Feelings of Fraudulence                             107
     *Janice Koch*

8. The Caged Bird Sings:
   On Being Different and the Role of Advocacy                     117
     *Barbara K. Curry*

9. Resisting Common Injustice:
   Tenure Politics, Department Politics,
   Gay and Lesbian Politics                                    127
      *Patricia M. McDonough*


PART III   The Process of Getting Tenure: Advice Along the Way

10. Writing and Publishing                                     147
      *Sandra Hollingsworth*

11. Teaching: Academic Whitewater Rafting                      163
      *Joanne E. Cooper and Sheryl E. Nojima*

12. Outreach in a New Light:
    Documenting the Scholarship of Application                 179
      *Pennie G. Foster-Fishman and Dannelle D. Stevens*

13. Reflecting on Your Journey:
    How to Keep a Professional/Personal Journal                203
      *Dannelle D. Stevens and Joanne E. Cooper*

14. Conclusion:
    Composing an Academic Life                                 225
      *Joanne E. Cooper and Dannelle D. Stevens*


*Appendix*
   *Tattered Covers: An Annotated Bibliography*                233

*Author Biographies*                                          239

*Index*                                                       243

# FOREWORD

*Meditation by the Stove*

In *PM/AM*, 1982 by Linda Pastan

I have banked the fires
of my body
into a small but steady blaze,
here in the kitchen . . . where a dim
brown bird dazzled by light
has flown into the windowpane
and lies stunned on the pavement—
it was never simple, even for birds,
this business of nests. . . .

Finding a home in the academy, settling in and attaining tenure, is much like the process of nest building. You look for the resources that will help you at your task: twigs and leaves, people and research projects. You build slowly toward your goal. You read the weather to see what is coming, and if you are very wise, you bank the fires of your body into a small but steady blaze. You pace yourself and try not to be too dazzled by the light. Still, the light of a tenured position in academe is sometimes too overwhelming. It is easy for women and minority faculty to be dazzled by the brilliance of their colleagues, stunned by the politics they encounter, enthralled with the life of the mind and all the rewards it holds. Sometimes, you end up on the pavement, stunned by some unexpected event. This book is meant to be a guide, to provide you and those around you with resources for the task ahead and to guide you away from the windows that look inviting and open but are really invisible barriers on your journey toward tenure.

Toward the end of her poem, Linda Pastan proclaims, "Today I feel wiser than the bird." It is our hope that all of you will come away "wiser than the bird," better equipped to handle the ups and downs you may encounter on your journey toward tenure.

# PART I

# Surveying the Landscape of the Sacred Grove

The landscape of the sacred grove, or that of tenure, is complex and multilayered. The complexity involves issues at the political, scholarly, pedagogical, personal, and interpersonal levels. Certainly in the case of women and minority faculty, it involves issues of gender and race. The purpose of this section is to give an overview of both the personal and professional issues that surround tenure. Obviously, granting someone tenure is an institutional decision, which means that the process varies across institutional type and depends on the individual institution's history and culture. Yet there are commonalities in the process that our authors disclose. This disclosure is valuable and necessary for new faculty because knowledge about tenure is often tacit, not explicit and is discussed in the hallways or behind the closed doors of promotion and tenure meetings. It is almost never written down, except in general terms. Thus, faculty, particularly women and minorities, are left with little explicit information about how to proceed and to succeed in their bid for the tenure prize.

This book is about issues new faculty encounter and strategies they employ as they move through the tenure process. In our first chapter, Joanne E. Cooper and Dannelle D. Stevens, the editors of this text, discuss research on the need for more women and minority faculty in the academy, both their absence and the ways in which they are undervalued in higher education today. It examines the barriers women and minorities face and outlines the rest of the text, which uses the literature of adult learning to frame the book. As society becomes increasingly diverse, the representation of that society in the academy should follow. To accomplish this, we need to have women and minorities succeed in breaking down the tenure barriers.

Chapter 2, by Joanne E. Cooper and Jacqueline B. Temple, describes several cases of minorities and women who have sought tenure. Their narratives reveal individual circumstances and yet provide a picture of the common experiences of faculty across institutions. In chapter 3, Phyllis Bronstein and Judith A. Ramaley place tenure in its current institutional context, describing both the variance across campuses and the particulars of the process. In chapter 4, William G. Tierney places tenure in its historical context, reminding us that its roots dwell in issues of academic freedom, not job security, although these two are inextricably intertwined. Together these four chapters survey the landscape of tenure issues for women and minorities as we enter a new century of higher education in America. They provide a description of the context in which women and minorities, as adult learners, struggle to understand and cope with their lives as faculty. Ideally, these faculty can move beyond mere understanding and coping to a place of growth and renewal as they join, in increasing numbers, the world of higher education.

# CHAPTER 1

# The Journey toward Tenure

## Joanne E. Cooper
## and Dannelle D. Stevens

This book is designed to help women and minority faculty navigate the path to tenure in the academy. This is not an easy journey. Bumps, barriers and sometimes boulders may block the way. Even after a journey of several years, qualified women and minorities are at risk of not receiving tenure (Aisenberg & Harrington, 1988; Padilla & Chavez, 1995; Turner & Myers, 2000). Often their work style preferences and career goal interpretations do not match the values that dominate and are rewarded in academe. Thus, the work of women and minority faculty challenges the current system. They are often viewed as "outsiders," unwilling to "play the game," and, subsequently, unable to enter the "sacred grove."

The title of this text refers to Aisenberg and Harrington's (1988) classic work *Women of Academe: Outsiders in the Sacred Grove*. While their original goal was to learn about the career pathways of women who had left the academy, they went on to study both those who left and those who remained. Remarkably, they found that both groups shared a generalized experience, even across institutions, disciplines, and social class backgrounds. There were gender-specific issues that include actual and perceived family/career tensions, greater use by women of qualitative research methods that require more time, and more passionate engagement with research content that interferes with an attitude of "playing the game." Aisenberg and Harrington did not have any women of color respond to the call to participate in their study, but subsequent works (Park, 1996; Antonio, 1998; Tierney & Bensimon, 1996) document a similar experience for minorities and people of color in the academy. This text extends the work of Aisenberg and Harrington by addressing the experiences of both these groups as they move along the path to tenure.

The academy has been characterized as a sacred grove (Aisenberg & Harrington, 1988; Packer, 1995). What is this sacred grove? *Sacred* comes from Latin *sacer*, "seen," and Latin, *sanus*, "sane" and in Greek *saos*, "safe." Sacred means a place devoted exclusively to a person or end; holy; inviolable. *Grove* is a "group of trees without underwood, planted or growing naturally" (*Websters New Collegiate Dictionary*, 1961). Thus, once you are in the grove, you can move around easily. The sacred grove, then, following the dictionary's lead, is a sane, safe, and open place that is holy and unable to be violated. This image includes a sense of elitism, distance, even holiness about the place. The sacred grove connotes the image of peace, separateness, and purity. The knowledge that would be generated in such a place must be especially pure, untainted by the dailiness, rawness, unpredictability, and dirtiness of real life. What happens, however, when outsiders enter the grove and challenge the very activities and values that the insiders develop and espouse?

This book is for the outsiders, people who have not had ready access to the sacred grove and those who, having gained access, are not sure they will be allowed to stay. It is for those who may need help, advice on how to survive, even thrive, in the sacred grove. For too long, access has been limited to White males. As our chapter authors delineate, women and minorities threaten these traditional occupants not only because they look different but also because their activities and values threaten to change what is sacred in the grove. Women and minority faculty may dispute what counts as knowledge (Tierney, 1997). They may challenge the dominant research paradigm through their interest in new kinds of research, new ways of knowing, and new topics heretofore unexplored. They challenge the traditional notions of advising as they begin to spend more time with their students. Finally, they challenge traditional ways of teaching, such as the "sage on the stage" image of a professor, by using a variety of student-centered teaching activities and techniques. Ultimately, these outsiders can become insiders through the tenure process. What is called "sacred" can change. Slowly, their voices can be heard, and they can make a difference in the quality of life in the grove. Yet attempting to enter this sacred grove and gain acceptance, while simultaneously adhering to identity and values that may challenge the status quo, is a delicate balancing act.

This book is for the untenured assistant professor and for those who might seek to mentor junior faculty, such as department chairs, deans, and faculty development officers. The book is a powerful ally along the path to the sacred grove. It guides you from the moment you accept your first faculty position until the day you receive notification of your tenure and promotion, serving as both partner and guide. It offers the sound advice of others who have gone before you, describing successes and possible pitfalls. It considers ways in which you must both discern and meet the expectations of your institution, from the perspectives of others like you (women, faculty of color, gays, lesbians, and bisexuals). We offer encouragement for the despairing, hope for the lost, strategies for the befuddled, checklists for the organized, and a wealth of reading material to support you on your journey.

As women who have recently completed the tenure process and who have spent time advising others along this path through research, writing, workshops, and programs, the editors feel uniquely qualified to help you succeed in this critical task. For example, we have conducted many training sessions for untenured women and minority faculty at various national conferences and have both helped to run junior faculty mentoring programs on our campuses. We bring along the advice of experienced others who set their contributions in the context of their own lives, simultaneously demonstrating both who they are and what they have learned. These chapter authors' combined wisdom should overcome even the most doubting and confused of tenure seekers. Ultimately, we seek to make the tacit overt and the hidden accessible. The more women and minorities understand the overt and tacit expectations, as well as the hidden norms of their new faculty roles, the more likely they will be successful in obtaining tenure, while retaining their core beliefs, values, and interests.

## PURPOSE OF THE BOOK

This book focuses on issues and strategies for women and minority untenured faculty, encompasses multiple perspectives on the tenure process, and underscores the interconnectedness of the personal and professional. Tenure was originally conceived as a means to protect academic freedom. As Tierney and Bensimon (1996, p. 25) state, "If academic freedom was the goal, then due process, tenure, and the evaluation of faculty work was the path to that goal." The United States has advanced from a time when no institution had a structured tenure system, to the present, when 85% of U.S. colleges and universities have some form of tenure for the protection of academic freedom. The tenure-track system has become the standard route to a respected position in the academy today.

Our chapter authors, who all address this issue in one form or another, represent a variety of perspectives across ethnicities, faculty ranks, positions, and institutional types. The authors include both junior and senior faculty, women, faculty of color, and a broad spectrum of administrative positions, including that of department chair, university president, and chair of a promotion and tenure committee. Since today's academy encompasses "competing definitions of reality held by different groups" (Tierney & Bensimon, 1996, p. 5), we sought to bring together this diverse group to share their expertise.

## THE KEY ISSUE: THE ABSENCE AND UNDERVALUING OF WOMEN AND MINORITIES IN THE ACADEMY

Both qualitative and quantitative data on faculty promotion and tenure describe the persistent and significant problem identified in the 1980s by Aisenberg and Harrington (1988): women and minorities are outsiders in the sacred grove. Even in the 1990s, women and minority faculty in higher education continue to experience both structural and personal barriers to tenure (Johnsrud & Sadao, 1998). Despite efforts to increase the visibility of women scholars in academe (Caplan, 1994; Johnsrud & Des Jarlais, 1994; West, 1995), women make up only 31% of full-time faculty in American higher education today, an increase of only 5% in the past 75 years (Hameresh, 1992; West, 1995; Trautvetter, 1999). Around the nation, the tenure rate for women has remained under 50%, while the rate for men is above 70% (Trautvetter, 1999). In the face of greater discrimination, women tend to leave the academy before they obtain tenure in significantly larger numbers than their male colleagues (Glazer-Raymo, 1999; Johnsrud & Des Jarlais, 1994).

Minority faculty have suffered a similar fate. Despite efforts to recruit and retain minority faculty in the past decade, the increase in their percentages has been small (Johnsrud and Sadao, 1998; "The Faculty," 1997). Often feeling unwelcome, unappreciated, and unwanted, minority faculty face continual pressure to prove that they deserve their positions (Johnsrud & Sadao, 1998; Menges & Exum, 1983; Reyes & Halcon, 1988). Their research may be under attack because of its focus on social change and minority issues and thus be labeled nonacademic or inappropriate (Astin, 1997; Banks, 1984). Like women, minority faculty face a number of barriers in the tenure review process, such as the holding of more split or joint appointments (Menges & Exum, 1983). Minority faculty tend to spend more of their time on teaching and service, such as student advising, and less time on traditional quantitative research, leaving them vulnerable to attack at the point of tenure and promotion (Turner & Myers, 2000; Antonio, 1998; Banks, 1984; Blackwell, 1996; McEvans & Applebaum, 1992; Nakanishi, 1993; Stein, 1994). In addition, minority faculty are often isolated, lack mentors, and receive promotion and tenure at a lower rate. In sum, minority faculty continue to be perceived as "other" and to suffer from institutionalized racist attitudes that reflect their differences as inferior to dominant White Western values and norms (Johnsrud & Sadao, 1998).

Although the numbers of women and minorities in the academy have increased slightly since 1972, the year affirmative action measures in academe were fully implemented, their progress has not been as great as expected (Glazer-Raymo, 1999; Park, 1996). Women continue to hold a much higher percentage of part-time and nontenure track positions than men and experience salary inequities within and across academic disciplines. In the fall of 1992, 41% of all female faculty were employed part-time, while only 29% of their male counterparts were part-time employees. In 1996, 22% of full-time women faculty were nontenure track, bringing the total of either nontenure-track or part-time female faculty to 62.4% (Glazer-Raymo, 1999).

Today women remain disproportionately located in the less prestigious community colleges (37.6%) and four-year colleges (29.3%). Across the country, the number of female professors has increased since the early 1970s, but the proportion of female faculty has remained the same, since the total number of faculty has also increased (Blum, 1991). Even when women manage to advance to the rank of full professor, the average salary of male faculty was 13 percent higher than the average female faculty salary (Busenberg & Smith, 1997). Women are clustered in fields such as the health professions and education. In 1995 women made up nearly all (98%) of the faculty in nursing and more than one-half (56%) of the faculty in education. In contrast, women made up only 6% of the nation's engineering faculty and 23% of the natural sciences faculty.

In addition, a closer look reveals that over the past two decades, predominantly White women have benefitted from affirmative action policies. Within the 36% of female instructional faculty employed by colleges and universities, 32% were White women and only 4% were women of color. While minority college and university female students constitute 13% of the student body today, they make up only 4% of the faculty, leaving few who might serve as role models or encourage students in their chosen professions (Busenberg & Smith, 1997). In spite of the progress that has been made, it is obvious that the need across the nation is still great for women faculty in general and women faculty of color in particular.

Faculty of color also continue to remain underrepresented in academe. Those who populate the grove do not proportionately represent the ethnicities outside the grove. For instance, in their study of midwestern universities and colleges, Turner and Myers (2000) report African Americans compose 3.7% of the faculty, while African Americans in the general population number 9.5%. Similarly, the most rapidly growing ethnic minority in the general population, Latinos, numbered 3% of the faculty in 1990, while numbering 9% in the general population.

For gay, lesbian, and bisexual faculty, the environment has improved over the years but often remains repressive in ways that can easily breed bitterness. Unfortunately, homophobia in the society continues to be echoed in the halls of academe as well (Tierney, 1997). McNaron (1997) states that "all lesbian and gay academics are called upon to occupy a difficult place, especially in North American culture. We are asked to inhabit a middle ground between exhilaration and watchfulness, between the beginnings of ease and the necessity for alertness, between appropriate gratitude to colleagues and administrators who are working to improve our environments and continued pressure on such people to do even more" (p. 213).

What are some of the barriers that minorites and women face as they attempt to enter and remain in the sacred grove? These barriers, which operate for both women and minorities, include isolation, lack of mentoring, occupational stress, and institutional sexism and racism (Antonio, 1998; Turner & Myers, 1997; Park, 1996). Other factors that impact minority faculty include the small and decreasing pool of minority Ph.D. candidates, (Solmon & Wingard, 1991; Jackson, 1991; Mickelson & Oliver, 1991; Washington & Harvey, 1989), the disproportionate tenure rates and rates of pretenure departure for minorities (Menges & Exum, 1983), and the devaluation of the qualifications of minority Ph.D.s not trained in the most elite, prestigious colleges (Mickelson & Oliver, 1991). When minority faculty are hired, they may face disproportionate advising and service loads because they are often the only faculty of color in a department. Their research may not be given the scholarly recognition it deserves if it focuses on ethnic minority populations (Reyes & Halcon, 1991; Garza, 1988; Tack & Patitu, 1992; Washington & Harvey, 1989; Frierson, 1990). Educational cutbacks combined with fewer tenure-track positions and more restrictive criteria for tenure and promotion have resulted in what Park (1996, p. 46) has termed the "revolving door phenomenon, wherein adjunct and junior faculty are rotated through entry level positions without serious consideration for tenure."

Park (1996) asserts that one of the ways sexism pervades academe is through the construction of its tenure and promotion processes. Current working assumptions about what constitutes good research, teaching, and service and the relative importance of each of these reflect and perpetuate masculine values and practices, thus providing another barrier for women in their reach for tenure. "Research is implicitly deemed 'men's work' and is explicitly valued, whereas teaching and service are characterized as 'women's work' and are explicitly devalued" (Park, 1996, p. 47). We must examine, according to Park, (1996, p. 47) "the ways in which sexism is embedded in the structures, norms, and policies of the university itself." Women of color face the double bind of institutional racism and sexism, both of which are deeply entrenched in the American university today.

While it is surely incumbent upon institutions of higher education to change these attitudes and practices, both women and minorities, in order to succeed in the academy, must know what they are up against and develop coping strategies that will take them beyond these barriers. It is our hope that as the numbers of women and minority faculty increase, the norms and values of the academy will change, recognizing the value-added nature of the work they do. This book is designed to assist those women and minorities on the tenure path. In so doing, our ultimate goal is to impact the larger institutions in which they work.

In considering the contribution of higher education to the current chilly climate for women and minorities, we remind the reader that it is the responsibility of these institutions to ultimately eradicate the elements of sexism and racism that are embedded in their norms and values and that contribute to the current barriers to tenure and promotion for women and minority faculty. We are not assuming that new faculty must learn to deal with their given situations while organizational cultures remain unchanged. We subscribe to what Tierney and Bensimon (1996, p. 37) term a "bidirectional scheme of socialization" in which individuals "influence and change the organization just as the organizational mores may influence and change them." By becoming a valuable part of the institution, women and minorities can begin to effect change (Antonio, 1998; Park, 1996). Thus, this book is designed to assist new faculty in becoming valued organizational members who will be able to work for change from inside higher education. To make a difference in these organizations, faculty must have knowledge of how the organization functions and which strategies are most successful.

## CHANGING THE LANDSCAPE OF THE SACRED GROVE

Will the presence of women and minority faculty truly make a difference in higher education? We believe so. While people of all colors and sexual orientations can be grasping, elitist, ego-driven, or power hungry, as a whole, a diverse faculty brings us closer to a representation of the world we live in. If universities are truly to serve the cities they inhabit and the larger world, if democracy is based on a sense of community and the discourse that community fosters, then we must strive to bring that world into being inside of our universities. If higher education is to help provide solutions to the world's problems, then it must know that world in all its diversity. And if the university is to live what it preaches, to embody what it proclaims, to realize the dreams of access and equity which are its clarion call, then the acceptance of women, people of color, and those of lesbian, gay, or bisexual orientation must be a powerful part of that community. If they are not, if they are excluded in significant ways, then our rhetoric is empty and our values corrupted.

Universities claim that the reason for their existence is the fostering of an educated and inclusive society. It is time we put our money where our mouth is, our actions where our words now fly safely into the air. We must rise off our cushions of comfort and take action, believing as we go that we can create a better society through the construction of a cacophonous and diverse society, rich in the traditions of many "others" and wealthier because of their presence. Rather than being expected to listen more than they speak and to survive with little support (McCall, 1995), new faculty must be encouraged to become valuable members of our academic conversations.

One way to meet the needs of women and minority faculty is to provide strategies and support for them in order that they might join the conversations they encounter. Since much of the knowledge about how to maneuver the rough waters of junior faculty life is frequently tacit, or deliberately hidden, a text such as this, with numerous resources and helpful advice from those who have gone before, will serve as a helpful guide or navigational tool.

The next section introduces a framework for understanding new faculty as they move along their tenure journey. Part of the socialization process is learning about oneself as well as about the expectations that the institution places upon its faculty. Thus, new faculty can be better understood through the literature on adult learning.

## New Faculty as Adult Learners

New faculty can be more clearly viewed through their role as adult learners. As new faculty move into new positions in the academy, they must "learn what their colleagues and students expect of them, acquire facility in dealing with organizational structures and processes, and grasp the history and traditions of their new institutional setting" (Whitt, 1991, p. 599). Menges and associates (1999) have organized these issues into three basic categories: establishing collegiality, clarifying expectations, and managing time. A massive amount of learning must take place in a short amount of time. As Whitt's title suggests, new faculty must "hit the ground running," working under a time constraint commonly known as "the tenure clock."

The literature on adult learners frames the efforts of faculty as they approach this massive learning task. Merriam and Caffarella (1999) remind us that the adult learner does not develop in a vacuum. Three general characteristics distinguish learning in adulthood from learning in childhood. Adult learners differ from children in terms of the context in which they find themselves, learner characteristics, and the learning process. In addition, these three factors together, in their distinctive and individual configurations, simultaneously interact to form a complex and interactive picture of learning in adulthood.

The context in which new faculty toil is important to the learning process. Merriam and Caffarella (1999) describe two dimensions, the interactive and the structural. The interactive dimension encompasses how the learner interacts with the context. As Jarvis reminds us (1992, p. 11), adult learning "is about the continuing process of making sense of everyday experience." We will be discussing various methods to aid faculty in this sense-making process as they move along the road to tenure, a road often littered with unspoken norms and ambiguous expectations. Journal keeping, for instance, can be a helpful tool for sorting through everyday experiences and making sense of them (see chapter 13).

The structural dimension of the context in which adult learners are embedded includes issues of race, class, gender, diversity, power, and oppression. As Merriam and Caffarella state, "It is no longer a question of whether in adult learning situations we need to address issues of race, class, gender, culture, ethnicity and sexual orientation, but rather a question of how we should deal with these issues" (1999, p. 396). As mentioned earlier, we want to underscore that we are not assuming that new faculty must learn to deal with their given situations while organizational cultures remain unchanged. Certainly, institutions must examine elements of sexism and racism that are embedded in their norms and values. This book begins to address some of the questions about how both faculty and institutions might deal with these issues.

The learning of new faculty starts well before they obtain their first tenure-track position. It begins in graduate school, where Fairweather (1996) asserts that their expectations about teaching, research, and service are initially developed. Like all adult learners, faculty bring with them to these positions rich life experiences; issues around intimacy, generativity, and integrity, and their need to juggle life roles, such as spouse, worker, and citizen (Merriam and Caffarella, 1999). Faculty have an added layer of juggling, in that within the work setting, they must juggle the demands of teaching, research, and service. It is not surprising then, that studies of new faculty indicate they experience high levels of stress and low levels of occupational satisfaction (Whitt, 1991).

According to Merriam and Caffarella, the process of learning must also be considered. The learning process takes place not in school, as it does for children, but amidst other life events. Mary Catherine Bateson addresses the integration of living and learning and the ways in which we often discount the complexity of the learning task: "Living and learning, we become ambidextrous" (1994, p. 9). Thus, new faculty live out their lives as spouses, parents, workers, and citizens, while they simultaneously grapple with the multiple demands placed on them by their institutions. In addition, they must contend with the ways in which forces such as sexism and racism contribute to the social construction of their identity in academe. In some cases, these constructions may be implicit, and in other cases, explicit. Moana Smith's experience of being labeled a "manipulative brown woman" by her department chair (discussed in chapter 2) provides us with an example of the explicit ways in which the forces of racism and sexism impact faculty work.

Finally, Merriam and Caffarella make the point that these elements, the context, the learner, and the process blend in adulthood, adding complexity to our understanding of adult learning in action. Previous experience, the sociocultural environment, the learner's personality, and many other factors contribute to one's self-concept, as well as to one's career development. All these factors converge in a complex blend that cannot be understood simply by describing each factor in isolation.

New faculty must attempt to make meaning of the careers they have chosen for themselves through the convergence of their accumulated life experiences, their current developmental concerns, both the sociocultural context and the departmental culture in which they find themselves, the current norms and expectations of their academic discipline, and the impact of technology on their work. This complex picture requires the ability to reflect critically on one's thoughts and assumptions, a particularly adult skill. This text is constructed to support that reflection and through it to enhance the success of women and minority faculty as they struggle with their new roles.

## REFERENCES

Aisenberg, N., & Harrington, M. (1988). Women of academe: Outsiders in the sacred grove. Amherst, MA: University of Massachusetts Press.

Antonio, A. L. (1998, Oct.). Faculty of color reconsidered: Retaining scholars for the future. Paper presented at the conference, "Keeping our faculties: Addressing the recruitment and retention of faculty of color in higher education," Minneapolis, MN.

Astin, H. (1997). *Race and ethnicity in the American professoriate, 1995–96.* University of California, Los Angeles (UCLA), Higher Education Research Institute.

Banks, W. M. (1984, January/February). Afro-American scholars in the university: Roles and conflicts. *American Behavioral Scientist,* 27, 325–339.

Bateson, M. C. (1994). *Peripheral visions: Learning along the way.* New York: HarperCollins.

Blackwell, J. E. (1996). Faculty issues: The impact on minorities. In C. Turner, M. Garcia, A. Nora and L. I. Rendon (Eds.), *Racial and ethnic diversity in higher education.* Needham Heights, MA: Simon and Schuster Custom Publishing, 315–326.

Blackwell, J. E. (1988). Faculty issues: The impact on minorities. *The Review of Higher Education* 11(4), 417–434.

Blum, (1991). Environment still hostile to women in academe, new evidence indicates. *Chronicle of Higher Education,* vol. 38, n. 7.

Busenberg, B., & Smith, D. (1997). Affirmative action and beyond: The woman's perspective. In M. Garcia (Ed.) *Affirmative action's testament of hope: Strategies for a new era in higher education.* New York: State University of New York Press, 149–180.

Caplan, P. (1994). *Lifting a ton of feathers: A women's guide for surviving in the academic world.* Toronto: University of Toronto Press.

Carter, D. J., & Wilson, R. (1996). *Minorities in Higher Education: Fourteenth Annual Status Report.* Washington, D.C.: American Council on Education, Office of Minoirites in Higher Education.

The faculty: Proportion of minority professors inches up to about 10%. (1997, June 20). *Chronicle of Higher Education.* A12–A13.

Fairweather, J. S. (1996). *Faculty work and public trust: Restoring the value of teaching and public service in American academic life.* Boston: Allyn & Bacon.

Frierson, H., Jr. (1990). The situation of black educational researchers: Continuation of a crisis. *Educational Researcher* 19, 12–17.

Garza, H. (1988). The 'barrioization' of Hispanic faculty. *Educational Researcher* 69, 122–124.

Glazer-Raymo, J. (1999). *Shattering the myths: Women in academe.* Baltimore: Johns Hopkins University Press.

Hameresh, D. (1992). Diversity within adversity: The annual report on the economic status of the profession, 1991–92. *Academe* 78, 7–14.

Jackson, K.W. (1991). Black faculty in academia. In P. G. Albach and K. Lomotey (Eds.), *The racial crisis in American higher education.* Albany: State University of New York Press.

Jarvis P. (1992). *Paradoxes of learning: On becoming an individual in society.* San Francisco: Jossey-Bass.

Johnsrud, L. K., & Des Jarlais, C. A. (1994). Barriers to the retention and tenure of women and minorities: The case of a university's faculty. *Review of Higher of Education* 17(4), 335–353.

Johnsrud, L. K., & Sadao, K. C. (1998). The common experience of "otherness:" Ethnic and racial minority faculty. *The Review of Higher Education* 1(4), 315–342.

McCall, A. L. (1995). Pressures for silence, opportunities to speak: Talking from a feminist perspective in teacher education. In Martin, R. (Ed.), *Transforming the academy: Struggles and strategies for the advancement of women in higher education.* Canyon Lake, CA: Graysmith Publications.

McEvans, A. E., & Applebaum, D. (1992, April). *Minority faculty in research universities: Barriers to progress.* Paper presented at the American Educational Research Association, San Francisco.

McNaron, T. A. H. (1997). *Poisoned ivy: Lesbian and gay academics confronting homophobia.* Philadelphia: Temple University Press.

Menges, R.J. and Associates. (1999). *Faculty in new jobs: A guide to settling in, becoming established, and building institutional support.* San Francisco: Jossey-Bass.

Menges, R. J., & Exum, W. H. (1983). Barrriers to the progress of women and minority faculty. *Journal of Higher Education* 54(2), 123–143.

Merriam, S. B., & Caffarella, R. S. (1999). *Learning in adulthood: A comprehensive guide.* San Francisco: Jossey-Bass.

Mickelson, M. L., & Oliver, M. L. (1991). Making the short list: Black candidates and the faculty recruitment process. In P. G. Altbach and K. Lomotey (Eds.), *The racial crisis in American higher education.* Albany: State University of New York Press.

Nakanishi, D. T. (1993). Asian Pacific Americans in higher education: Faculty and administrative representation and tenure. In J. Gainen and R. Boice (Eds.), *Building a diverse faculty* (pp. 51–59). San Francisco: Jossey-Bass.

Packer, B. B. (1995). Irrigating the sacred grove: Stages of Gender equity development. In L. Morley & V. Walsh (Eds.), *Feminist academics: Creative agents for change* (pp. 42–56). London: Taylor and Francis.

Padilla, R. V., & Chavez, R. C. (1995). The leaning ivory tower: Latino professors in American Universities. Albany: State University of New York Press.

Park, S. M. (1996). Research, teaching and service: Why shouldn't women's work count? *Journal of Higher Education* 67(1), 46–83.

Reyes, M., & Halcon, J. J. (1991). Practices of the academy: Barriers to access for Chicano academics. In P. G. Altbach and K. Lometey (Eds.), *The racial crisis in American higher education.* Albany, NY: State University of New York Press.

Reyes, M. De la Luz, & Halcon, J. J. (1988). Racism in academia: The old wolf revisited. *Harvard Educational Review* 58, 229–314.

Solmon, L. C., & Wingard, T. L. (1991). The changing demographics: Problems and opportunities. In P.G. Albach and K. Lomotey (Eds.), *The racial crisis in American higher education.* Albany: State University of New York Press.

Stein, W. (1994). The survival of American Indian faculty: Thought and action. *The National Educational Association Higher Education Journal* 10, 101–114.

Tack, M. W., & Patitu, C. L. (1992). *Faculty job satisfaction: Women and minorities in peril.* Report No. 4. Washington, D.C.: School of Education and Human Development, George Washington University.

Tierney, W. G. (1997). *Academic outlaws: Queer theory and cultural study in the academy.* Thousand Oaks, CA: Sage.

Tierney, W. G., & Bensimon, E. M. (1996). *Promotion and tenure: Community and socialization in academe.* Albany: State University of New York Press.

Trautvetter, L. C. (1999). Experiences of women, experiences of men. In R. J. Menges & Associates (Eds.), *Faculty in new jobs: A guide to settling in, becoming established, and building institutional support* (pp. 59–87). San Francisco: Jossey-Bass.

Turner, C. S. V., & Myers, S. M., Jr. (1997). Faculty diversity and affirmative action. In M. Garcias (Ed.), *Affirmative action's testament of hope: Strategies for a new era in higher education.* Albany: State University of New York Press.

Turner, C. S. V., & Myers, S. M., Jr. (2000). *Faculty of color in academe: Bittersweet success.* Boston: Allyn & Bacon.

Washington, V., & Harvey, W. (1989). *Affirmative rhetoric, negative action: African-American and Hispanic faculty at predominanatly white institutions.* Report No. 2. Washington, DC: School of Education and Human Development, George Washington University.

West, M. S. (1995, July–August). Women faculty: Frozen in time. *Academe* 81(4), 26–29.

Whitt, E. J. (1991). Hit the ground running: Experiences of new faculty in a school of education. *Review of Higher Education* 14(2), 177–197.

# CHAPTER 2

# Case Studies:
# Learning from Others

## Joanne E. Cooper
## and Jacqueline B. Temple

### INTRODUCTION

In this chapter the authors attempt to flesh out real problems encountered by faculty across the country as they move along their tenure journeys. We present case studies of both women faculty and male and female ethnic minority faculty from a variety of disciplines and institutions who have successfully negotiated the tenure process. It is within the individual case that issues of sexism and racism, the personal, the professional, and the political converge, providing readers with a glimpse of the complex interaction of these forces within the academy. We believe that the complexity of these cases and the potentially familiar elements within them are of particular value to individual readers. The details of individual circumstances embedded in distinct campus cultures and different academic disciplines might prove most instructive. In some cases, circumstances may vary as widely between disciplines on the same campus as they do between campuses in disparate geographical areas. In addition, circumstances may vary according to the gender or ethnicity of individual faculty members, who may encounter dissimilar treatment even within the same department. Despite these differences, we will attempt to synthesize common elements across these cases and extrapolate suggestions for the new faculty member. However, readers are encouraged to be alert for elements that may be similar to their own particular circumstances that may not run across cases.

Case studies are valuable, asserts Merriam (1998) because they faithfully represent how others make sense of their experience. In addition, they "uncover the interaction of significant factors characteristic of the phenomenon" (1998, p. 29). In our case, the interaction of the personal and the professional elements of faculty lives can be underscored by using case studies. Case studies deal with information in a complex, holistic, process-oriented way that can mirror the actual lives of participants (Wilson, 1979). They depict the nonlinear, complex realities of professional life and in that complexity, enable new faculty to more thoroughly understand the intricacies of the tenure process. Because case studies extend and refine personal and experiential knowledge, rather than simply providing new faculty with linear, rational, cause-effect explanations (Stake, 1994), they are particularly useful for our purposes.

In order to learn from case studies, it is necessary to first understand the individual case and then to synthesize elements across cases, applying conclusions from one set of circumstances to another. Some of the elements of these cases that readers may want to consider are the technical, political, cultural, and moral (Merriam, 1998). For example, new faculty may be struggling with technical guidelines, political issues within their departments, both individual and organizational elements of culture, and the moral questions that surround professional identity and integrity.

These cases describe the actual experiences of both male and female junior faculty from diverse backgrounds. They come from fields such as education, foreign languages, and engineering in various public institutions across the country. They are Japanese American, African American, Latino, and Caucasian. Others are of mixed race, and some were born in countries other than the United States. All currently hold tenured positions in U.S. colleges and universities. Their departments may be small or large, congenial or unfriendly, with a variety of tenure and promotion guidelines. Some found the process a nightmarish struggle; others had an easier time reaching their goal. Their individual and collective journeys provide reflective yet insightful perspectives and valuable lessons. Often living in two worlds, their professional and cultural identities frequently collided, revealing warring ideals and strivings. However, their resilience, their tenacity, and their strength helped them to persevere and succeed.

As a group they have much to teach us about unraveling the often tacit knowledge necessary to gain tenure and about believing in yourself and your ability to contribute to higher education's goals and values. As Nyquist and colleagues (1999) have asserted, higher education must be concerned about the academy's current values and structural organization and about whether the academy is adequately preparing the kind of innovative, committed, and thoughtful faculty members needed in this millennium. The following stories of faculty provide beacons that may guide new generations of scholars who can bring innovation and energy to the sacred grove.

THE CASES

*Setting Priorities*

Eldon Kenjo is an Asian American faculty member in an engineering department of a large, public research university. He has a doctorate from MIT and is currently the chair of his department. His greatest challenge as a new faculty member was to achieve a balance between his research and his teaching. He says, "I thought teaching would be easy, until I went to class." Thinking it would be similar to giving a conference presentation, he discovered that it was much harder. He started out with lecture notes at least a month ahead of the class, but as demands on his time increased, to set up a lab and get started on his research program, he found himself only about one and a half lectures ahead. What have I gotten myself into, he wondered. His colleagues were advising him to focus on his research, but he realized all the students were depending on him and that he needed to take care of them first. Eldon decided to finish his lecture notes for the whole semester and then turn to his research.

Eldon says his decision to focus on his teaching came from asking himself what would matter to him on his deathbed. At that point, he realized, having a long list of publications wouldn't matter much, but helping people would. So, even though he realized he might not get tenure, he decided to live with that consequence.

The struggle to manage his time has remained with Eldon. If he worked hard long enough, he thought he would reach a point where he would have more free time. But that point has never come. Now, as department chair, with small children at home, he still wishes there were more hours in the day. He says he has learned that if you work hard, you will probably always work hard, that you choose to do this, and in the end it can be both satisfying and enjoyable.

When Eldon entered the department, he found one faculty member he felt he could trust. "Sometimes," states Eldon, "the ones who let you be are your true allies. If they're too friendly, it might not be in your best interest, particularly if they want your loyalty. Don't be paranoid, but just be careful." Other colleagues may give you advice you don't want to hear, such as "work harder in this area" or "attend more conferences." Eldon says it may sound like personal criticism, until you begin to fill out your tenure application. Suddenly you realize everything you were told was for a reason, not just personal criticism.

Eldon became embroiled in a political conflict in his department soon after he arrived, when a crucial vote on which the department was split came up. The department is half Caucasian and half Asian but was not split along ethnic lines. Eldon voted his conscience, and while he worried about relationships between himself and potential tenure committee members, he felt the best advice he was given was, "You cannot argue with facts. The burden of proof is on you. Show concrete evidence of your own research program and your publications and you [should] be fine."

Eldon has remained committed to his teaching. He states, "If your students are not learning, part of it could be your fault. Do not only blame the students, because we are here to help them." He firmly believes if students lose hope, they lose interest. He recommends that new faculty find out the tenure criteria for their departments, not only what is stated, but what it means. How does the department feel about the importance of teaching? Check on the relative importance of journal publications, conference presentations, and grant funding. What is your department most interested in? Finally, Eldon stresses the importance of social skills in interdepartmental relationships: "Be humble" and "try not to be too opinionated." "Do speak up for yourself," but "rather than criticizing, try to talk more about solutions." And be careful what you say. "Alliances can change," he warns. New faculty can make it a lot harder for themselves if they do not attend to rules of common courtesy.

### Dancing in a Snake Pit

Moana, who has just received tenure, describes her experience in higher education as "one of dancing in a snake pit." She says it has been necessarily cautious and constrained. She "wouldn't wish these last three years on anybody," yet her fortitude and "kick ass" attitude have helped her not only to persevere, but to succeed despite great odds. As she approached the tenure review process, Moana thought her application would be relatively straightforward. She had served on her department's personnel committee on several occasions and was aware of the criteria for tenure. She also knew the quality of dossiers that, in recent years, had been deemed as deserving of tenure. As such, Moana felt she met the standards that were expected of her. In keeping with department personnel policy and procedures, she had a sound research agenda, strong service contributions, and an outstanding teaching record.

Yet her personnel endeavors were not straightforward. Two years earlier, at the point of contract renewal, her department chair criticized her for having too much service and too few publications. In the formal written review, the chair also failed to mention that Moana had been recognized by the university for her excellence in teaching. At that time, Moana returned the review and asked the chair to document the teaching award. In the following year's contract renewal review by the chair, the excellence in teaching award was again omitted. For a second time, Moana asked the chair to include it. At this point, Moana also noted that the chair had "recommended" a minimum number of publications necessary for her to be awarded tenure. This recommended number was greater than the actual number of publications of some peers who had previously been successful in their tenure applications.

It was clear to Moana that the relationship between her and the department chair was becoming both strained and dangerous. Once, in reference to Moana's request to the dean for a teaching reassignment, the chair told Moana that "brown females who go crying to the dean can get anything they want." The chair, who had opposed the reassignment, was angry that the dean had supported Moana. It was at this point that Moana realized she would need to prepare carefully and strategically for her tenure application.

Knowing that her department chair would not support her tenure application, Moana asked several other department chairs in the college to review her dossier and write letters evaluating its merit. She also asked other well-established researchers and administrators at the university to provide objective reviews of her dossier. Just prior to completing and submitting her application for tenure, Moana heard that the chair of her department had discussed her personnel matters with a person outside of the department. Apparently, the chair had mentioned that she was considering writing a negative review of Moana's application for tenure. Moana, who was still in the process of putting her dossier together, says she felt betrayed by a system that was meant to ensure equitable treatment for everyone. Moana knew that if the allegation were true, the chair's actions were a serious breach of department policy and procedure.

In frustration, Moana called the faculty union. The union representative took a neutral position as he listened to her story. At first, Moana felt he could have been more reassuring, more supportive, more of an advocate. But, as the conversation continued, she began to understand the importance of approaching the problem in a clear and logical manner. She was reassured when the union representative informed her that hers was not an isolated case. Following the advice of the representative, Moana sought a resolution that she described as having "the perfect outcome." The university responded to her concerns, and for the first time in nearly three years, Moana felt that she would receive fair and equitable treatment in the tenure review process. She was reassured that her tenure papers would be reviewed by experienced individuals who understood the importance of impartiality. She said that this was all she wanted—nothing more and nothing less.

Moana received tenure. She felt particularly pleased that members of the universitywide tenure and promotion review committee were unanimous in their support of her tenure application. "I feel tired, I feel relieved. But most of all I feel vindicated! What a sad commentary! But now I can get on with my work without the constant fear of sabotage," she said. Moana's advice to other junior faculty is to know the system and its requirements and to network with faculty beyond your own department. She advises, "Be gutsy enough to stand up for yourself. When you are attacked, adopt the attitude, 'Stuff you! I've worked hard!'" She describes the wearing effect of having to be at her office and how she prefers to work at home. She says, "It is hard to stay in your office and get beaten up by a power freak. It is tiring watching your back at every minute of the day!" But too much time away from the office may result in colleagues complaining that you are not a "team player." Balance is the key. She adds, "The best thing about being tenured is that you can get on with what you enjoy most—education!"

Moana believes that her teaching duties helped keep her sane. But one of the biggest challenges has been finding time to write. Moana's classes are very large due to her reputation as an excellent teacher. This keeps her busy during the school year, so most of her writing is accomplished during the summer. Moana says that another saving grace was the terrific opportunity she had to work with an established researcher from her department. She said, "My colleague, who has my utmost respect, is highly acclaimed in national and international arenas." Together, they have established a strong research agenda. Her colleague also introduced Moana to her national and international network of colleagues and was helpful in many ways. She said that during the roughest times, her colleague provided her with support and encouraged her to channel her energies into productive endeavors. Moana also brought to the partnership a network of indigenous women scholars from across the country and around the world. All of these forms of networking have been helpful to her. She says, however, that her department chair's "campaign of terror" has taken its toll on her professional reputation. Moana feels that some faculty have adopted the attitude that she and her research needed to be "rescued." This Moana believes is yet another form of oppression in the academy. "But, when it comes down to it," Moana says, "you learn to sort those who have a clue from those who don't! You dismiss the latter."

At this point Moana has established a fine reputation as a scholar and a teacher. She finds comfort in the understanding that her ordeal was not about her lack of merit as a scholar; rather it was about an individual who was ill qualified to undertake the responsibilities of a department chair. While these last few years have been intense and exhausting, Moana says her refusal to be a victim and her sense of humor have helped her to survive.

## Is It Time?

Lynda is of Asian ethnicity and is an associate professor of Japanese and international studies at a public university in the western part of the United States. She began her academic career as an instructor, prior to the completion of her doctorate in 1991–92. Upon completion of her Ph.D., she signed a document stating that the year in which she was working to finish her degree would not be counted toward tenure. Unfortunately, her department chair was unaware of this. Thus, in the summer of 1995, she received a memo from her chair stating that it was time for her to prepare for tenure. Her mentor, from whom she sought support and advice, was out of the country and could not be reached. Feeling extremely alone and in a state of panic, Lynda began preparing her application and dossier with no guidance. In doing so, she realized that her career was somewhat erratic; she had no coherent line of research and did not have the national connections she thought she needed. To further complicate matters, in the midst of everything, the document she had signed stating that the 1991–92 academic year would not count toward tenure was found. However, it was too late. She had already submitted her dossier. Lynda had no choice but to keep her fingers crossed and wait. She was successful in achieving tenure but states that "the process was mentally exhaustive and anticlimactic. It was like my whole life was being judged and then . . . I was thrown into hell. Confused and frustrated, I felt like I had to make a decision without being fully informed. I was told I had a strong case, but I had no idea what that meant. . . . In my perception, my strong point was just the hard work. During the ordeal I needed to vent my concerns to those I felt I could trust. Needing to be heard was crucial."

## Am I Smart Enough?

Maria Rendon, a first-generation college graduate, was advised by her professors not to seek a doctoral degree. With this sort of colonial psychology ingrained in her brain, she doubted her intellectual capabilities. At one point she found herself wondering aloud to her husband, "Am I smart enough?" His response was, "You've done a lot of other things in your life. This is just one more." Working through the decolonizing baggage, she earned a Ph.D. in foreign languages. She is now the chair of the ethnic studies department at her institution.

A political and social activist, this Latina woman began the first phase of her tenure journey from assistant to associate professor in 1983. Although Maria had published several articles, she was heavily involved in governance, teaching, and all kinds of university service. She was not heavily involved in writing. "I wasn't writing. I was reluctant and afraid. I didn't believe that I could write things people would want to publish. I was doing the other stuff. I was acting like a good mother and housewife, the caretaker for the department. Although my teaching and service records were outstanding, I did not have the academic record. [I was] serving the university and the Latino students . . . this hidden work didn't count. The hidden work that we do is valuable to us personally, but is not thought of as having promotion merit. It was not equal to academic work. Faculty of color often have immense responsibilities to their communities, and yet this work is not valued by the academy. We bring so much to the institution. We bring our souls and give generously to the institution. We have to believe that this is for us . . . that we do make a difference. Yet we are always measured by their measuring stick. This is a constant dilemma."

She describes her experience reaching tenure: "[It was] the most devastating and humiliating thing I've ever gone through. Nobody likes to fail. This was major failure, and everybody knew it. The message was, 'You really don't meet the publication requirements of the University.' Because my publication record was so weak, I was tenured but not promoted. This meant I couldn't get fired, but I was not promoted to associate professor at that time." Resentful but undaunted, she persevered. The next year she focused on writing, made her case for promotion, and got it.

In 1990 the second hurdle from associate to full professor began. This time Maria was mentored by a Chicano woman who helped her to become more professionally active and consistent in her writing. They published collaborative papers and made conference presentations. Maria also published many articles on her own and was working on an edited book. She felt confident and secure in her academic record. Assuming she had the support of her chair and the department, she put herself forward for promotion. In her department, the decision was in her favor by one vote. However, she was turned down at the college level. Upon the advice and support of the dean, she resubmitted her portfolio, once the book was published. At that point, Maria was promoted to full professor.

*Juggling Three Departments*

John Rogers, an African American academic, came to his current institution as a tenured associate professor. With seventeen years in administration, he has held positions from assistant vice president to associate dean, yet his goal to "make a change in the ways kids are educated" was the catalyst for his transition into a faculty appointment. The appointment also provided the impetus for his "get out of town promotion experience." John's new position was an interdisciplinary appointment between three separate departments. In this capacity he juggled numerous meetings and encountered many ambiguities and confusions regarding which procedures and guidelines to follow. Despite repeated attempts to meet with the dean and his department chairs for clarification, all were condescending, vague, or evasive. Nor did anyone delineate how his skills were to be utilized or how his performance was to be evaluated. Thus, upon submission of his portfolio for promotion to full professor, his application was deferred. The reason given was that his scholarship was scattered and lacked coherence. However, the real message to him was, "You're not welcome here."

On an emotional roller coaster, his self-confidence and tenacity were marred, his beliefs daunted. Yet, refusing to be defeated, he took a sabbatical in an administrative position at another university. During this time, he did a lot of reflection and reassessed his situation. His confidence was restored and his perseverance renewed. He has since returned to his home institution and plans to resubmit his promotion dossier.

## Starting Over

Lucille Robyn, a lesbian academic, is going up for tenure for the second time. Having obtained tenure after a long struggle at a public university in the Midwest, she quit her job and moved west with her partner, effectively starting over as a part-time faculty member and then an assistant professor in a tenure-track position in the Department of Kinesiology. The second time, Lucille stated that she didn't "feel pressure in quite the same way. It is more of an on-going part of how you live in a university. If you do what you love," she says, "the rest of it will come."

Lucille's first tenure process was a "horrible experience." She was attacked by two of her colleagues in her first year as a new faculty member. They disapproved of what she was doing, complaining to the dean that she was lowering the department's standards because she criticized the department's observational instrument for student teachers. Although Lucille was using the instrument, she made the mistake of publicly critiquing it to students in one of her classes.

The dean called her into his office and handed her a first-year evaluation that stated she had "limited probability of success" as a faculty member, and he urged her to find another institution. Lucille refused to sign the evaluation, stating that what he had written was based on hearsay and had no factual basis. At that point, with her dean enraged because she would not sign her evaluation letter, Lucille resolved to find a niche for herself and to establish a scholarly record that would be beyond reproach when she came up for tenure.

Eventually, she was both tenured and promoted. The two women who had originally attacked her both received tenure but not the promotion to associate professor. While her first response was to gloat, she says, "After a while, it didn't matter." She received her tenure and promotion letter alone in her office: "It was nothing more than a piece of paper."

Now Lucille takes the long view. She focuses on doing what she loves and the emphases of her work is on what her students are learning. She describes her teaching, research and service as "infinite loops that come back on themselves." She feels she is working to make the world a better place and focuses everything she does on social justice and gender issues. All her work is a piece of this whole. Ironically, as she looks back, she believes that leaving her tenured position to start over was the best thing that could have happened to her. She is much more confident as a result of that, believing that she can do what she did not believe was possible before. Like Eleanor Roosevelt, she believes, "You must do the thing you think you cannot do."

## CONCLUSION

What can we learn from the stories of these faculty? First of all, their experiences underscore the fact that many bright, competent women and faculty of color are marginalized in the academy because they are unaware of the tenure politics and processes at their university. As these cases have demonstrated, these scholars go on to have fine, productive careers when they get the information they need to negotiate the tenure process. However, if they are unaware, misguided, or simply have no guidance, the academy loses valuable, talented people who can make important contributions to higher education. While their presence enriches the experiences of all faculty and students, it is especially important to other women and faculty of color. As we mentioned at the beginning of the chapter, these cases synthesize the personal and the professional, the technical, political, cultural and moral. Within these individual cases are embedded lessons learned about the complexities and dilemmas that lie at the intersection of these elements.

The following strategies arose from the experiences of junior faculty in our cases and provide sound advice on steps to take from the first day you enter the door through the last dotted "i" on your tenure dossier.

1. Set priorities for yourself as a new faculty member. Given your own sense of identity, your values and your understanding of depart-

mental priorities, develop a plan for juggling the three major responsibilities of all faculty—teaching, research, and service. Boice (1992) has found that because teaching provides immediate feedback and rewards, new faculty often turn the bulk of their attention to their teaching responsibilities. Eldon is not alone here and in fact, may be typical. The danger is that teaching may consume one's time, leaving junior faculty without the needed research agenda and publications when they apply for tenure.

2. Seek out colleagues within your institution that are trustworthy and supportive. Network both within and across departments and build informal relationships. Listen to the advice of the colleagues, and, like Eldon, try not to take their advice as personal criticisms. Often, they are simply offering you the benefit of their own experiences and insights that arise from their tacit knowledge of departmental norms. (See chapter 8 for more on mentoring and self-advocacy.) This networking can prove valuable when you receive conflicting advice, as Lynda did. Talk to others who have obtained tenure previously in your department or college, as well as across campus. Find out what was expected of them, what their experiences were, and what advice they might have for you. Finally, get connected nationally, as well as locally. Connect with faculty in your field at other institutions and take advantage of campuswide networking opportunities. Have someone evaluate your curriculum vita honestly, with constructive feedback.

3. Be in close contact with your department chair. Know what is expected of you. Be sure to obtain both your department's and your college's written tenure guidelines. Lynda could have saved herself a lot of grief if she had had clearer lines of communication with her department chair. In some cases, such as John's, even repeated attempts to clarify departmental expectations were not successful. Being a member of three departments is just too much. Avoid split appointments if you possibly can.

4. Seek formal avenues of support within and outside of the institution, as well as within and outside your department. Hopefully you will not need to enlist the support of the faculty union, as Moana did, but knowing where you can get the support you need is crucial. Take advantage of any structured mentoring opportunities available through faculty development offices. In seeking a mentor, what characteristics do you look for, and what type of support do you need if you find yourself the only person of color in your department? Spend some time reflecting on what you need and then look for people who can provide that. Studies of mentoring indicate that

most people do not find a single mentor who can meet all their needs but instead enlist the help of various mentors along the way, each providing help according to his or her expertise.

5. Attend closely to your reports of yearly service or other formal feedback you receive from your department. These are official summaries of your work that constitute an established record of your progress toward tenure. They often contain hidden clues about departmental perceptions of your record. Pay careful attention to what is not said, as well as to what is said. Ask questions if you don't understand what is written. Here Moana had some clues to her future difficulties. If you cannot work out the problems with your chair, you will have time to set up a supportive network elsewhere, as Moana did. In conversations with colleagues and your chair, take as many opportunities as you can to talk about your work. This includes informal conversations with senior members in your department, local and national conference presentations, and so on.

6. Decide how you will maintain your sense of value and self-worth in spite of adversity. Although spouses, as in Maria's case, are helpful, they may not be enough. Moana, for instance, really needed the support of other department chairs in the college. Try to establish a broad range of supporters who can reaffirm your sense of self-worth when you begin to have doubts. Getting away, as John did, is sometimes helpful to regain your sense of perspective. However, getting away can also have its drawbacks, as Moana cautioned. People need to see you as a "team player." Don't succumb to the temptation to just stay home or to hide in your office and write. Develop a support system; find allies in the organization. Be cautious; be aware of the climate in the environment.

7. Finally, enjoy yourself. Be sure to play on occasion. Take breaks. Exercise regularly to maintain your mental and physical health. Use a journal to "keep your rudder in the water" as Joanne states in chapter 13. Being a faculty member can be a satisfying and wonderful career, one in which you are perpetually learning about yourself and others. It is a profession that allows you to "make the world a better place," as Lucille stated, and it affords women and minorities the opportunity to welcome other newcomers into the academy.

## REFERENCES

Boice, R. (1992). *The new faculty member*. San Francisco: Jossey-Bass.
Merriam, S. (1998). *Qualitative research and case study applications in education*. San Francisco: Jossey-Bass.

Nyquist, J. et al. (May–June, 1999). On the road to becoming a professor: The graduate student experience. *Change*, 18–27.

Stake, R. (1994). Case studies. In N. K. Denzin & Y. S. Lincoln (Eds.), *Handbook of qualitative research* (pp. 236–247). Thousand Oaks, CA: Sage.

Wilson, S. (1979). Explorations of the usefulness of case study evaluations. *Evaluation Quarterly* 3, 446–459.

# CHAPTER 3

# *Making the Persuasive Tenure Case: Pitfalls and Possibilities*

## Phyllis Bronstein
## and Judith A. Ramaley

To be successful in their career, pretenure faculty must do two things. The first is to pay very careful attention to the institutional culture in which their career will unfold. Starting from when they first arrive, they need to notice the ways in which their own values and experiences shape their responses to the culture within their department or program as well as within the institution as a whole. The culture of the academy creates possibilities and barriers that inexperienced newcomers need to identify and manage. Often, however, these things are so implicit or so familiar to others that no one thinks to mention them—or their existence may be unacknowledged, or even actively denied. It is especially important for women and faculty of color, who may not share the world view that is built into the priorities, expectations, and reward structures of mainstream institutions, to understand these issues. The second important thing that junior level faculty need to do is to utilize this understanding in very planned and systematic ways, so that they can achieve the ultimate goal of receiving tenure without having to compromise their values, their long-term visions and plans, or their emotional or physical well-being.

In this chapter, we offer a guide to understanding those issues and to applying that understanding in a very practical way. In the first part, Judith Ramaley, from her broad perspective as a university president, presents a theoretical description of changing cultures within the academy and the ways to identify the transitional phase an institution may have reached, particularly regarding its commitment to diversity. In the second part, Phyllis Bronstein, a faculty member who has chaired her college's tenure and promotion committee, done research on institutional climate and retention, and run groups and panels to provide information and support for pretenure faculty, offers a practical and personal guide for the journey down the tenure track.

## UNDERSTANDING INSTITUTIONAL CULTURES
### (Judith Ramaley)

An overarching factor that shapes an institution's structures and priorities is its mission. In the traditional academy, especially within universities where basic research is an essential part of the mission, success in teaching, advising, community service, committee work, and even applied research is often not as highly rewarded as success in obtaining sponsored funding and acquiring a national reputation for basic research in one's field. In other kinds of institutions, such as community colleges, small liberal arts colleges, or community-focused urban universities, the institutional mission may generate greater emphasis on excellent teaching, applied research, professional service, and good campus citizenship. Sometimes there is an unstated mission that is different from the stated one. For example, during the hiring process, new faculty might be told that a key part of the institutional mission is research, only to discover upon arrival that most of the faculty do not publish and that newcomers are expected to be more involved in teaching and service. It is essential, therefore, for new faculty to find out which forms of scholarly work are valued, and to learn whether innovative teaching and successful community and professional service are viewed as scholarly work at all.

Another important aspect of an institution's culture is a kind of code that defines acceptable faculty social and political behavior, within the department as well as in campus life overall. Much of this code is unwritten so that the boundaries of acceptable behavior are not clearly delineated, but they are nonetheless real and must be understood. Newcomers unfamiliar with the ground rules of a new culture may unwittingly stray across these boundaries, either of their own accord because of strongly held values and aspirations or in response to pressures placed upon them by students, community members, or difficult-to-refuse service duties on search committees or task forces. What is expected and rewarded in one department may be discouraged in another, so it is also important to recognize specific departmental "customs" as well as campuswide criteria, in particular, the norms for demonstrating competence and quality in the areas of teaching, research, and service. In addition, it is essential for new faculty to be clear about whether the culture of the institution and the social and political boundaries within that culture are compatible with their own interests and motivations. Reports and "survival guides" based on the experience of women and minority faculty at traditional research universities may not be helpful to new faculty at other types of institutions, such as regional public universities, community colleges, tribal colleges, historically Black or Hispanic institutions, or urban institutions serving inner-city populations.

To the above cultural components that new faculty need to understand, I must add an increasingly important set of variables: the institution's definition of diversity, and the phase the institution or some component of it has reached in the process of attaining multiculturalism. Women and minority faculty may find themselves being pressured to play a role in accomplishing institutional diversity goals, causing them to channel precious time and energy away from their own scholarly pursuits. In addition, such pressure may lead them to feel that there is an insufficient commitment by the faculty as a whole to take on this challenge; one faculty member of color said to me recently that she was tired of teaching all the rest of us what we ought to have figured out on our own. The perception that diversity goals rest mainly on their shoulders, and that those goals are not central concerns of the faculty as a whole, can lessen women and minority faculty members' sense of safety and increase their sense of marginality. Thus, it is important for new women and minority faculty be aware of these issues and possibilities.

Manning and Coleman-Boatwright (1991, p. 367) have provided a useful definition of multiculturalism to describe what an institution may aspire to achieve:

> A multicultural organization is one which is genuinely committed to diverse representation of its membership; is sensitive to maintaining an open, supportive and responsive environment; is working toward and purposefully including elements of diverse cultures in its ongoing operations; and is . . . authentic in its responses to issues confronting it.

A multicultural environment cannot be achieved easily. Different parts of an institution may be in different phases, and groups of people may make progress and lose ground many times before creating together a campus-wide intellectual and social environment that sustains and nurtures diversity.

Recently, the Association of American Colleges and Universities (1999) outlined five phases that a predominantly White institution may pass through as it seeks to become genuinely multicultural. It is important for junior-level women and faculty of color to know which phase their institution has reached, because strategies for building a successful academic career will need to be adapted to reflect that campus context.

These phases, as they apply to the faculty experience, are described below. Specific ways to address the challenges each phase presents will be discussed by Phyllis Bronstein in the second part of the chapter.

### Phase 1: Good Intentions

The campus focuses on affirmative action, seeking to recruit women and people of color as faculty, staff, and students, in an effort to open up higher education to underrepresented groups. Diversity is generally viewed as a matter of social justice or economic necessity. In this phase, very little thought is usually given to helping new faculty to adapt to the campus environment or to promoting the professional development of newcomers, who may be likely to have difficulties functioning within a predominantly White, male culture. In such an environment, a new faculty member must be alert to the need to learn the new culture. An important initial task is to find trustworthy mentors who can explain what the "rules" are and who will assist the newcomer in understanding and meeting the expectations of colleagues.

### Phase 2: Attempts at Acculturation

Noting that women and minority faculty are getting tenure less frequently than their White male colleagues and that minority students are less likely to graduate, the institution begins to focus on retention through the creation of special academic and social mentoring programs to support new "at-risk" students and faculty. These programs are usually based on the assumption that the newcomers have academic deficiencies that must be addressed and that they will not automatically understand the standards and expectations of the academy. The goal is acculturation to the dominant cultural norms—that is, to help women and people of color learn about the majority culture and become successful on its terms, rather than to facilitate their contribution to a shared or multicultural environment.

In this phase, a key challenge for new faculty members may be figuring out how to retain their own values and goals while working within a dominant culture that is based on different norms—and still create a professional path that will be accepted by the dominant culture. Faculty facing this challenge may feel forced to lead bicultural lives, with a clear division between their attempts at assimilation in the workplace and their adherence to their own values and cultural norms in their personal lives. In addition, they may interpret the attempts to acculturate them and address their presumed deficiencies as evidence that they are less qualified and capable than their colleagues, which may further undermine their chances for success.

An opposite kind of problem can occur when new women or minority faculty members have very traditional values and scholarly interests, which are in fact consistent with those of the dominant culture, yet they are presumed to be fully invested in promoting gender or multicultural issues. In such an environment, they may find that colleagues or administrators expect them to speak for all women or all faculty of color. In my own experience, I have frequently been the first woman to hold a variety of faculty leadership roles and administrative positions, and, in each instance, I have been expected to have a special sensitivity and desire to advocate for women's concerns. This expectation has sometimes been problematic, because it has not recognized my desire, responsibility, and full potential to provide leadership for a much broader constituency. Similarly, acculturated faculty who are perceived in this limiting way may come to feel that their potential for making a contribution on their own terms is not being sufficiently recognized or valued. A key task for such faculty is to figure out how to honor their own interests and goals within a cultural context that is giving them very mixed messages about their expected roles and behaviors.

### Phase 3: Improving the Climate

At this point, the campus begins to realize that the major goal is not simply to recruit a diverse group of people and give them the resources to be successful in the dominant culture, but also to create, in a predominantly White institution, an environment that will nurture all faculty, staff, and students. The institution begins to work on changing its climate and culture and to promote a set of common goals, including concepts such as respect, openness, and diversity. These efforts to build better and more respectful working relationships do not yet extend to the core of academic life, namely, individual scholarship or the content of the curriculum.

In this phase, women and minority faculty face an interesting dilemma. Although the values of embracing diversity are being promoted in good faith, and fewer incidents of overt bias may occur, the content and goals of exemplary scholarship are still defined according to the values of the majority culture. This can create a difficult paradox, in which women and minority faculty are pulled between the need to meet the majority culture requirements for scholarship and the wish to foster the growing attention to diversity and multiculturalism in other aspects of institutional life. Campus expectations pressuring them to contribute disproportionately to achieving these goals exacerbate the dilemma, in that yielding to them will leave less time for scholarly work.

## Phase 4: Adding Multiculturalism to the Curriculum

At this point, the disparity between efforts to promote diversity and the continuing influence of the dominant culture on the intellectual life of the institution becomes apparent. The campus community begins to reframe the challenge of diversity as one of academic and curricular reform. New fields of study and new programs are developed; new material on multiculturalism and research from different world views are introduced into the curriculum and recognized as legitimate scholarly work. This shift is generally driven by a growing realization that the institution needs to change its collective perspective and acquire a new set of competencies in order to achieve genuine diversity and to prepare its students to be successful in an increasingly multicultural/global environment.

In many cases, this effort takes the form of a diversity or race and culture requirement in the curriculum that many students resent. Achieving this well-meaning but often poorly developed goal of exposing students to issues of diversity and culture can divert the energy of the faculty who have the expertise to teach such courses, often women and minorities, from pursuing work that is still more highly valued by the institution. Most White male faculty remain uninvolved; it is easier to assume that only individuals who are personally affiliated with the issues can authentically offer instruction in that area—for example, that only women can teach women's studies.

## Phase 5: Transformation

In the most advanced phase, institutional transformation is truly underway, generated by a rethinking of the educational mission and a revisiting of the principles and goals of scholarship. A genuine engagement with diversity and with issues of equity and social justice begins. Opportunities are made available for all members of the campus community to acquire a stronger base of multicultural competence, which is now seen as a necessary condition for academic excellence in teaching, research, and service. At this point, multiculturalism and diversity become integral to the educational purposes and are prized as vital intellectual resources by the institution. They become an essential and accepted aspect of campus life.

In this phase, faculty are still held to rigorous standards of scholarship. However, scholarship is no longer defined according to the old norms that rewarded basic but not applied research. The new definitions are much broader, allowing for the integration and application of knowledge in ways that will directly address community concerns and improve the human condition.

Most colleges and universities are still in the early phases of the process of seeking diversity, and most institutions still operate within a traditional "White male" frame of reference for judging the quality of faculty work (Knowles & Harleston, 1997). Under such conditions, women and people of color are particularly likely to stray across the boundaries of expectations for faculty at their institution. Because of their research and teaching interests and their desire to serve the community with which they strongly identify, they may pay the "cultural tax" of being an embodiment of the diversity that the campus seeks. They are likely to be regarded as doing too much applied and community-based research, spending too much time working with students, or participating too much in outreach and professional service activities.

It is important for new faculty members, whatever their background, to think about the cultural context in which they find themselves. They need to examine their own interests, motivations, and goals, and to work out clear strategies for being true to them, while understanding and meeting the dominant cultural expectations within their department and institution. The next section will address this process more specifically. The advice it provides is based on the premise that most institutions have not yet reached phase 5. This is our "how to" section. It speaks directly and personally to pretenure faculty, who may need help in furthering their careers in majority-culture institutions that ascribe to more traditional notions of scholarly productivity.

## THE TENURE JOURNEY:
## MOVING AHEAD AND STAYING ON TRACK
### (Phyllis Bronstein)

When you have been hired on a tenure-track, the journey toward tenure starts on the day you begin your new job. To reach the ultimate destination, it is useful to start out thinking of yourself as the engineer on this journey, and not as a passenger along for the ride. This means looking out for your own interests, planning your route carefully, and making sure not to get side-tracked or derailed along the way. You might think of this journey as divided into two stages—the long haul of building your academic career and your place in the institution, and the final, intense preparations as you approach your destination. I have divided the discussion below into those two stages, with references to other chapters in the book that discuss particular topics in more depth.

### The Long Haul: Building Your Career

All faculty members know that they will be evaluated for reappointment, promotion, and tenure (RPT), as well as for raises in salary, in the three categories of scholarship, teaching, and service. However, as Judith Ramaley mentioned in the first part of this chapter, institutions vary widely in regard to their requirements within each category and the relative importance of those categories. Further, there are often intangibles not found in faculty handbooks or RPT guidelines, which may be referred to as "collegiality," "fitting in," "being a team player," or "being a good citizen," that also figure in evaluation processes. Thus it is important to attend to both the stated and the unstated requirements for advancement in your department and institution.

**Scholarship**  If you have been hired in a tenure-track position in a research-oriented institution, your department obviously believes that you have excellent scholarly potential, based on the work you did beforehand. Your first task is to find out what level and kind of scholarly productivity will now be expected of you. If you are in a scientific field, you may be expected to begin applying for external funding, and receiving funding may be an important factor in the ultimate tenure decision. If you are in the humanities, you may be expected to publish your dissertation as a book. For many fields, ongoing publication in refereed journals is the primary indicator of scholarship.

In all instances, however, one route to success is to capitalize on what you have already done, while launching yourself into a new project. Obviously, if you have not yet completed your dissertation, it is essential to do so immediately. Then it is time to mine it for publications; even if you are intending to publish it as a book, you may be able to produce several shorter pieces in article form. All dissertations can yield at least one article, and some will generate three or four—perhaps a theoretical piece or an extensive literature review and one or more articles focused on research questions. Further, even if you have been out of graduate school for several years, you may want to look over the projects and papers you did during that period, as some of them may be worthy of publication. Chapter 10 in this volume provides a thorough guide for writing and getting your work into print. The latter process can be discouraging; the most prestigious journals in some fields have over an 80% rejection rate. However, there are specialized journals, lesser-known journals, and journals in related fields that may be receptive to an interesting of piece work that doesn't quite fit the criteria of the most prestigious ones in your field.

In terms of preparing yourself for tenure, it is important to submit your work for publication as early as possible and to keep track of its progress. It may take as long as 10 months before a journal editor responds to your initial submission, and if you are invited to revise and resubmit, it may be well over a year before the article is finally accepted or rejected. My policy is to call or e-mail the editor to inquire (politely) if I haven't heard anything after three months and to try to get an indication of how long the initial review will take, which I hope will prod the process along. I have also learned not to revise an article that has been rejected by one journal before submitting it to another. In my experience, the new reviewers may have a very different perspective from the initial ones, with very different recommendations—which I am happy enough to follow if they have indicated a willingness to reconsider the paper. The important message here is to get your work out early and to keep it circulating until it finds a home. Last year, an article of mine that I thought was an important piece of work was published—in the fifth journal to which I submitted it. All faculty, including the most famous in their fields, have had articles rejected for publication, and some articles that have come to be regarded as classics in their field were submitted to a number of journals before finally being accepted. Persistence and a thick skin are essentials in this aspect of tenure preparation.

Many junior faculty submit proposals to conferences, based on the idea that this will help move them toward publication. They reason that a commitment to present their work will force them to analyze their data and write up the findings and that publication is simply one step beyond that. Unfortunately, it usually doesn't work that way. Conference presentations take a substantial amount of time in their own right—preparing slides or poster illustrations and traveling to distant places—and in research-oriented institutions, such presentations will not be sufficient to earn you tenure. I have found, over the years, that it is more productive to prepare an article for publication, and then to submit a conference proposal based on it while it is under journal review. It is usually easier to trim an article down to presentation size than to build a presentation into an article—and it is all too easy to get into a pattern of presenting at conferences and never quite finding the time to write the material up for publication.

The content of your scholarship is another factor to consider in preparing yourself for tenure evaluation. Ten years ago, women and faculty of color, many of whom focused on feminist or sociocultural issues in their research, had a difficult time gaining acceptance for their work both in their institutions and in the mainstream journals in their field. Since that time, there have been enormous changes, with much more opportunity to teach feminist and multicultural courses and to pursue and publish research in those areas. However, in institutions that have not reached phase 5 in their journey toward multiculturalism, there is still a mindset regarding what Foster-Fishman and Stevens refer to (in chapter 12) as the "limited notion of scholarship as discovery"— that is, as separate from the integration and application of knowledge, particularly as it relates to social change. They provide a guide for documenting the scholarship of professional service as one way to build a tenure case. Additional approaches that I and other social activist scholars have taken is to try to pursue our research questions within a more traditional framework, or in addition to a more traditional line of research. For example, my deep concerns about sexism have been channeled into investigations of gender role socialization, within a larger framework of research on parenting and adolescent development. In addition, I have maintained an entirely separate line of scholarship writing articles and chapters (such as this one) related to gender and sociocultural issues in the academy, and some of those writings have reported quantitative research, which is particularly valued in my field. When I have been evaluated for tenure and promotion, I have made it clear that outside reviewers need to be chosen in each area, and they need to be informed that my body of work in that area represents only one-half of my total scholarly productivity.

I mentioned above the necessity for launching into new research, as well as writing up previously completed research for publication. RPT committees will be impressed with numbers of publications related to your dissertation, or to work done with your graduate school or post-doctoral mentor, but they will invariably ask what you have been doing since then. They will look for evidence of new, independent directions. If you continue to do ongoing research with your mentor, it is important to be able to demonstrate how the work is now going in a new direction that you have originated, or else to show that you have started up a new line of work that is entirely your own. If you continue doing research on your dissertation topic, you will need to show that you are investigating new questions or devising important new ways to explore the original ones. The senior colleagues who evaluate your work will want to know that you are moving forward in your research and not merely spinning in place. One way to facilitate your involvement in new research is to find someone at your institution to collaborate with; working with a productive, compatible colleague can increase your enjoyment and double your output. Finally, given the length of time it takes to go from conception to publication, it is a good idea to have several different projects going at once, at different stages of development. Thus, while you are waiting for a response to an article submitted for publication, you can be analyzing the results of a second study and collecting data for a third.

**Teaching**    Chapter 11 provides valuable information for honing your classroom teaching skills. However, other aspects of teaching may also be important. Your department may expect you to supervise graduate

student research or clinical training or to oversee undergraduate intern-
ships, independent study, or honors theses. Although there are inherent
rewards in training and mentoring scholars-to-be, it is also essential to
keep in mind that this area of job performance is part of your preparation for tenure. Two aspects in particular need to be considered: your
time and your relationships with students.

In regard to time, it is very easy for new faculty to give unlimited
time to individual research supervision. You may be flattered when a
number of students come to you with proposed projects, and knowing
that such supervision is valued in your department, you may readily
agree to it. If you are the only faculty of color in your department, you
may feel particularly pulled to oversee the projects of any students of
color who request it of you. More experienced faculty with strong
research and publication agendas seldom do this. They are more likely
to invite students to participate in a project of their own—perhaps des-
ignating or adding a piece that will be a student's particular project—
and thus are able to further their own work while supervising student
research. I have tended over the years to organize research teams con-
sisting of graduate and undergraduate students, who have different levels of involvement and responsibility. They help one another with such
tasks as data collection, scoring, and entry and learn from one another
as well as from me, with graduate students or experienced undergraduates sometimes overseeing the work of novice undergraduate members.
They enjoy being part of a team and get to see a large research project
at work. In such endeavors, it is important to have stringent criteria for
the undergraduates you include, so that you know that your research
subjects or materials will be in responsible and capable hands.

If you do agree to supervise theses or dissertations on topics that are
not part of your own ongoing research, it is a good idea to make a clear
agreement beforehand that the students will make every effort to publish when finished, and if they don't, that you may do so, with second
authorship. In this way, you will be encouraging them to take themselves seriously as researchers and also provide yourself with the possibility of additional publication credits. Relationships with students are a
more delicate matter. In addition to enjoying the collaborative aspects
and the pleasures of mentoring, you will need to keep in mind the positive and negative possibilities related to tenure. The positive possibilities
are that you will have a grateful and loyal following of past and present
students who will be happy to write glowing letters describing your
supervision and mentorship. These letters can give a vivid picture of the
valuable role you play in your department and can provide a moving testimony of the ways you have affected students' lives. The negative possibilities are that there may be rough spots that you encounter with some

students, who may complain to other faculty and then put their complaints in writing when you come up for tenure. Students who are feeling disgruntled or oppressed because of the department's climate, or who are having their own difficulties in the world at large, are more likely to vent their anger at "safer" targets than at the senior faculty who wield the power in the department; thus junior-level women and faculty of color can be at risk for these kinds of negative reactions.

There are some ways to safeguard yourself against such outcomes. One is to be very clear about expectations, timelines, and consequences in setting up your working relationships with graduate students. After discussing these thoroughly, it is a good idea to provide students with a copy of the agreed-upon points, which can be referred to at a later date if needed. Another is to maintain careful professional boundaries. As much as graduate students may seem like junior colleagues just a few years younger (or even older) than you are, it is important to be conscious of the power differential between you and the psychological accoutrements of your roles. Because they know that their professional fate in the program is to a large extent in the hands of the faculty (in terms of course requirements, allocation of resources, publication credits, performance evaluation, and letters of recommendation for fellowships and jobs), graduate students usually have a great deal of caution and concern about their relations with faculty. Treating them as your equals within this system denies the reality that they are experiencing and will usually lead to mistrust. Because they look to you for expertise and guidance, they may become confused and anxious if you take a totally noncritical or "democratic" approach to their work or discuss your personal problems with them. Newly arrived junior faculty, who may be imbued with feminist ideals of openness, collaboration, and equality, need to recognize and function within the hierarchical power structure that shapes faculty-graduate student relationships in academic departments.

If you begin to sense trouble in dealing with a student, there are several useful things you can do. The first is to talk to the student as gently and nonaccusingly as possible, asking questions about your own behavior in a puzzled way: for example, have you perhaps miscommunicated or misunderstood about an expectation or timeline, or have you done something to make the student uncomfortable in your work together? At this point, it is best to listen nondefensively to whatever feelings or complaints there may be and to invite the student to keep talking and explaining, so that she or he will feel heard. After appreciating the student's candor and apologizing for any oversights or thoughtlessness on your part, you might try to do some renegotiating of the problem area. But you may at this point want to arrange to continue the conversation later when you have had time to think about it and perhaps get some guidance and support from a trusted senior colleague. If this approach does not take care of the problem, it is important to consult with your program director or department chair, who may also be able to advise you. But more important, you will have provided a context for any complaints the student might bring so that your director or chair will be less likely to be drawn into making hasty judgments about you. One approach I have developed in recent years in dealing with graduate students around such things as poor class attendance and noncompletion of work is to send them e-mails stating my concerns and the consequences, with copies forwarded to the program director. This defines the problem in terms of the roles and hierarchical context of the program and helps to keep it out of the personal realm.

**Service**   There are many different kinds of service which will fulfill the requirements for tenure, although those requirements will differ across institutions. In institutions that have not reached phase 5, you will probably be expected to show a record of service within your department and within the larger institution, with regional or national service being a bonus but not a requirement. However, if service counts much less than scholarship and teaching in your overall evaluation, as is the case in research-oriented institutions, you should allot your time to it accordingly. The most important thing is to be a good department citizen: carry out your committee assignments dutifully and cheerfully, attend events to welcome prospective students or to honor graduating seniors, and come regularly and on time to faculty meetings. If the call goes out for a few faculty needed to do summer advising, and the task will not be very time consuming, volunteer. On the other hand, try to avoid committees and tasks that demand some of your time every week throughout the academic year.

Within the institution, try to get involved in a committee or task that interests you and allows you to network with people who can write letters of support for you during the tenure process. This might include committees related to women's studies or ethnic studies or the promotion of racial equality and justice, as well as more traditional committees such as those concerned with the overall curriculum or undergraduate honors. As discussed earlier, because of the need to provide gender balance and cultural diversity in faculty governance, junior-level women and faculty of color in particular may find themselves on so many committees that they have little spare time to pursue their scholarship. When you are invited to join an additional committee, one thing to consider is whether it will increase your visibility and connection to a key person in the tenure process—for example, if the committee reports directly to the dean or provost. But in most cases, it is important to develop tactful ways of saying no.

**Life Priorities**    The pretenure years may require considerable rearrangement of your life priorities and goals. For faculty wanting to begin a family, the tenure clock and biological clock are ticking simultaneously, and difficult decisions will have to be made. Many institutions will now grant a year's extension of the tenure timetable for childbirth or adoption, but apart from that, the requirements remain the same and do not take into account the reduced amount of time and energy new parents have to build their record of scholarship. Thus, having a family may put your chances for tenure more at risk, and you may decide to postpone it. Chapter 6 explores these issues and provides suggestions for thinking about and prioritizing work and family goals. Within the professional sphere, the goal closest to your heart may be to use your expertise to help underserved populations within the community, or to combat racism within your institution and create a diverse and welcoming environment. However, until you have the job security that tenure provides, it is usually best to limit your involvement in activities that don't build your record of accomplishments in areas your colleagues will value and to keep a relatively low political profile. A certain level of campus political involvement (particularly through official committees) is certainly acceptable, but you don't want to find yourself on the front page of the local paper, arrested during a takeover of the administrative offices. At institutions that are wary of change, campus political activism may be viewed as adversarial, with negative consequences for junior faculty. It can lead to a reputation for being a troublemaker, which gets translated into terms such as *lack of collegiality* or *not a team player* in the tenure review.

**Gathering Support**    Although a well-developed support system is not a requirement for tenure, it is an extremely important factor that can affect both the process and the outcome. The three domains where it is most important are your department, the institution, and your professional field. Within your department, you may experience a tendency to isolate yourself, working behind a closed door and taking a 10–minute lunch break to eat a sandwich at your desk, while your senior colleagues hang out in the coffee lounge, joke in the hallways, and go out to lunch together. You may do this out of a general sense of urgency about your work overload, or a need to maximize workday hours before going home to family responsibilities, or perhaps a social timidity based on your low position in the academic hierarchy, exacerbated by an absence of overtures from your colleagues. It is important, however, to resist the temptation to keep to yourself and to make deliberate efforts to establish cordial social relations within the workplace—for example, stopping to chat on your way back from the mailroom, inviting people to go out to lunch, and attending (and helping to organize) department social functions. Not only will such relations make your work environment seem more pleasant and welcoming, but they may provide you with important information about department politics and create allies who will want the department to retain you when it is time for the tenure decision.

Within your institution, you may of course develop friendships with faculty or staff from other departments and collegial working relationships with people you have worked with on committees. However, it is a good idea to try to connect with faculty groups that share your values and goals, perhaps joining committees related to women's studies or ethnic studies or becoming part of a faculty women's caucus. Here you are likely to find people who can give you political advice from a perspective outside of your department and who can mentor you through the tenure process if such mentoring is not available within your department. In addition, there are often networks that can influence the process at different stages. For example, if a feminist scholar is evaluated unfairly by her department, and her situation is known to feminist faculty on campus, there may be people who will keep a protective eye on her case when it comes to the college or university RPT committee. This brings me to another reason to get involved in such networks—to help elect to RPT and grievance committees faculty who actively support diversity. At my institution, a colleague and I started a faculty women's caucus a number of years ago, an informal group that, in addition to other forms of advocacy, nominates and endorses candidates for these key positions in faculty governance.

Networking within your professional field can also be invaluable. One benefit can be opportunities for collaborative research and publication. Early in my career, I joined a teaching interest group in a feminist psychology organization and also a division of the American Psychological Association devoted to the psychology of women. These led to my participation in task forces and symposia with feminist colleagues who had similar interests and eventually to invitations to write chapters for their books—as well as to two edited books of my own.

Another benefit is that you and your work will become known to people in your field; if they know you personally and value your work, they may be very pleased to attest to its quality as external reviewers during the tenure process. Although close friends and mentors are generally not regarded as acceptable reviewers in tenure cases, there is usually little objection to professional acquaintances familiar with your work serving in that capacity.

A final benefit is a political one. There are people out there who have undergone all sorts of struggles and if needed can provide the kind of guidance and support that may not be available on your campus. Years ago, when I was going through a very rocky tenure process with little active support, the people most helpful to me were two feminist faculty of color who had gone through horrific struggles at other institutions. One of them was able to give me useful input about the kinds of attacks that have all too often been directed at feminist scholars and scholars of color and to provide advice about "paper trails" and the tone to take in making my case. The other was wonderful at modeling courage and reminding me that I was a valuable person doing important work, which helped me to stay afloat emotionally. It is also not unusual for members of a professional network to rally around a colleague who is embroiled in a tenure struggle, writing letters and petitions, and even raising money for legal assistance.

**Pretenure Evaluations**    At many institutions, faculty are evaluated once or twice for reappointment during the pretenure years and may be evaluated annually as well. As you approach your destination, you will want to pay particular attention to the most recent of those evaluations, to see whether you are gliding along smoothly or whether you have gotten sidetracked along the way, and whether it looks like there may be some attempts up ahead to derail you. If a problem area was flagged in an earlier evaluation, and you have taken care of it, you need to make sure that a later evaluation explicitly acknowledges that the problem was resolved. If an area needing improvement is cited in a later evaluation, you need to make every effort to attend to it so that you can document in your tenure dossier that the required improvement has occurred. If an annual or reappointment evaluation at any stage along the way underreports or undervalues your accomplishments or includes unjust criticisms, you must challenge it at that time, using whatever negotiation or appeal avenues there are for such processes at your institution. It is essential not to let misinformation about you stand as unquestioned truth, because it may be part of a developing negative "story" about your career that is being created by political agendas in your department or by the kinds of unaware sexism, racism, antisemitism, ageism, and/or classism that keep institutions from moving ahead to phase 5 in their multicultural development. Specific ways to construct such appeals will be discussed below, in the section dealing with the tenure process. Further perspectives on dealing with these kinds of formal feedback can also be found in chapter 9.

*Approaching the Destination: Preparing Your Case*

Going through that final stage can be very stressful. Unlike job situations in the world outside of academia in which your boss evaluates your performance, you are now going to be evaluated by hordes of people—your peers in your department, past and present students, committees and administrators within the institution, and prominent scholars in your field. If you have never had evaluation anxiety or feelings of fraudulence, you are likely to develop them now. Further, you will not be evaluated, as you would.be in most other jobs, for your performance on an assigned task but on work that is mainly of your own design and that comes out of your own deep interests and life goals. Thus, it can feel like being evaluated for who you are as a person—a measuring of your basic identity and worth. On top of that, of course, is the knowledge that a negative outcome is likely to impede your career.

On the other hand, going through the tenure process is also an opportunity to showcase your accomplishments, take pleasure in how much you have achieved, and very possibly receive the recognition and reward that you deserve. Try to keep this proactive perspective in mind when preparing your case. The other essential things to do are to gather information and support, start early, do more than is necessary, and blow your own horn loudly.

**Gathering Information and Support**    Every department and institution has standards regarding qualifications for tenure, which may be written out or implicit. They may be followed to the letter, or they may sometimes be ignored or manipulated depending on the politics of the case. If you are aware of these standards, it is easier to make sure that you have met or exceeded them and to make your case with confidence. Chapter 9 provides advice on obtaining this information.

It is also essential to gather support during the final tenure preparations, which can be very isolating. Because of confidentiality requirements, even department colleagues who are supportive of your case may not speak to you about it, and if the outcome is in doubt, people may deal with their discomfort by acting as if the situation does not exist. In order to maintain the confidence and positive energy needed to put your dossier together, you will need to reach out for personal support to any available department members, to colleagues in the larger institution and in your professional field, and to friends and family members. It is a good idea also to seek some sort of individual or group counseling at this time, to help you deal with the fears, self-doubts, and sense of isolation that may come up.

**Gathering Materials**    For this final stage of your journey, it is best to get going early. If the completed dossier must be submitted to your department in October, it is not too soon to start planning the process with your chair as soon as classes end in the spring. This will allow ample time for your chair to solicit external reviews of your scholarship and for you to have the summer to gather resources and give thoughtful attention to your self-presentation.

The selection of external reviewers is an extremely important part of the process. Selection procedures vary across institutions and often across departments within institutions. In most instances, the tenure candidate has some say in who will be solicited, and you should use that say to your best advantage. Much as we like to believe that the established scholars who take on the reviewing task will provide unbiased evaluations, this is often not the case. People's standards are shaped by their own adherence to a particular school of thought or methodology, by the standards of their own institution, by their social and political biases, and by their own life experiences and personality. A recent case I am familiar with involved a reviewer who harbored old resentments toward the tenure candidate's graduate school mentor, and these feelings, judging by the inappropriate harshness of the evaluation, apparently spilled over into the review. In short, it is important to try to guard against negative bias and to ensure that some of the bias will be in a positive direction.

This may take some inquiry on your part. If you are given any veto power over reviewers your chair or department has selected, try to eliminate anyone whose theoretical or political stance is very different from yours or who might feel competitive toward you. If you know very little about some of the people on the list apart from their published works, use your professional network to find out whether they are known to be supportive in their interactions with colleagues—or overly critical or arrogant—and, if relevant to your case, whether they are receptive to feminist or multicultural scholarship. If you are given the opportunity to suggest reviewers, use the same network and criteria to come up with a list of people likely to be supportive of your kind of scholarly work. It is also a good idea to provide more names than are actually required, because some people may decline or not respond. Further, if there are no strict limits on the number of reviewers, it is better to have more of them, if they are of your own choosing. Twelve positive external evaluations are more impressive than four or five, and if there are one or two negative or equivocal evaluations, they will carry less weight among all the positive ones.

Similar principles apply in the solicitation of letters from current and former students. Departments may invite all current graduate students to submit letters, or they may target only students who have worked with you. A good strategy is for you to ask for letters to be solicited from a list that you provide of your biggest fans, which might include graduate and/or undergraduate students—and the more the better. One way to prepare students for this eventuality is to let them know, when they are appreciative of letters of recommendation you have written for them, that you may be asking for something similar from them in the future. In my mentoring of students, I try to communicate that they can help in creating a more diverse and multicultural environment by supporting faculty who are working toward those goals. However, it is important not to pressure students into doing something they are not comfortable with and to avoid blurring the boundaries between your roles by focusing too strongly on your needs.

**Making Your Case**    Chapter 8 provides a guide for successful self-advocacy, so I will make only one key point. Leave nothing to chance. Specifically, do not assume that your chair or department tenure committee will write an accurate and complete report that recognizes and appropriately extolls all your accomplishments. I have learned from experience on my college's RPT committee that chairs vary widely in their ability to present a strong case for tenure. Thus, you will need to make your own very thorough, well-documented, and convincing case. For example, include important aspects of your numerical teaching ratings and verbatim excerpts from positive student comments, and include a complete listing of all the students you have supervised and mentored, with a tally of their projects, theses, dissertations, conference presentations, and publications. These kinds of very specific details may in fact aid your chair or tenure committee in completing their report. And be sure to go over that report with a magnifying glass, as there are often inadvertent (and not so inadvertent) errors and oversights.

**Trouble on the Track**    Despite your best efforts to build an excellent record in the areas under consideration, you may find at the end of your journey that there are obstacles blocking your way. These may be things you caught glimpses of much earlier, or they may have loomed suddenly without warning. Whatever the case, it may become clear that there are forces or individuals within your department or institution who do not think you should be awarded tenure. Perhaps you have fewer publications than the department's tenure guidelines specify, or perhaps you have continually scored below department averages on student ratings of your teaching. If one of these is the case, your only option may be to try to buy more time to rectify the situation; institutions anxious to retain women and minority faculty may be willing to add an additional year to the tenure clock, based on a growing awareness of such things as acculturation issues, family demands, and the debilitating effects of sexism and racism in the academy.

However, many cases involving tenure difficulties for women and faculty of color are not based on inadequate scholarship or teaching, although there may be a concerted effort to create that impression. What has become clear to me, after surveying faculty at a research university (Bronstein & Farnsworth, 1998), helping junior faculty at different institutions through the process, and comparing observations with senior colleagues who have served on RPT committees is that sometimes there are discriminatory forces operating. Here are some examples:

> One third of the dossiers for women considered by an RPT committee contained strong imputations about the candidates' character—either that they were difficult, noncooperative and highhanded, or that they were dishonest or unethical. None of the dossiers for men mentioned such problems.

> Two men in a department were up for tenure at the same time, one European American and the other a foreign-born person of color. It was clear from the former's self-presentation that he had been well mentored, and his chair further extolled his accomplishments, never mentioning the strong empirical evidence of a deficiency in classroom teaching. The latter, on the other hand, submitted only his *curriculum vitae*; obviously no one had bothered to tell him what sort of self-presentation was needed. Further, he was referred to by the chair as an "adequate" classroom teacher, when student ratings of his teaching were in fact excellent.

If, in your department, the way you are treated leads you at any point to suspect you are headed for tenure difficulties, there are a number of things you can do, in addition to the general suggestions provided above. First, keep copies of all written evaluations, as well as quotations and detailed notes describing any verbal feedback on your performance so that you can provide documentation if needed. For example, if you can document that your job performance in all three areas was rated as excellent in your last annual evaluation, it is difficult for your department to make a convincing case that you do not meet its standards for tenure. Second, in addition to challenging any unfair evaluations (as discussed earlier), don't accept smaller unfairnesses that may later be used to build a case against you. For example, if you feel you have been unfairly evaluated by a senior colleague sent to observe your teaching, you need to provide a nondefensive written response to the evaluation and to request additional observers. If a student lodges a complaint against you, you are entitled to know the details and to present your own written perspective on the situation. Third, keep a journal with dates and times and a careful recording of any interactions that you think may be part of a pattern of discrimination. And fourth, begin to create a "paper trail." For example, if your chair unfairly criticizes some aspect of your performance or demeans your character, record the exchange as completely as possible in your journal. Then, in a respectful tone, frame a memo to him or her repeating the conversation, explaining what the implications seem to be and your concerns about them, and concluding with a request for clarification if you have misunderstood. You don't necessarily want a response—although an apologetic clarification would be welcome. But no response means that, in effect, your reading of the situation is undisputed and now on record. Further, you have established yourself as someone to be reckoned with; such memos signal that you do not take discrimination lightly and that you know the kinds of documentation necessary for taking legal action. A word of caution here: don't use e-mail. You want to keep this kind of communication formal and deliberate and not a spontaneous exchange that can easily lapse into emotional excess.

If it happens that you are turned down for tenure, and you believe the decision was unjust, there are a number of things you can do to try to reverse it. Your course of action will depend, to a large extent, on the structure of the tenure process at your institution. In almost all cases, the process is multitiered, and a negative decision at a lower level can be reversed at that same level or at a higher one. Thus, for example, you may be entitled to ask your department to reconsider a negative decision or to appeal to the dean or provost if the RPT committee has turned you down. You will need quickly to learn all the possible avenues of reconsideration and appeal and to adhere to the procedures and timelines that are provided.

In challenging an unjust negative decision, you need all the support you can muster. Now is the time to make full use of the networks you have been building during the pretenure years. It is all too easy to internalize the disapprobation and to feel overwhelmed with shame and helplessness. To contradict these feelings, you need to have people reminding you continually of the importance of your contributions, your value as a person, and the injustice of what has occurred. You also need people skilled in handling institutional politics to help guide you through the struggle. In particular, this means seeking out senior faculty allies at your own and at other institutions. Writing an appeal is a difficult and painful process in that you have to read and re-read negative allegations about yourself in order to understand and deal with them. You may react with depression or rage at what seems to be distortion, misrepresentation, and even complete fabrication of the facts. If you can channel your feelings into a kind of controlled, outraged indignation, you are likely to feel most empowered to do what is needed. And it is important to have someone close by when you are working on the appeal; if you are alone, it is too easy to sink into hopelessness and despair.

In writing an appeal, it is best to take a firm but puzzled tone, as if there has clearly been a misunderstanding or a mistake, which can easily be rectified. Avoid sounding emotional, accusatory, defensive, or sarcastic; understatement can be much more powerful than overstatement. Your opening might be similar to the following: "I appreciate the careful consideration my colleagues have given to my tenure application, but given the data documenting my accomplishments, I am puzzled by some of the conclusions they have come to." Then proceed to cover each of the points for which you have been underrated or criticized and any areas of accomplishment that were ignored. An effective way to do this is first to quote or paraphrase a dismissive or critical allegation and then present the actual data that refute it, followed by a brief conclusion noting that the allegation is unsupported or contradicted by the data. For example, if your publication rate has been deemed inadequate, you might be able to document that it is equal to that of other faculty who recently were tenured in your department. Or if it is stated that a number of faculty have heard negative reports about your dealings with students, you may be able to point out that no documentation has been provided to substantiate these reports and then quote from positive student letters that have been submitted on your behalf. If there actually are one or two negative student letters, you can respond thoughtfully and respectfully to their concerns, point out that it is difficult to be liked by everyone, and then perhaps cite the much larger number of positive letters that were submitted. It's good to keep expressing surprise or puzzlement as you compare each allegation with the data; you want to convey, in an understated way, that once people have had a chance to review all the facts, they will of course agree with you.

You will need to deal with any procedural irregularities in the process in a similar way, first spelling out the event that occurred and then presenting evidence that it did not follow the standard procedures in the RPT guidelines or faculty handbook or did not match procedures used for other tenure cases in your department. For example, a woman in a service-oriented department found that her chair, who was trying to build a negative case against her, had gotten his friends in several state organizations to write critical letters about her nonparticipation in those groups, although they had no knowledge of her work or interests. In another instance, students of faculty who were opposed to a woman's tenure were encouraged to submit written complaints about her, although they had had very little contact with her. In both of these cases, the attempts to collect "data" were not within the prescribed guidelines or the traditions of the department and were clearly manipulations of the process in order to produce negative information.

Challenging a negative tenure decision is best handled within the institution, using the available appeals processes. The campus affirmative action officer and the ombudsperson usually have no power to intervene, and discrimination complaints at state or federal levels rarely have much effect. By all means consult a lawyer who has dealt successfully with academic discrimination cases, who can help you construct your appeal and apprise you of the possibilities for redress. But be very hesitant about taking legal action; tenure cases are rarely won. Some institutions have deep pockets, so a case can drag on for ten years and cost you your life savings, your career energy, and your emotional well-being. Class-action lawsuits have a better chance of success, if you think there is a pattern of discrimination in the institution that can be documented.

## SUMMING UP: A FINAL POSITIVE OUTLOOK

To summarize our advice for how to build a faculty career during this period of institutional transitions, we offer some key points. On the broader level, it is important first of all to understand the often unspoken values and expectations that underlie the priorities, programs, and reward structures of your institution and then to use this understanding in planned and systematic ways to build a strong case for your own advancement. In particular, this means finding out what forms of scholarly work and campus citizenship are valued and whether innovative teaching and successful community and professional service are regarded as legitimate scholarly work. It also means coming to understand the institution's unwritten codes for faculty social and political behavior, both within your department and in campuswide affairs. You will need to learn the ground rules that shape collegiality in those domains, which will affect how people react to you and ultimately judge your performance and contributions. In addition, as a new faculty member, you will need to examine the cultural context in which you find yourself—in particular, the extent to which the institution has adopted principles of diversity, equality, and social justice, and consider your own interests, motivations, and goals in relation to the realities of how other people view diversity issues.

On a more specific level, you will need to attend to both the stated and unstated requirements for advancement in your department and institution, in particular any that apply to publishing and obtaining external funding. To demonstrate your capabilities as an independent researcher, and to begin to establish a reputation within your discipline, it is a good idea to initiate your own program of scholarly activity, in addition to publishing work that you may have begun elsewhere. However, to lighten your load, increase your output, and feel supported in your efforts, it makes good sense to find a colleague or two to collaborate with—as long as the contribution of each is made clear from the outset—and to involve students in your research, rather than supervising multiple individual projects.

In terms of more personal issues, it is essential to focus on getting tenure, even if it means putting some of your social activism or altruistic life goals on the back burner for a while. Choose service commitments within your institution that are meaningful to you but also ones that allow you to network with people who are likely to be supportive of your advancement, and above all, learn to say no to service overload. It is also important to build professional networks within your field, which may lead to opportunities for collaboration and also allow you to connect with senior colleagues who may be called on later as external reviewers of your tenure dossier. Work to build collegial relationships within your department; keep your door open, and keep reaching out, even if no one seems to be leaping at the chance to spend time with you.

In regard to the tenure process, there are a number of things you should particularly attend. In the years leading up to your review, keep records of all your accomplishments (e.g., committee work, teaching evaluations, community service, media interviews). Also, pay close attention to (and save) all periodic evaluations of your performance, making sure to correct any deficiencies, challenge any unjust criticisms, and document any improvements, and be sure to request regular feedback if it is not provided. When it comes to preparing your case, give careful thought and all the input you're allowed regarding the selection of external reviewers. Then, when writing up your accomplishments, present them in great and immodest detail. If the process does not go smoothly, be sure to use whatever channels that are available to you to rebut unjust criticisms and challenge unfair procedures. Finally, get personal support throughout the process and professional support from colleagues and a lawyer if needed.

The good news to keep in mind throughout all this, is that even though women and faculty of color are still being tenured at lower rates than their White male peers, their numbers are growing, and their increased presence can only open the doors wider for others. In addition, institutions are moving—some rapidly, some slowly—toward phase 5 transformation. As more and more campuses incorporate multiculturalism into all aspects of their culture, the narrow, traditional values of academia will be replaced by ones that view diversity as a vital intellectual and interpersonal aspect of campus life. And as this transformation progresses, institutions will value more deeply the diverse perspectives and talents that men and women of all backgrounds bring to their research, teaching, and service. Many of the issues that occupy our attention today will diminish and then disappear. In the meantime, we hope that the material we have provided will help pretenure faculty assess the campus cultural norms and values that affect how their contributions are evaluated and that set the bounds of expected and rewarded conduct. Our campus communities today call upon us to be both very conceptual in our thinking and very practical. We have tried to offer both perspectives.

## REFERENCES

Association of American Colleges and Universities (1999). Diversity Website http://www.inform.umd.edu/EdRes/Topic/Diversity/Response/Web/.

Bronstein, P., & Farnsworth, L. (1998). Gender differences in faculty experiences of interpersonal climate and processes for advancement. *Research in Higher Education* 39, 557–586.

Holland, B. (1997). Analyzing institutional commitment to service: A model of key organizational factors. *Michigan Journal of Community Service Learning* 4, 30–41.

Knowles, M. F., & Harleston, B. W. (1997). Achieving diversity in the professoriate: Challenges and opportunities. A report to the American Council on Education, Washington DC, 25 pgs.

Manning, K., & Coleman-Boatwright, P. (1991). Student affairs initiatives toward a multicultural university. *Journal of College Student Development* 32(4), 367–374.

# CHAPTER 4

# Tenure and Academic Freedom in the Academy: Historical Parameters and New Challenges

## William G. Tierney

Two suppositions guide this chapter.* On the one hand, although *tenure* and *academic freedom* are inextricably linked terms, some might wonder at face value how affirmative action relates to academic freedom or tenure. On the other hand, in the recent past, I have heard commentary that questioned whether the current attacks on tenure were in some way linked to the increase of women and minority faculty in the academy. Is it merely a coincidence, some have wondered, that just as women and minority faculty begin to get a toehold in academic life, individuals begin to question the worth of tenure?

I take issue with both suppositions. My argument is that no organizational structure is color blind or neutral to gender differences. A meritocracy did not exist when tenure came about at the start of this century, and it does not exist in the academy today. Who has populated tenured positions is not mere coincidence or happenstance. At the same time, one ought not draw a causal distinction and suggest that it is because there are more minority and women faculty in academe today that tenure is under attack. Such an argument, I will suggest, is historically mistaken and puts those of us who support affirmative action in a defensive posture when more proactive policies are warranted.

---

*An earlier version of this chapter was presented at the Keeping Our Faculties conference in Minneapolis, MN, October 18–20, 1998.

Accordingly, this chapter has three parts. I first outline the historical parameters of tenure and academic freedom. I then turn to a discussion of the problems some critics have with tenure and outline the solutions they have suggested. I conclude by offering suggestions about what colleges and universities might do should they desire to increase the presence of faculty of color and women faculty in the academy and improve faculty work and productivity in general. As will become clear, I will argue that tenure forms the framework for basic faculty protections; within such a framework, vast leeway exists about the kinds of practices that might be developed to help increase the presence of diverse faculty in the academy.

## TENURE AND ACADEMIC FREEDOM

Tenure came about actually in part due to issues of race but not so much in a manner that many would approve of today. Stanford University's president, David Starr Jordan, hired Edward Ross, a young economics professor, in 1893. In many respects Dr. Ross mirrored the new wave of academics that increasingly populated academe at the turn of the century. He was a popular teacher, a noted researcher, and a public intellectual. President Jordan noted, "I do not know a man in this department in whose future I have more confidence. I think, of all the younger men in the country in this line of work, Dr. Ross is the most prominent. He shows himself entirely free from either political prejudices or the prejudices of books" (Elliott, 1937, p. 331). What Ross was not free of was racial prejudice.

As an economics professor and a socialist, Edward Ross looked on Asian immigration as a mistake. He was an advocate for workers, but he defined workers as white. He gave a series of speeches about how Chinese immigrants would pollute California's shores. "It would be better for us," he charged, "if we were to turn our guns upon every vessel bringing Japanese to our shores rather than to permit them to land" (Bromberg, 1996, p. 116). At another time he stated, "The Oriental can elbow the American to one side in the common occupations because he has fewer wants. . . . We are resolutely determined that California, this latest and loveliest seat of the Aryan race, shall not become, if we can help it, the theater of a stern wolfish struggle for existence" (*San Francisco Chronicle*, Nov. 15, 1900).

To be fair, he also championed other controversial causes, such as the free coinage of silver, the municipal ownership of public utilities, and the railway union strike of 1898. Many individuals had problems with his points of view. One of those individuals was Mrs. Leland Stanford, the benefactor and sole trustee of the university. Although she did not appreciate many of his viewpoints, his comments about Chinese immigrants were particularly repugnant. She thought such virulent racism was unbecoming of a professor at a university that bore her name and was an insult to the memory of her husband. "I am grieved to the depths of my heart," she wrote. "This movement is but a repetition of the old prejudice against the Chinese" (Bromberg, 1996, p. 116). By the fall of 1900 Mrs. Stanford demanded and received President Jordan's acquiescence; Ross was fired.

The removal of Ross sowed the seeds for a policy that ultimately became the idea of academic freedom and the structure known as tenure. Although in hindsight one would have chosen a more admirable example on which to base the case for tenure, one might also make the analogy to free speech in the larger society. The citizenry protects free speech of those with whom the broad majority often will disagree and find repugnant, whether it be the speech of the Ku Klux Klan advocating racial hatred, Howard Stern denigrating women, or Louis Farakahn excoriating gays and lesbians. However hurtful the speech may be, the courts have argued that ultimately society must find other ways to address hurtful speech than curtailing it.

The premises of academic freedom are similar. Academic freedom has become a core value in this century in American postsecondary education. Broadly stated, academic freedom pertains to the rights of the individual to study and teach whatever he or she desires without threat or sanction. In the well-worn words of the American Association of University Professors' statement of 1940: "Tenure is a means to a certain ends; specifically, (1) freedom of teaching and research and of extramural activities, and (2) a sufficient degree of economic security to make the profession attractive to men and women of ability. Freedom and economic security, hence tenure, are indispensable to the success of an institution in fulfilling its obligations to its students and to society" (AAUP, 1985, p. 143).

Ironically, when faculty are questioned about academic freedom today, the refrain is often that a Marxist should be able to teach Marxism without being fired, or that simply because someone studies feminist theory his or her career should not be derailed. However true such comments are, the roots of those ideas extend back to an individual who lost his job in large part because of his racism and promulgation of White superiority.

The import of academic freedom and tenure has been continually supported throughout much of this century. Indeed, the Supreme Court has written:

> The essentiality of freedom in the community of American universities is almost self-evident. . . . To impose any straightjacket upon the

intellectual leaders in our colleges and universities would imperil the
future of our nation. . . . Teachers and students must always remain
free to inquire, to study and to evaluate, to gain new maturity and
understanding; otherwise, our civilization will stagnate and die.
(*Sweezy v. New Hampshire*, 1957, p. 250)

One cannot emphasize enough the basic premises that the Supreme
Court has outlined here. The Supreme Court does not want a "strait-
jacket" on academics; to do so compromises the nation. Academic freedom helps keep society free. Without the professorate's freedom to
stretch boundaries and limits, society is at peril. Undoubtedly, some
individuals will never employ the principle of academic freedom
throughout their academic career; others such as Edward Ross will use
it in ways that one or another of us will disdain. Ultimately, however,
the principle of academic freedom has served as the essential totem for
the purpose of the academic enterprise in the twentieth century.

## TENURE'S PROBLEMS AND PROPOSED SOLUTIONS

### Problems

Critics of tenure have pointed out six problems that ostensibly exist
because of the faculty reward structure. First, colleges and universities are
currently experiencing fiscal problems. Some individuals argue that the
largest outflow of cash goes to personnel and that a system such as tenure
rigidifies positions. From this perspective tenure imposes an inflexible
financial burden upon institutions. One cannot move resources around to
more appropriate areas if they are committed until the individual retires or
leaves the institution. As Chait and Ford have commented, "To tenure a
classicist is to tenure classics" (1982, p. 6). At a time when businesses stress
the importance of flexibility, tenure appears to make change difficult.

Second, and perhaps the most prominent of the criticisms about
tenure, is the concern over "deadwood." Tenure presumably protects
unproductive faculty. An individual receives tenure, and there is nothing
an organization can do to remove the individual if he or she is no longer
productive. Accountability is impossible with a tenure system, argue the
critics. "The procedures for ridding the profession of misfits" note
Bowen and Schuster, "are so arduous and so embarrassing that few
administrators are willing to take the time of themselves and the faculty
to prosecute the case. The procedures take on the flavor of a trial for
murder" (1986, p. 243). Thus, if tenure were removed, then the problem of unproductive faculty would recede.

Third, tenure has made individuals risk-averse. Ironically, tenure
was supposed to create the conditions for experimentation, but appar-

ently it has done the opposite. Rather than create an atmosphere of innovation, tenure has created a system that stultifies creativity, while junior faculty rush to publish. Similarly, since most institutions are risk-averse, the individual who wishes to experiment will have less chance than those individuals who conduct more typical work because the university does not want to tenure someone who may never produce results.

Fourth, tenure devalues teaching. State legislators and other interested parties frequently see tenure as the main reason why faculty do not spend more time teaching. If tenure were removed or changed, then presumably a greater focus on student needs would be possible. It is true that in all kinds of institutions except community colleges, faculty are more rewarded for research than teaching (Fairweather, 1993). The assumption of the critics is that somehow tenure inevitably privileges those who do research, to the detriment of those who teach.

Fifth, tenure does not protect the untenured. The structure was created at a time when there were not so many nontenured, part-time and adjunct faculty. Those who do not have tenure have to conform to the whims of senior faculty. Although academic freedom was meant for everyone, tenure actually protects only those who have tenure. Thus, if the desire is to extend academic freedom, then tenure needs to be reconfigured.

Finally, academic freedom is no longer as important as it once was to some individuals. The assumption is that tenure might have been needed at the time of Edward Ross, but today such protections are no longer necessary. Individuals have other means, such as the courts, to protect their ideas and speech. Everyone also does not need tenure, claim the critics, because not everyone uses his or her academic freedom. That is, academic freedom may well apply for the faculty member in the humanities, but it seems unnecessary for the professor in engineering. If that is true, then the structure that was created to protect academic freedom—tenure—is unnecessary.

Thus, the critics arrive at the conclusion that tenure is no longer needed. As I have noted elsewhere, "The portrait that the critics draw is of an organization with a cumbersome structure that restricts institutional choice and ability to respond to the needs of the day" (Tierney, 1998a, p. 44). If tenure restricts organizational action, depresses individual creativity, and protects unproductive faculty, then why not change the system?

## Proposed Solutions

Given the problems that I have outlined, the critics have offered four solutions. The first proposal pertains to contracts. One might create long-term contracts that are renewable after a particular length of time, such as five or six years. The strength of this proposal is that it creates flexibility for the institution and enables the organization to get rid of unproductive faculty. If the institution decided that a particular area was no longer necessary, or another area was vital to the strategic plan of the institution, then presumably resources could be shifted and departments and programs could be downsized or closed.

A second solution concerns salary definition. Some have argued that tenure should be decoupled from one's salary. Rather than tenure being the equivalent of 100% of an individual's salary, an institution might substitute what economists call "x-y-z" funding. The "x" of the scenario is the base pay that the individual will always be paid; the "y" is what the individual is expected to bring in through external support such as grants, and the "z" is a bonus. The result is that the organization is no longer responsible for 100% of a tenured faculty's salary. For example, at Southern University in Louisiana, the administration cut the salary of seven professors by 25% when it changed the terms of their tenure contracts from 12 months to 9 months. The administration's argument was not that the faculty were poor performers but that the fiscal health of the university would be better off if tenure's fiscal parameters were rearranged (Tierney, 1998b). Again, the institution has greater fiscal flexibility, and there is greater accountability with regard to individual productivity.

Where tenure resides is a third possible solution. At most institutions tenure exists at the organizational level. Thus, if a unit or a branch campus is closed, the individual still has tenure somewhere else in the organization. If tenure were given closer to the unit in which an individual worked and the unit were closed, then the organization would not have to carry the burden of the tenured faculty member. The organization will have greater flexibility, and individuals will be more entrepreneurial.

Finally, there has been increased discussion about posttenure review. Some systems have adopted quite severe interpretations of posttenure review to the extent that if someone is judged negatively, he or she could conceivably lose tenure. Other systems think of posttenure review as a way to gauge faculty work and improve performance. The driving rationale for it is to increase productivity and ensure that deadwood have some form of accountability.

### Responses to the Proposals

There are immediate responses on the part of tenure's supporters to the criticisms and proposed solutions that individuals have put forward. There is no evidence, for example, that postsecondary organizations have any more deadwood than a business. If colleges and universities have as productive a group of individuals as a business, then the problem is not one of tenure with regard to deadwood; instead, the problem is a human resources issue.

Similarly, although not every individual with tenure will stretch the limits of experimentation, one can also look at the preeminence of American universities with regard to scientific breakthroughs throughout this century. One ought not suggest that tenure precludes innovation, argue some, when the evidence exists that some of the century's major changes were discovered by professors with tenure.

A standard response of the AAUP about tenure's protection of the untenured is that those who have tenure have a moral responsibility to ensure that the climate exists for all faculty to be protected. Further, many cases still exist today where someone's academic freedom has been threatened. Tenure is needed in order to maintain academic freedom; simply because every individual will not call upon academic freedom during his or her career does not mean that tenure should be abolished. An analogy might be that many citizens will not test the limits of free speech, but no one suggests that we should get rid of the First Amendment.

Further, none of the suggestions that have been proposed to alter tenure in any way offer similar or greater protections to academic freedom. Contracts essentially void the import of academic freedom; to speak of tenure without economic security makes a mockery of the idea of tenure. What is tenure if it is not some form of job security? If posttenure review means that tenure can be voided, then whither academic freedom?

## USING TENURE'S FRAMEWORK TO INCREASE MINORITY AND WOMEN FACULTY

As I noted at the outset of this chapter, there are those who might suspect that these recent criticisms of tenure have come about because more women and people of color are populating tenure-track positions. Of course, one would be hard pressed to describe the increase of diversity in academe as a tidal wave or an onslaught that necessitates the wholesale elimination of tenure. Colleges and universities have a long way to go before equity is reached in tenure-track positions.

Moreover, the criticisms of tenure that I have outlined here are not new. Similar discussions took place in 1973 (Commission on Academic Tenure) where criticisms and solutions appeared that are not particularly different from what one hears today. At my own institution, for example, the University of Southern California, an administration-sponsored committee was formed in 1972 to review alternatives to tenure. The final report, states James McBath, "contemplated serious inroads in the tenure system through fixed-term renewable contracts" (1992, p. 18). One can find similar critics and criticisms in the 1960s, as well as calls for the elimination of tenure in the 1950s because it protected "Communists" during the McCarthy era. Thus, tenure has vexed particular individuals almost since its very inception.

To be sure, there is no magic bullet that one might use to fix the problems that exist with tenure codes or to increase women and minority faculty in the academy overnight. However, from previous work I have done (Tierney and Bensimon, 1996; Tierney, 1999a), there are at least four issues one might consider with regard to retaining minority and women faculty. Assuming that tenure will remain, the following topics need to be addressed more forthrightly.

## Graduate Student Socialization

If one assumes that colleges and universities function as organizational cultures, then of necessity ideas pertaining to socialization need to be taken into account more seriously than they have in the past. Some of the problems that women and people of color face relate to anticipatory socialization (Tierney and Rhoads, 1993; Turner and Thompson, 1993; Antony and Taylor, forthcoming). Anticipatory socialization pertains to how nonmembers take on the attitudes, actions, and values of the group to which they aspire.

Graduate training is where students begin to acquire the values, norms, attitudes, and beliefs associated with their discipline and the profession at large. For aspiring faculty, graduate training serves as a significant force in socializing students into the roles and expectations associated with faculty life. Such a task is particularly important with students of color and women (Clark & Corcoran, 1986; Turner & Thompson, 1993), and the work of socializing such students ought not always fall on the shoulders of minority and women faculty.

Further, anticipatory socialization for female and minority students—indeed, with all students—does not begin in graduate school. The undergraduate years also serve to introduce individuals to the prospective roles and expectations of various professions. However, women faculty and faculty of color report that they were less often encouraged as undergraduates to pursue graduate work (Olsen, 1991). Blackwell noted that one-third of all doctoral students receive assistantships, but only one-fifth of minority doctoral students receive such positions (1984). Thus, one concrete step is to concentrate on those who are potential scholars.

*Cleaning up the Tenure Process and Mentoring*

There are two significant ways to increase the pool of tenure-track women and minority faculty. One route is to increase the pool in a manner suggested above. The second route is to maintain those scholars who are already in the pool. That is, one needs to create a process that enables faculty of color and women faculty who are on the tenure track to succeed, gain tenure, and be promoted to full professor.

In order to improve the chances of women and minority faculty succeeding, there are two overall tasks that need to take place. First, the mentoring process of junior faculty needs to be formalized and improved. In a study conducted at the University of Wisconsin, for example, support for faculty was reported as a major factor in attrition (Rausch et al., 1989). A key ingredient in the support system is mentoring. Few Black academicians benefit from a protégé-mentor relationship (Frierson, 1990). Only one in eight Black faculty members identify themselves with a mentor (Blackwell, 1988; Washington & Harvey, 1989). Thus, college and university leaders need to develop a better awareness of what mentoring is, how it is done, and what kind of formal and informal networks might be created that succeed in supporting assistant professors in general and assistant professors of diversity in particular.

The second key issue to tackle is cleaning up the tenure process. My previous research has highlighted how the tenure process is far too often a guessing game where individuals are unclear about what they need to do to gain tenure. To be sure, the conferral of tenure on an individual is an intellectual process that cannot be reduced to a system of bureaucratic points and numbers. I am not suggesting that an institution reduce its tenure guidelines to stating that if an individual writes "x" articles of "y" page length, then he or she will receive tenure. However, the mystery that currently clouds the tenure process can easily be changed and improved.

*Alternative Criteria within Sectors*

At present, a one-size-fits-all approach exists at traditional colleges and universities. That is, as I observed above, for all institutional types except community colleges, research is more valued and rewarded than other forms of academic work (Fairweather, 1993; Tierney & Bensimon, 1996; Tierney, 1999b). Although one certainly supports the idea that critical research is done by some individuals in some institutions, I suggest here that in the twenty-first century, we need a more robust approach to academic work.

If the twentieth century was one where sector assimilation took place, then the next century ought to be one where sector differentiation occurs. The key point here is to ensure that the multifaceted tasks that occur in an organization are equally honored and recognized. One ought not call on, for example, some faculty to engage in community-based projects if that means they will not be recompensed in a manner akin to their counterparts who conduct research. However, society needs faculty to undertake a multitude of tasks, rather than merely emphasizing one to the exclusion of others.

Such a suggestion implies that different systems will develop different criteria for rewarding faculty work rather than moving toward similar statements about what it takes to get tenure. Indeed, not every individual may need to be on the tenure track. As I pointed out earlier, tenure is inextricably related to academic freedom. If tenure is merely a means to job security, then it loses its purpose and meaning and is nothing more than a sinecure for intellectuals. Thus, if tenure is related to academic freedom, institutions need to question actively rather than passively if the positions that they hire individuals for are ones where tenure-track positions should be awarded. There are probably some positions that are better defined as *fixed term*. My main concern is that such decisions are made in a forthright, conscious manner, rather than the way they appear to be done now, where tenure-track positions evaporate one by one as an administrator tries to balance his or her budget by reduction.

## Performance Contracts

If the faculty are to safeguard academic freedom, then until a better system comes along, tenure must remain. However, it is also the obligation of the faculty to accept responsibility for dealing with the issues raised by critics of tenure. Some individuals do undertake research to the detriment of their teaching. Some faculty do achieve tenure and then become unproductive. Such problems, however, do not of necessity suggest that tenure must be eliminated.

Instead, on-going forms of assessment need to be created where faculty and administrative leaders (e.g., department chairs and deans) are able to engage in annual discussions about one's performance over the past year and what one hopes to accomplish over the next one. Yearly, formalized dialogues with one's colleagues enable an academic community to create communal contracts with one another that deepen, rather than lessen, individual obligation and responsiveness. I by no means intend to suggest that such dialogues will be easy or without conflict. Indeed, the kind of discussions that need to take place undoubtedly suggest the importance of training for department chairs and deans about how to engage in such interactions. And yet, however difficult such conversations may be, they are imperative if academe is to reform itself to meet the challenges of the twenty-first century.

## CONCLUSION

The academic world is undergoing vast changes. Although I do not subscribe to a "great man" theory of organizational change, I also reject the assumption that colleges and universities are little more than organized anarchies buffeted and swayed by external forces. To be sure, if there is no collective will, if shared governance is a myth rather than a reality, then academe will be directed by external forces. What I have suggested here, however, are points to consider that enable colleges and universities to develop unique missions that help provide the culture, structure, and reward system for faculty in general and faculty of color and women faculty in particular to flourish. If we are able to enact such cultures, structures, and reward systems, then we are providing faculty with the possibility of helping create a more diverse, equitable, and productive society.

## REFERENCES

American Association of University Professors. (1985). Academic freedom and tenure: Statement of principles, 1940. In M. Finkelstein (Ed.), *ASHE Reader on Faculty and Faculty Issues in Colleges and Universities*. Lexington, MA: Ginn Press, 143–45.

Antony, J., & E. Taylor. (2001). Graduate student socialization and its implications for the recruitment of African American education faculty. In W. G. Tierney (Ed.), *Faculty Work in Schools of Education*. Albany: State University of New York Press, 189–210.

Blackwell, J. (1984). *Increasing access and retention of minority students in graduate and professional schools*. Paper presented at Educational Testing Service's Invitational Conference on Educational Standards, NY.

Blackwell, J. (1988). Faculty issues: Impacts on Minorities. *The Review of Higher Education* 11(4), 417–34.

Bowen, H., & J. Schuster. (1986). *American professors: A national resource imperiled*. Oxford, England: Oxford University Press.

Bromberg, H. (March/April, 1996). Revising history. *Stanford*, 116.

Chait, R., & A. Ford. (1982). *Beyond traditional tenure*. San Francisco: Jossey-Bass.

Clark, S. M., & Corcoran, M. (1986). Perspectives on the professional socialization of women faculty: A case of accumulative disadvantage? *Journal of Higher Education* 57(1), 20–43.

Commission on Academic Tenure in Higher Education. (1973). *Faculty Tenure*. San Francisco: Jossey-Bass.

Elliott, O. (1937). *Stanford University: The first twenty-five years.* Stanford: Stanford University Press.

Fairweather, J. (1993). Academic values and faculty rewards. *The Review of Higher Education.* 17(1), 43–68.

Frierson, H. 1990. The situation of black educational researchers: Continuation of a crisis. *Educational Researcher* 19(2), 12–17.

McBath, J. 1992. Salute to an economist in faculty governance. *International Journal of Social Economics* 19(7), 15–23.

Olsen, D. 1991. Gender and racial differences among a research university faculty: Recommendations for promoting diversity. *To Improve the Academy* 10, 123–39.

Rausch, D. et al. 1989. The academic revolving door: Why do women get caught? *CUPA Journal* 40(1), 1–15.

San Francisco Chronicle. (November 15, 1900). *The Address That Caused the Trouble,* 1. Sweezy v. New Hampshire, 354 U.S. 234, 77 S. Ct. 1203 (1957).

Tierney, W., & R. Rhoads. (1993). *Enhancing promotion, tenure and beyond: Faculty socialization as a cultural process.* ASHE-ERIC Higher Education Report No. 93–6. Washington, DC: George Washington University.

Tierney, W., & E. M. Bensimon. (1996). *Promotion and tenure: Community and socialization in academe.* Albany: State University of New York Press.

Tierney, W. (Ed). (1998a). *The responsive university: Restructuring for high performance.* Baltimore: Johns Hopkins University Press.

Tierney, W. (1998b). Tenure matters: Rethinking faculty roles and rewards. *American Behavioral Scientist* 41(5), 627–638.

Tierney, W. (Ed). (1999a). *Faculty productivity: Facts, fictions and issues.* New York: Garland.

Tierney, W. (1999b). *Building the responsive campus: Creating high performance colleges and universities.* Thousand Oaks, CA: Sage.

Tierney, W. Forthcoming. *Faculty of education in a period of systemic reform.*

Turner, C., & J. Thompson. (1993). Socializing women doctoral students: Minority and majority experiences. *The Review of Higher Education* (16)3, 355–70.

Washington, V., & Harvey, W. (1989). *Affirmative rhetoric, negative action: African American and Hispanic faculty at predominately white institutions.* ASHE-ERIC Higher Education report 89–2. Washington, DC: George Washington University.

# PART II

# Faculty as Individual Learners: Sharing Personal Perspectives

While the larger institutional context dominates the previous section, this second section tells the stories of individuals who have negotiated the tenure process. It focuses on the individual adult learner, struggling to understand and cope with issues of age, race, gender, class, and sexual orientation within higher education today. These are the stories of women and minorities who have negotiated tenure and been successful. Yet they are often not without their bruises and certainly not without advice for others. The nature of the text in these chapters is more conversational and includes thick descriptions of individual experiences, which invite discussion among and between readers and authors. As with most stories, we learn to understand the perspective of others and have an opportunity to understand ourselves better by walking in their shoes. Chapter 5 by Joanne E. Cooper, Anna M. Ortiz, Maenette K. K. Benham, and Mary Woods Scherr is largely written as a dialogue among women who do not fit the typical academic profile. Our writers are Native Hawaiian, Latina, and midlife women. The conversations tell their stories and provide insights about creating a home in the academy. In chapter 6, Michelle Collay tells the stories of women who are balancing work and family as they climb the academic ladder. In chapter 7, Janice Koch, and chapter eight, Barbara K. Curry, share particular issues that they faced: coping with the fear of fraudulence and becoming a self-advocate. In chapter 9, Patricia M. McDonough addresses the personal issue of being a lesbian in the academy and shares her advice and insights from her current position as department chair.

These personal narratives were chosen because narrative knowledge, it has been argued (see Polkinghorne, 1988), is more than mere emotive expression; it is a legitimate form of reasoned knowing. This type of knowing "captures in a special fashion the richness and the nuances of meaning in human affairs" (Carter, 1992, p. 6). This section of the book relates the personal stories of diverse women and minority faculty because we believe that the narrative mode carries a multiplicity of meanings, which accommodate ambiguity and dilemma as central features or themes. They help construct our personal identities and reveal life changes, enabling us "to organize, articulate, and communicate what we believe . . . and to reveal, in narrative style, what we have become as educators" (Jalongo, 1992). Thus, through narrative or story, the authors in this text share the complexities of their own personal stories in ways that can frame the foundation, collect the wisdom, and shape present and future knowledge of the tenure process in higher education.

Additionally, there is a growing body of literature that supports story as an essential component of understanding how educators think (Pagano, 1990; McEwan & Egan, 1995; Jalongo & Isenberg, 1995; Carter, 1992). In part, it is through stories that we, the authors and the women and minority faculty whose stories are present in this book, have been able to navigate our own discoveries regarding professional and personal identity, as well as look to balance the paradoxes of living both on the margin and at the center.

## REFERENCES

Carter, K. (1992). The place of story in research on teaching. *Educational Researcher* 22, (1), 5–12.

Jalongo, M. R. (1992). Teachers' stories: Our ways of knowing. *Educational Leadership* 49(7), 68–73.

Jalongo, M. R., & Isenberg, J. P. (1995). *Teachers' stories: From personal narrative to professional insight.* San Francisco: Jossey-Bass.

McEwan, H., & Egan, K. (Eds.) (1995). *Narrative in teaching, learning and research.* New York: Teachers College Press.

Pagano, J. (1990). *Exiles and communities: Teaching in the patriarchal wilderness.* Albany: State University of New York Press.

Polkinghorne, D. (1988). *Narrative knowing and the human sciences.* New York: State University of New York Press.

CHAPTER 5

# Finding a Home in the Academy: Confronting Racism and Ageism

## Joanne E. Cooper, Anna M. Ortiz, Maenette K. P. Benham, and Mary Woods Scherr

For several years now we have been contemplating the meaning of trying to find a home the academy (Cooper et al., 1999; Cooper, Benham, & Martinez-Aleman, 1997). Questions emerge about the wisdom of trying to find a home in the workplace (can you even build a home at work?) and about the fraught meaning of the term *home . . . homemakers*, women who have been spending their adult lives trying to escape the nightmare that was their childhood home, and so on. In discussing this concept, many women academics talk about finding or forging, if not a home, then "welcome ground." One friend said she thinks of her campus as her "neighborhood." Whatever the term, the connotation is one of a place that is friendly, rather than hostile, one that counters the chilly climate image about which Sandler and Hall (1993) have written.

Harris (1996) talks about home as both a political and a biblical image, political for those in exile who are finally able to return to their homelands, and biblical in the stories of Ruth, Naomi, and Jesus. She describes home also as "an extraordinarily personal image, full of power and feeling" (1996, p. 58). It is a place where we learn to care and be cared for, a place where loneliness can be relieved through community, a place for love making and people making. While love making is not something commonly found in the halls of academe, people-making could certainly be legitimately described as a central function of educational institutions. In fact, the early idea that colleges functioned *in loco parentis*, in the place of parents, extends the idea that they carry on the making of educated citizens, begun in the home. Finally, there is the idea of coming home to oneself, an idea Scherr explores in her conclusion that she is now more at home in the academy because she is more at home with herself (Cooper et al.,1999).

Benham, in our earlier work (Cooper et al., 1999), whose work has taken her far from her homeland, Hawaii, talks about carrying her home with her, turtlelike, as she moves through differing climates and cultures. Harris (1996), too, shares this thought, quoting the diary of Etty Hillesum, a young Jewish woman who lived in Amsterdam and died in Auschwitz in 1943. In the last two years of her life, Hillesum (1983, p. 176) learned this about finding a home, " We *are* at home. Under the sky. In every place on earth, if only we can carry everything within us. We must be our own country."

Granted, it is possible, perhaps even advisable, that we carry our homes with us, that we "be our own country." However, our job as academics, in forging welcome ground not only for ourselves but also for those who come after us, is to create a more welcoming environment in the academy. In considering the journeys of doctoral students, those who make up the future professorate, Nyquist and colleagues (1999) have underscored our responsibility to reform higher education in ways that create a place that future academics might consider making their professional home. They ask, "As universities and colleges face rapidly changing external contexts, demanding competition, and high expectations from students and the broader public, are we willing to let some of the best and brightest of our graduate students slip quietly off to other occupations?" (p. 27). We would add that not only graduate students but also the best and brightest of junior faculty may be leaving the profession because we cannot find a way to make the tenure system more welcoming, developmental, collegial, and supportive of the work they want to do. The problems with the culture of institutions in higher education have been documented by men as well as women, White faculty, as well as faculty of color. Concerns about the lack of collegiality (the ability to all "get along") and faculty isolation and fragmentation have been discussed for years (Bennett, 1991; Massy, Wilger, & Colbeck, 1994). Women and minority faculty thus face a double layer of complex and interconnected conditions that create a chilly climate for them. First is the lack of collegiality in higher education, with its accompanying sense of isolation and fragmentation. Second are the forces of racism, sexism, ageism, and homophobia that add considerably to the burdens women and minority faculty face. The thoughts that follow address some of these issues, outlining the forces that still pervade the halls of academe, the responses to these forces, as well as the efforts of diverse women and men not only to survive but to thrive in higher education today.

First we hear from Maenette and Anna. Maenette is a newly tenured professor in educational administration (focus in K–12 educational leadership). She taught in K–12 schools for 15 years and has been a member of the academic academy for 6 years. Anna is in her third year as an assistant professor in educational administration (focus in higher education and student affairs). She has held positions in higher education administration and has done extensive work in the area of cultural identity among college students.

Using their own faculty experiences as a case study, they examine the politics of race/ethnicity, gender, and culture identity in the academic grove.

## THE DIALOGUE

MAENETTE. I am Brown woman! I'm pretty clear about this. When I was growing up, I think it was when I turned 13 or 14, I remember attempting to mask the features of my skin color with makeup, hair color with dye, and eye color with blue mascara—all to disguise my nativeness. I yearned to be more like my light-skinned classmates because they seemed to get all the attention and the "boys!" I looked like a caricature out of a Dorothy Lamour movie fitting every stereotype of an exotic Native Hawaiian girl. This camouflaging experience has taught me several lessons: masking the features considered by the mainstream as loathsome breeds self-hate; masking the inner self denies the rich consciousness of history, lineage, and the multiplicity of self; masking color and gender silences the divisive and bifurcated perceptions of identity that are based on overgeneralizations; and the act of masking by people (especially women) of color allows for color blindness and politeness.

ANNA. When I was growing up I never had the experience of being told or understanding that being Mexican was a bad thing. My friends and I were very aware of our ethnic heritages, and we would frequently make derogatory remarks toward each other about them, but it was definitely equal access hazing. When I went to college I began to learn what it felt like to be different in a way that others either didn't value or overvalued in some way. I became the diverse other that was sought after for student leadership positions, at the same time I discovered that being White, affluent, with the correct cultural capital was the way to be. That being so, I embarked on a voyage, not to change the way I looked, like you Maenette, but to acquire the cultural capital I thought necessary to fit in with my White peers and their communities. So my college years were filled with learning more about Western civilization, its history, its music, its art, and ultimately, its values. In the framework of the ethnic identity models that inform my research, I experienced a reverse process of resocialization. I didn't resocialize myself toward a positive ethnic identity as a Mexican American, I was educating myself on what was most prized in American society. Ironically, my K–12 education educated me quite nicely on the history of diverse others, especially Native

Americans and Latino/as, but seriously left a gap in what I knew about things Western. My rural high school didn't seem to value the traditional high school curriculum that my college classmates received.

MAENETTE. What appears to be an interesting difference between our experiences, Anna, is that because of the "Americanization" that Native Hawaiians have experienced for over 100 years, we have had to relearn, that is, reach back into our memories and sit at the feet of elders to understand the *mana'o* (the power and meaning) of Hawaii. We've had to resocialize. Learning to "mask," as I mentioned earlier, had become so ingrained into our daily lives. I never understood, until recently, that "masking" is an element of the hegemony of the master narrative that both privileges and oppresses. For example, in Hawaii we tell many "ethnic," often derogatory, jokes that serve to oppress the "other" (the Hawaiian, the Samoan, the Portuguese, the Filipino, and so forth). In most of the jokes, the "White" person is always smarter while the "other" becomes the brunt of the joke. Yet, in Hawaii, you'll hear the rhetoric of diversity, that is, pride in being the "rainbow" state where everyone gets along and there is no racism. This attitude, I believe, has allowed for the thinking that because skin-color/ethnicity is not mentioned as an issue, we are color blind, and therefore, we are enlightened. I don't see it that way.

ANNA. Maenette, I'm struck by the persuasiveness of colored blindness as an enlightened view of how higher education and society [think] about race and ethnicity. The recent reversals of affirmative action policies in our "enlightened" states on the West Coast help to institutionalize color blindness as a higher form of thinking and being. My experiences in the academy tell me that it is a compliment for another to see me with color blind eyes. To be judged as excellent without considering my ethnic heritage is quite a coup in higher education. What this does, though, is announce to me that diverse others are routinely judged as being "good . . . for a Chicana" and that in the eyes of the majority, others are always judged through the sieve of affirmative action. Fortunately, for me, these experiences were relatively infrequent occurrences as I became educated in universities. When I was a student I had very positive experiences, strong role models, women who believed in my abilities and potential. I call these women my "academic mothers," my "womantors." With their guidance and support I felt nurtured, safe, and secure. It was as if they were shielding me from the nasty ugliness of color blindness and other acts of discrimination.

MAENETTE. Your "womantors," Anna, appear to have the insight of acknowledging and mentoring you as a woman, a higher education scholar, a Chicana, a critical thinker, an administrator, a teacher and adviser, a friend, a daughter, a sister, a colleague and peer, and so on. This action says to me that there are caring people in academe who value the richness and depth of what an individual brings to the academy. Unfortunately, for many of our colleagues across the United States, the politics of identity, within the academy, is a divisive and bifurcated road. The symbols and rituals of the institution continue to define a woman (or a man) who is different because of a combination of race/ethnicity, age, gender, sexuality, class, disability, and so on as a caricature that reflects a single element of color or gender or discipline or whatever. This accounts for your "good . . . for a Chicana" observation. Being an overgeneralized caricature dismisses us from our skin down to our soul.

I see this dismissal in the suppression of issues of difference and diversity in our educational courses. I'm not talking about your classes or mine, as I believe difference and diversity sit at the core of what we do, but I am implicating graduate courses in education in general. To not address difference, for example being color blind, is to say to people of color that their contributions and who they are [are] not recognized, therefore, defined as a deficit in academe. It also, I believe, stigmatizes the White student. That is, because they are not challenged to look beyond themselves or the boundaries of the institution, they are deprived of the opportunity to critically analyze institutional tensions and to confront (both personally and professionally) injustices.

This is a long way of saying that I believe the "grove" in the academy is sometimes too shaded, a place where we have become too relaxed and indifferent. To be color blind results in mythologizing difference, which is plainly social ignorance. We, as faculty of the academy, must model what your womantors exemplified in more explicit and sustainable ways.

ANNA. Maenette, what you say about the shady grove in academe is so relevant! When I think of a shady grove, I too think of ease and comfort almost to the point of being lazy (after all, who doesn't enjoy a nap in the shady grove?). And when I think of most classrooms, graduate classrooms being just as guilty or even guiltier than undergraduate classrooms, I see the same laziness about the issues. There is a sense of ease that comes from ignoring rather than confronting difficult issues. Comfort is afforded the majority students in the class when their provincial views are not contested. Students of color "nap" just so they can get through another lecture or class discussion that discounts and minimizes their experiences.

You were right in saying that our teaching is different, that our core beliefs, communities, ethics, and personal values do not allow us to facilitate the norm. However, I believe that we and others like us (especially the untenured, the "color"ed, and the gendered) risk harm to our professionals selves in doing so. When I step before my classes, I am acutely aware that my students see me as a woman, a minority, and too young to be a professor. My struggle to establish credibility with them is an uphill battle no matter what the topic. However, when I first approach issues of difference or inequality, I see my credibility as a target at the end of the firing range. The more and more I push students, the less credible I become. I am soon judged to "favor" the students of color. White students (men especially) think any grade other than a 4.0 is a reflection of their color and gender rather than the quality of their work. When I give honest feedback about a student needing to work on his or her tolerance for diversity, I am threatened with a trip to the ombudsperson. My student evaluations also reflect these judgments. They are often "littered" with comments about the overly politicized nature of the class.

In defense of my teaching ability, even the most critical students eventually come around and see the value of learning in an authentic environment, but the weeks or months that pass between these points in time are ones of intense anxiety for me because I am untenured. I am worried that uneven teaching evaluations will become focal if there should be a senior colleague or a member of the tenure committee who does not like or agree with my line of research. Again, Maenette, you and I are more fortunate than most of our colleagues across the nation. You earned tenure this year with high accolades from our colleagues. We are in a college that values the very unique type of work we do. But there are countless faculty of color who have to sensor what they teach, what/who they challenge, and what they research. The shady grove is a very dark one for these faculty.

MAENETTE. What has complicated my life tremendously is geography. I have lived and worked in California, Texas, Washington State, Hawaii, and Michigan. To better understand the educational dilemmas that each community had to address, I have had to learn how to communicate, especially how to listen, to parents, community leaders, and school leaders. As a preK–12 school educator and administrator, knowing the cultural and political dynamics of the community that I served was essential to doing my job effectively and fairly. Although I had not been "socialized" to the world of postsecondary education, I felt that my rich history in K–12 education would help me take on almost any challenge. I believed that regardless of the context of the situation, I could "Kulia e loa'a ka na'auao strive to obtain wisdom."

I, too, found that the shady grove can be dark. I entered the world of academe, but not in the traditional way. I was hired, at no risk to the faculty, as a visiting minority assistant professor. I was the only woman and the only person of color who was full-time faculty in a K–12 educational administration unit. My first two semesters, as a visiting professor, found me sitting in on "antler scraping" meetings during which my invisibility created much pain in my soul. My passion, as a citizen of the academy, was to create a space for transformational learning and leadership, a place where men and women could gather to challenge and resolve tough school issues, a home where both student and professor might seek the spirit. What I observed were tensions between the individual commitments of faculty members and the work to create community that sought social transformation. I also observed my own madness in the cacophony of academic noise. This was like a Jack and the Beanstalk experience. That is, I was looking down on the terrain but could not move for fear of falling. I found myself shifting between the woman of color, the Hawaiian woman consciousness and the predominate White consciousness of the institution. I felt both privileged and oppressed at the same time!

In short, being a visiting professor means that there are certain bargains that one makes all in search of the tenure-stream position. It's not that

I behaved or made decisions that maintained policies and procedures that were unfair, but it's that I didn't speak out against them. Ah, Anna, this is what hurt the most! Oh, the feeling of betrayal, of being the oppressor and the oppressed at the same time. What madness! I almost quit. I remember that day vividly. I shared with a senior colleague, who I believed at the time was the only male colleague I could trust, how broken my spirit was. He began by berating me for my silence and fear, which had created a mask that shielded my soul. He asked me who I was. I remember being quite angry with him, but I responded by saying, "I am Hawaiian." You know, that one statement made all the difference in the world. Being Hawaiian means that you "live aloha." I don't mean this in a superficial way. Our elders teach that coming to a situation with aloha, of giving and loving and embracing the breath of life, opens the heart and soothes the mind.

Shortly thereafter, I won a tenure-line position. After working hard to be invisible to survive, I recommitted myself, with the support of key senior colleagues, mentors, and womantors, to live my passion. I took on a great deal of responsibility, and I struck a bargain. I would be the workhorse, and in exchange I would get the support I needed to teach and do the scholarly work that I believed was important. The downside of this, as a junior faculty member, is that I have worked extremely hard—much harder than I perceive that some White men and women in junior faculty positions work or have worked—to be of service to my colleagues and to my students. I have risked tenure by taking on students (who happen to be of color) that other faculty want no part of. I have taken on increasing amounts of administrative work, which cuts into my writing work, thereby jeopardizing my chances of tenure. And, like you, I have taken unpopular positions in classes (and in faculty meetings). I appreciate your sharing of fear in regards to student comments and the possibility of senior faculty *not* valuing your perspective. Yes, we're always looking and analyzing 360 degrees around ourselves, aren't we?

Anna, it seems that many women of color experience this invisibility and masking (an injurious craziness) early on in their professional careers, and perhaps throughout their professional lives. I think we are just beginning to learn how to navigate this terrain, how to locate our womantors and mentors, and how to come to our voice, which is not a gesture of resistance but is really an affirmation of who we are and the lives we live.

ANNA. Maenette, your passage makes me wonder about the bargains I have struck since I began my work in the professorate. Having just finished my second year, I doubt I have the full benefit of reflection and time to judge just how precisely my spirit has been compromised. I have made little bargains along the way to get to teach the courses which are important to me, and I bargain for favored assistantships and scholarships for students of color. But I think my loss of voice is the hardest bargain I have struck, and I think it is one that benefits most of my colleagues. I frequently feel as if I can only push my colleagues so far on issues of diversity and equity. I fear that by exposing acts and unwritten policies as having racial bias I risk my favored status among my faculty. I give up the privilege of my skin color; that I am a "good" person of color is an asset to my faculty. I have gone out on the limb a couple of times, but it has been lonely out there! And I must admit that I did not spend a long time there. I have also been rebuffed by colleagues that expect me to take others to task for their biased points of view. Those colleagues undoubtedly forget what it is like to be an untenured professor. The ultimate bargain I strike is this loss of voice. If I remain silent and polite, I get to do the kind of research I want to do, and if I do enough of it, I get tenure. I so often envy the voice you now get to use since you were awarded tenure. I think, Look out now guys, you're gonna get it, and can't wait until, I too, can wrestle up controversy in those faculty meetings.

I think we were supposed to write about creating or finding a home in the academy. I think we have spent a good amount of text relating the ways in which the academy is not a homelike environment for us, but I do think we have each found a home here. I remember in a conversation we had recently we decided that achieving tenure institutionalizes our home in the academy, because home really resides in us as internal phenomena. Home is created and maintained inside each of us. When tenure is earned, we as faculty experience the academic freedom that allows us to be true to our cultural histories, the liberation of our communities, and the integrity of ourselves. As a pretenured faculty member (and through my other roles in the academy), I have found a home with the support of others. Womantors and academic mothers have taken care of my "soul" by guiding me, running interference when necessary, and by giving me the space to enact home in small, more intimate circles. Even with that support I know that my home is temporary, that there are still house rules under which I must abide. Violation of those rules puts my home in jeopardy.

Maenette, I wonder if you now feel closer to home? One of our colleagues recently said that her road to tenure was so filled with compromise that once she achieved tenure she found that she had lost the sense of who she really was; she had forgotten the reasons she wanted to do this work. Has it been the same for you?

MAENETTE. Anna, using *home* as a descriptive term to describe the academy has been somewhat problematic for me, as you well know. It is a troublesome analogy if we see home as a "bounded place" where particular events and processes occur (e.g., nurturing). My home in Hawaii has not always been nurturing. As I shared earlier, I suffered the consequences of stereotyping, and recently, because of the privilege of education, I have slowly become disconnected, both voluntarily and involuntarily, from family and friends. What is home then, is not a place, but more a spirit space that for me is grounded in the values of Hawaiiana, for example, in aloha (*alo* meaning "to embrace" and *ha* meaning the "breath of life," so, to embrace life). So, with tenure do I feel more at home in the academy?

Well, I feel very much at home with my spirit. This is not attributed to my recent tenure, but with age and time. Being a citizen of the academy (from the day I started in January of 1993) is just a small part of my life journey. So, given my perspective and my growing knowledge of my spirit, I am at home. The question for me has always been this: How can I come from the core of my home, my spirit to engage in and across institutions that might have different values and beliefs from my own?

I've been successful in the academy, because like you, Anna, I have made bargains along the way. I have reserved or silenced myself to be polite. Because I have been pragmatic, I have survived. I have also, and you might want to consider this too, been silent in order to heal. Silence for contemplation and reflection is extremely important and leads, I believe, to compassion (you know, I've heard it said that silence can be loud). So listen to the silence. In exchange for the bargains, I have been rewarded with increasing authority and power and have wiggled my way into a place where I can more effectively be a voice of reason and change. I mourn the fact that untenured professors have to "self-edit," and I want to work to reclaim the conversation for all of us.

Anna, I think we need to remember that we are changing the language and the culture of this institution, you, me, and our many colleagues of different race/ethnicities, sexuality, national origin, mother tongue, and so forth. We need to teach both the veterans and the neophytes in this institution that getting a "terminal degree" (the Ph.D. or Ed.D.)—which by the way is so "death" oriented—is only the beginning of (a birthing really) an important journey. Higher education is in a space in time during which great change will need to occur to ensure the institution's viability. In our little corner, educational leadership, new voices are emerging, and new knowledge is being valued. So how do you see your home in the academy, Anna?

ANNA. I very clearly see my home in the academy from a perspective much larger than the institution in which I currently work. I feel connected, grounded, and surrounded by care when I consider higher education as professional field and discipline—the "academy." I define home as a place (within) where I feel comforted, safe, and valued. Home for me is a network, not so much a place, of womantors, academic mothers, supportive colleagues, and mentors, too. I so much value the network of academicians and practitioners who have supported me on every step of my journey. These are the folks that always think I'm brilliant and doing important work when I'm in the depths of feeling a fraud. They nurture my soul and being because they know *me*, not the silent or polite untenured faculty member working hard to survive.

One of my favorite womantors and dissertation chair was at a recent conference where I was presenting with one of my students. Although she had a very tight schedule, one not in her control, she managed to break away to attend my session. When she arrived (early) she immediately came to the front to meet my student, at which time she said with the widest of grins, "See what we have here is another generation; there is me, there is Anna, and now there is you!" Connectedness is critical to my home in the academy, and my womantor very directly brought those connections to life. I am awed at the miracle of academic mothers. I do see how early, ground-breaking women in the academy have cleared the way for those to come. I see how actively they support their students, when they are in their immediate care and beyond.

See Maenette, it is through this connectedness that I see the greatest potential in changing the academy and empowering individuals. We select, nurture, and challenge the students who have different voices, whose presence needs to be felt and heard in the academy. We create a legacy not only through our own work, but through the work of these students who become agents of change. Our message and spirit passes to others through them. It is a great feeling to be a part of something so vibrant, so "aloha." My institutional home has the trappings of home—a place where both good and bad happen. But my home in the academy stretches across miles, connecting those who are in community with my spirit. In this home I accept all of the benefits but very few of the liabilities. One of the most important benefits is knowing that when I feel most alone, I am not. For an extroverted person like me, this is truly a gift. Networking is something that is so twisted as a concept. The word conjures up images of "glad handers" working a crowd for his or her own personal benefit, thus bastardizing one of the critical tools faculty of color need to survive in the academy. There are few places in the academy where we are in community with others like us in our departments or colleges. We need those external connections so that we don't experience the craziness that you spoke about earlier in this piece.

Isolating faculty of color or women serves to diminish our impact in the academy. Through our networks, we can work to combat such a divisive way of life.

MAENETTE. Anna, I believe you and I have hit upon many important themes, and I am hopeful that others will find meaning in our dialogue that will help them to sustain and strengthen their spirit and their connections with others. We talked about the patterns of domination that exist for untenured faculty of color, for example, contested curriculum and content, instructional methods, relationships and communication styles, and the complicated and multiple issues of voice. I think we have recognized the power of our own intellectual process, that is, to define truths that can be applied to social and cultural constructs to increase insight and meaning. And we have acknowledged our inclusive networks, which is home, that includes the support of family/kin relations, kindred friends, academic mothers (womantors and mentors), colleagues and peers, and our students. The lessons learned are many and varied, but I see that we both have a consciousness of self and a strength of spirit that grounds our commitments to the work that we do as women, as scholars, as teachers, as eldest daughters, as women of color, and as citizens of the academy. I believe that if we can sustain our soul through our family and friends, and if we continue to strengthen our networks, our voice of compassion, inclusivity, team building, ownership, and justice will always have a home.

This second dialogue, between 2 tenured professors, 1 in her sixties and 1 in her fifties, addresses the issue of ageism in the academy. Mary taught English in high school for 7 years and then part time in a community college for over 15 years. For 10 of those years she served as a school board member in a unified school district. When her youngest daughter was a senior in high school, she enrolled in a doctoral program. Joanne was a speech therapist in the public schools; she was a faculty member and a department chair in a community college; and she has been a higher education faculty member in a large public research university for 10 years now.

JOANNE. As I recall, Mary, you told me you were 52 when you finished your doctorate and then began a tenure-track position 5 years later.

MARY. That's right. I worried that I wouldn't get a job at my age, and then when I did, I worried that I wouldn't get tenure.

JOANNE. Although I was 12 years younger, I can relate to some of the fears you describe, Mary. I worried that if I didn't hurry up and find a job, I would be too old to be considered a viable candidate. To my delight, after I was hired, my department chair, who was a vigorous and energetic 64-year-old, kept introducing me as one of the "young" new faculty members. It wasn't until one of my colleagues said, "Oh, so you'll be 50 when you get tenure, too?" that I began to realize that the rest of the world might not think of me as young and full of promise.

MARY. Shortly after becoming a professor and meeting with potential doctoral students, I realized how relative age can be. When a serious young woman earnestly asked, "Do you think I can manage the statistics course when I haven't had any math for over 10 years?" her strained expression prevented even the slightest smile on my part. I vividly recalled my own anxiety before the GRE test. I hadn't had a math course in 30 years. My own experience and the experiences of my doctoral students enable me to assure applicants that they aren't too old to succeed in a doctoral program. Universities talk about life-long learning, but some graduate schools do not admit older students and do not hire older professors. Older professors can demonstrate with their own lives that life-long learning means learning far beyond the ages of youth.

JOANNE. Yes, the irony in this prejudice is that we live and work in institutions that support life-long learning for their inhabitants. As the baby boomer generation hits retirement and turns to the nation's institutions of higher education to fulfill their dreams of learning new and exciting things they've always wanted to pursue, will we be ready for them? Will we welcome their talents and curiosity? Or will we simply operate on ancient stereotypes about the capacities of older adults to be active and productive students as well as professors? Unfortunately, I don't think most large, public research universities, such as the one I'm in, are centrally concerned about fostering the growth and development of either graduate students or new faculty. Most universities tend to valorize research and scholarship, often at the expense of attention to teaching and service. From my vantage point in a public research one institution, they are chiefly concerned with garnering more grant funding and improving their national reputation. Individual faculty then become focused on using their graduate students to advance their careers and reputations, rather than helping to nurture the next generation of new faculty. Older faculty, who have already built their careers, may then bring a much-needed concern for the growth and development of their graduate students and their junior colleagues. In addition, they model, through their own professional lives, the fact that they continue to learn and grow throughout their careers.

MARY. It seems that beginning professors often anticipate that after two to three years they'll become proficient, not realizing that after ten to twelve years many professors are still striving to become the professionals they want to be. Their concept of the professor's role evolves as the result of their own experience, ideas received from students, personal reflection and analysis, and studying the expanding body of research on how learning occurs—for adults as well as for children. As a result they realize the complexity of the teaching role: a challenge but also the source of intellectual stimulation, leading to a satisfying professional life.

JOANNE. I agree, Mary. I believe that in many ways, we teach what we most need to learn. I know I learn every time I teach. I learn more about the subject matter, more about my students, and more about myself. I believe that one of the great bonuses of teaching is the sense of self-development, of improving as one matures. If we are able to achieve some measure of maturity through the act of teaching/learning, then it would follow that we can be greater gifts to our students as we mature. Not that the young don't have something to offer, a sense of energy, enthusiasm, great hope, perhaps, but those on the other end of life's journey have gifts, too.

For me, one of the gifts of age comes from simply having taught successfully for 20 years now. I have a greater sense of confidence in my ability to make things go right in the classroom. I have done it over and over, and even though what happens in the classroom often seems like magic, it is a magic I can realistically hope for. It doesn't always happen, and there is often the fear that it won't. Teaching takes a lot of courage. Every time I stand in front of a new class, I feel the need to reinvent myself for the eager souls waiting in rows in front of me. They are so touchingly biddable, and yet in the world of education, I often face a sea of veteran teachers who have great expectations and high standards for me as a teacher. I have learned to live with the terror and take great satisfaction in the reinvention of myself and others as we move through the semester together.

Another strong source of satisfaction comes from the opportunity to express one's commitment to the future. Generativity is a strong motivator. Although we think of this concept in relationship to the child-rearing years and those years of giving birth to new ideas, we actually have the time to reflect on the importance of generativity and the world we want for the next generation when we are older. One of the most meaningful ways to engage in generativity is to continue teaching or working with others—work based on the hope for the future—the hope for the next generation, the nurturing of ideas for peace and justice in the global community.

MARY. For me, that hope for the future, my own as well as that of my younger colleagues and my students, is a powerful motivation. I became a university professor because I wanted to foster self-development, after majoring in adult development, and because I fervently believed that classrooms were the most stimulating places to spend one's days. I continue in a university classroom because it continues to be the most stimulating environment that I know, and I therefore consider it a privilege to be a professor.

JOANNE. I agree with you Mary. We may have entered the profession at a time when our adult development stage meant we were interested in discovering what we could accomplish, but as time passes, there are increasing satisfactions in helping to foster the growth and development of others. Unfortunately, this is not the central concern of most universities, or at least not most research one institutions, such as the one I'm in. My work today is centrally about helping both students and new scholars to define their own goals and reflect on what might be meaningful in their own lives, not just adopting wholesale the values of an institution that at times seem to be badly misguided. Aren't we about fostering the growth and development of future generations, both in our classrooms and in the halls of academe? I think that's where we started, but I'm not sure that is where we find ourselves today. This is the one goal I believe we often lose sight of, in our frantic effort to enhance our reputations through research and publication. Where is the sense of generativity? Where is the work to increase diversity? One of my recent doctoral students, who just graduated after a long struggle to produce a fine dissertation in what was not her first language, wants to go back to her island home in the Pacific and be a gift of talent and caring for her people. She will never gain a national reputation as a scholar in higher education. Does this mean she is not worth our time and energy? In my experience, those students defined as "the best" according to the values of the academy may simply be the most competitive, the least able to foster a sense of generativity for those that follow them. What is the old saying, "You reap what you sow?" What are we sowing here?

MARY. I believe that we cannot change the culture of our institutions alone. We need a few friends within or close to our own generation; need colleagues who value our insights; and need friends who share our values and who understand our ancient references to past history. If we're completely honest, we may admit to ourselves and to our close friends that sometimes a holiday without children or grandchildren, a special day with one's own generation, can be a rewarding experience. Or maybe this is a 60s experience that doesn't affect you in your 50s?

JOANNE. Living in Hawaii, I feel painfully separated from my children, who live in the Northwest. I don't know if that's a function of age or geography.

However, I do believe that we need friends in the academy, colleagues who value our insights, whatever their age may be, and who share and understand our desire to make a difference for our students. Many of us long for closer relationships, for a community of scholars that is willing to grapple with fundamental questions, especially in the areas of teaching and curriculum. However, I believe these faculty can be of any age. In fact, I think conversations across generations may be the most fruitful. A new faculty member in engineering talked to me recently about the pressure to conduct research at the expense of his teaching. He found himself asking about what would matter to him on his deathbed, not a question frequently asked by the younger generation but an extremely important question nevertheless. The answer helped him to sort out where he wanted to put his energies, into teaching first and then research. So we need friends, young or old, who can help clarify our responsibilities to those who will come after us.

MARY. Those friends can act as role models as well as be sources of support for the work we do. I collect examples of older people who are highly productive into their late eighties or early nineties. There are growing numbers of creative, valued professors who teach beyond their sixties, as well as growing numbers of people who live beyond 100. The media publishes more and more accounts of those who are productive into their 90s. Peter Drucker, for example, is still teaching at the Claremont University Graduate School of Executive Management at the age of 89 and continues to write books.

JOANNE. One of the things these people do for me is to help me think about how I want to grow older. Watching others go before me gives me a sense of possibilities. When they talk to me about the choices they are facing, they are not only good company but help me think about my own future. That I will grow old is a given; it's a question of how.

MARY. We need to practice mindfulness when it comes to aging as a buffer against the strong youth culture in this century. Mindless aging refers to accepting all the old stereotypes regarding age: inability to learn new concepts and skills, gradual loss of memory, and declining physical health. Mindful aging means actively pursuing physical health, concern for nutrition and experience, and maintaining a positive attitude towards mental growth and the advantages of age. When we age mindfully, we create new possibilities instead of following a predetermined downward path. We become more like a free-flying bird.

JOANNE. Wow! That is great. I like the idea of growing old, mindfully, rather than mindlessly. As we baby boomers age (I'm right on the cusp), the idea of aging mindfully will become more and more important. Actually, some of my childhood friends are retiring now, having taught 30 years, and I wonder what they will do now with their lives. I am sure they want to actively pursue physical health, keep a positive attitude towards mental growth, etc. Perhaps they will want to go back to school, pursue more learning. Here is an area I feel the academy must be alert to. As I watch my doctoral students, some of whom are my age or older, I realize that many of our practices must change. We must find ways of teaching that include adults in their 50s and 60s and their styles of learning.

These students often perform better than the young. Some of these older students are much more able to digest the material and connect it to new and innovative ideas because they have had so many more experiences in life. They are able to connect what they are learning to their own experience and understand it at a deeper level. For instance, one of my doctoral students is studying the experiences of Pacific Island students in an American research university. Although she is Caucasian, she has spent years in the Pacific as a Peace Corps volunteer and trainer. These experiences help her to understand the Pacific Islands and its people in deeper ways than someone with no experience in this area at all.

MARY. Fortunately, developmental theory is now recognizing and including the growth of wisdom in the accounts of aging. The Spanish language has the word *vieja* for an old woman, one advanced in years, but another word, *anciana*, that means an old woman who has grown with all the years and has value. If we're fortunate, our life will be a long journey, and we'll become wise, old women whose experiences will be valued, and we'll then be known as someone who is *una anciana*.

JOANNE. Sounds great! I like the idea of a lifelong journey. I think reflecting on our life journeys helps us to put our fears and our values in perspective. It helps me to ask, "What is really important here? Over the long haul?" What kind of conclusions have you come to about aging, Mary?

MARY. Upon reflecting about my own experiences as an advisor to graduate students, I realize that age is relative. Women of 30 can be as insecure about starting graduate work as women of 50. I realize that a woman's age can be a major source of concern. Although we talk of *growing* older as if we have indeed grown with the years, some women will avoid giving their age—even admitting that they are reluctant to tell the age of their children for fear it will reveal their own age. These efforts to mask their age are understandable in institutions known for practicing subtle, if not overt, ageism. Yet, unless women admit their age, I don't think we'll ever succeed in gaining respect for age and the wisdom that can accompany a long life of experiences.

As a professor who teaches adult development, I've very much aware that institutions accept stereotypes regarding aging more easily than they reflect current research on adult learning. We talk of life-long learners, but do our policies on admission, recruitment, and promotion reflect a belief in life-long learning?

JOANNE. Do you think the academy will ever value age more than the general society? I do hope so. One way is for us to be conscious of older women in history who have made valuable contributions and to continue to tell their stories. For example, did you know that in the first wave of feminism in this country and in England, angry women in midlife and older were marching and visible? Emmeline Pankhurst, for instance, was 59 when she marched to King's Gate and was arrested. I have a friend who makes a deliberate effort to mention her hot flashes simply to combat her own invisibility as an older woman in society. By discussing older women in history and our own lives more openly, we can begin to combat the ageism so prevalent in our society today. The title of Barbara McDonald's (1983) book on old women, aging, and ageism articulates one singular request we may all have, *Look Me in the Eye*. In other words, don't render me invisible by looking past me or through me. Acknowledge my presence as a valued member of society. As we enter the next century, isn't that what universities should be about, the acknowledgment of others as valued members of society and the fostering of the growth of all citizens regardless of age?

MARY. I often remind myself that I'm the one who needs to be understanding of younger women—their anxieties and concerns over age—because I've been there. They haven't had the benefit of my experiences and the support of my friends and colleagues who have helped me reach what I call "one more step on the path toward authenticity" by voluntarily stating my age whenever appropriate.

JOANNE. I know that has been a help to me, Mary. I have always admired you for your energy and enthusiasm. I look ahead to my 60s and think, if Mary can do it, I can! However, if I didn't know that you were in your 60s, I wouldn't have the promise of possibilities that your honesty has brought me. All I can say is thank you, Mary, for all that you are and all that I might some day become.

## CONCLUSION

It appears, after reviewing both our conversations, that we are all working to create an academic life that is "whole." That is to say, we are each working to create a balanced professional life that values "who" we are, to include embracing our race/ethnicity, age, and our diverse and rich professional experiences. In addition, "wholeness" means that we are also working to create an academic life that uplifts us spiritually as well as enlightens us intellectually and that supports us to meet our commitments to both our family and community(ies) as well as maintain our physical health. Another theme is embodied in Tierney and Bensimon's (1996) concept of "welcome ground" and the creation of a truly diverse community in the academy. Each one of us has made a commitment to engage students, colleagues, and peers in learning environments that honor diversity of thinking and sharing of multiplicities (e.g., language, history, gender/sex, class, etc.). Although we each struggle within our own structures/organizations, we are very resourceful women. So, what's next? What can we do within our own institution to transform it? Perhaps we might begin by creating places (space and time) within our institutions and at professional association meetings that encourage soul, body, and mind connections. Perhaps we might include, in faculty development seminars, discussions that seek to respond to the following questions: How can we behave as caring, respectful mentors and womentors? How can we behave as trustworthy teachers and colleagues? As the numbers of women and minority faculty begin to grow across the administrative ranks we may now look to the following question: How do we now transform the institution's policies and procedures so that equity is actualized.

## REFERENCES

Bennett, J. B. (1991). Collegiality as "getting along." *AAHE Bulletin*, October, 7–10.

Cooper, J., Benham, M., Collay, M., Martinez-Aleman, A., & Scherr, M. (1999). A famine of stories: Finding a home in the academy. *Initiatives* 59(1), 1–18.

Cooper, J., Benham, M. & Martinez-Aleman, A. (1997). A famine of stories: Searching for a home in the academy, a focused dialogue presented at the annual meeting of the Association for the Study of Higher Education, Albuquerque, NM.

Harris, M. (1996). *Proclaim jubilee.* Louisville, KY: Westminister John Knox Press.

Hillesum, E. (1983). *An interrupted life: The diaries of Etty Hillesum 1941–1943.* New York: Pantheon Books.

Massy, W. F., Wilger, A. K., & Colbeck, C. (July–August, 1994). Overcoming "hollowed" collegiality. *Change* 26(4), 10–20.

McDonald, B. (1983). *Look me in the eye: Old women, aging and ageism.* San Francisco: Spinsters.

Nyquist, J. et al. (May–June, 1999). On the road to becoming a professor: The graduate student experience. *Change*, 18–27.

Sandler, B., & Hall, R. (1993). The campus climate revisited: Chilly climate for women faculty, administrators, and students. In J. S. Glazer, E. M. Bensimon, & B. K. Townsend (Eds.), *Women in higher education: A feminist perspective* (175–204). Needham Heights, MA: Ginn Press.

Tierney, W. G., & Bensimon, E. M. (1996). *Promotion and tenure: Community and socialization in academe.* Albany: State University of New York Press.

# CHAPTER 6

# Balancing Work and Family

## Michelle Collay

> Women have been regarded as unreliable because they are torn by
> multiple commitments; men become capable of true dedication
> when they are either celibate, in the old religious model, with no
> family to distract them, or have families organized to provide sup-
> port but not distraction, the little woman behind the great man.
> But what if we were to recognize the capacity for distraction , the
> divided will, as representing a higher wisdom?
> —Bateson,1989, p. 166

As I type, I listen for my 18-month-old son to wake from his nap and
feel the movements of another child due to be born this summer. I smile
ruefully at the note I got from Joanne several months ago about writing
this chapter. She said, "We need a chapter about balancing work and
family, and you're the most qualified right now." I am just beginning to
understand how qualified I am. I also know one doesn't need children
to understand the challenges of balancing work and family—in my years
as a member of the Special Interest Group: Research on Women and
Education (SIG), I have learned that academic women face special challenges because of women's multiple roles in society. All women have
extended families or partners who place expectations on them, or to
whom they offer family support. This chapter is about all women academics with all kinds of family responsibilities.

The women who speak about their lives, both from existing literature and from data collected for this study, move us from the continuum
of work versus family to a more holistic "composing a life." It is critical
that findings from feminist inquiry take their place within decades of
work decrying personal and psychic losses incurred by women who have
entered masculine domains. Let us acknowledge what is unhealthy

about the institutions to which we have finally gained entree—and offer other perspectives on their evolution. The women in this study add their voices and wisdom to an evolving literature and give us hope that we might compose a life of both family and scholarly satisfaction.

The voices in this text represent some from the literature about academic women making meaning of multiple roles and multiple commitments. Interspersed with the existing literature are the voices of eight recently tenured women from the field of teacher education: four are minority women, and four are white, including myself. The majority are first-generation academics and the first in their families to attend college or graduate school. Participants include African American, Native American, Latina, Native Hawaiian, and European American women. Three are in same-sex relationships. Voices from existing literature are cited as such. The participants from this study are introduced with a pseudonym and their institutional context the first time, then by name and ethnicity after that. I learned about these women and many others from professional contacts throughout North America. Approximately 20 women were invited to interview by telephone—those not represented felt they didn't meet the criteria or were unable to meet the time line. I hoped to collect interviews from recently tenured women and from those who were turned down or who chose different paths.

Rereading the literature about women and tenure reassures me that I share the path with many. Even as an academic who chose career first and bore children later, I still fit the profile offered in the statistics. As a married woman, I was divorced the year I got my Ph.D. and left my first, tenure-track position after three years, so my new partner and I could live in the same community. As midlife new mom, I now relate to challenges and woes of balancing family and work on a new level. Even though Von, my first child, was born when I was 42, I have not yet achieved tenure. After he was born, I chose to leave a well-paid administrative post and take a tenuous term appointment as a faculty member in another state. While that story is more complex than the changes wrought by the birth of a child, I completed a crash course on the politics of mothering and its risk to advancement in that particular academy before I left. I was resensitized to lessons learned when I was hired as a "minority," a woman drafts"man" working for the federal government in the mid-1970s. My story evokes empathy for many women within and beyond the academy.

The challenge of composing a life is not just about raising children. Many of my colleagues and some of the participants in this study have life partners who live in distant states, a common phenomena for junior faculty seeking first and even subsequent academic positions. Some have same-sex partners and may or may not have grown children. Others have no birth children but carry responsibility for the children of others, their siblings, and parents. Family must be understood in the broad terms outlined by Grappa and MacDermid (1997), who "define family to include single- and dual-parent homes, cohabiting couples, people living alone, same-gender parents, step-families, and intergenerational families." The authors remind us, "During their careers, employees are likely to experience several of these diverse family structures" (1997, 2). No faculty woman can ignore the complex interweaving of family and work as she makes meaning of her career.

In some ways, current thinking about women and tenure looks depressingly similar to the work that appeared 20 years ago. Authors of other chapters address this literature and update the readers on which issues have remained the same and which have evolved over time. Fortunately, other more feminist and postmodern world views are making their way into the literature as exemplified by Bateson's opening words. When family responsibilities are reframed as a critical, imperative part of a well-lived life, those who despair of "balancing" work and family are now posing a healthy challenge to the academy. My task is to focus on the multiple roles women have as academics and family members and the implications of family responsibilities on tenure. As an activist, however, I am delighted to contribute to the pro-active side of the literature and hope this chapter adds an important dimension to the breadth of current advice about obtaining tenure. Participants in this study give vital meaning to Mary Catherine Bateson's *Composing a Life* (1989) as they advise junior faculty to do the same.

## BECOMING SOCIALIZED AS "OTHER" INTO THE ACADEMY

As the academy begins to reflect greater society, those who are different from the previous generations are reshaping its culture and policies. Women and minorities are still the outsiders, but their presence is changing business as usual to a business that has been forced to recognize faculty as human beings with families. One of the greatest challenges women face on the road to tenure is that the engineers of the highway were men of privilege, and the expectations of academic performance reflect that social status. Paula Caplan's detailed and thorough *Lifting a Ton of Feathers* (1993) is a no-nonsense review of myths about the academy and guide to women seeking tenure. As with many others in this text, she reminds us that the academic career, time line, and social structure were designed by and for male academics with wives. For women academics, time spent doing child care and household tasks also drains time, energy, and concentration from both teaching and publishing, and women remain far more likely to do the lion's share of family-related care. She details how women's quest for tenure can be confounded because of the following: "women who stay in academia are either single or childless; that married women are even less likely than other women to be hired into the tenure track; that the average professor works 55 hours a week but those who have major child-care and home responsibilities work 70 or more hours per week; and that marriage tends to be a depressant of women's academic productivity but a stimulant for men's" (1993, p. 185).

She captures the dilemma many women feel about acknowledging their status as partners, mothers, or caretakers: "A woman who refuses to take a job that would mean living apart from her partner, children, or elderly family members doesn't take her job seriously, but a women who is prepared to make such a move is uncaring and unwomanly" (p. 67). This assumption frames many experiences shared by participants in this study. Adelle, a white Jewish woman with two young adult daughters, recalls her early socialization into the profession as the only mother in her work place. "I did not know any woman who was a mother and a professor. I knew only single women, lesbians without children, and older women who had come back to do their work when their kids were in college. I did not have a single cohort among other women who had to run from faculty meetings to the daycare center, or to the kid's play at three, or to figure out how to get the kids to the dentist."

Lest one think that, beginning the new millennium, it is not as great a liability to be female or minority, old notions die hard. There are still only 24 hours in a day, and the majority of women, whether married, with partners, childless, or single, still carry the larger burden of immediate and extended family responsibility. This is especially problematic for junior women faculty giving birth. A recent *Chronicle of Higher Education* entitled *Timing Is Everything: Academe's Annual Baby Boom*, describes the challenges of childbearing for full-time faculty women:

> Scheduling a summer delivery is important, say academic women, because maternity policies at many colleges leave a lot to be desired. Although all institutions must abide by the Family and Medical Leave Act and offer employees up to 12 weeks of unpaid leave, institutional policies regarding paid leave vary enormously . . . negotiating with department heads can be a difficult process for women who are untenured and may be reluctant to push too hard because the decision making is so decentralized. "You are at the mercy of your chair," says an associate professor at a research university, who asked not to be named. I don't think as a junior woman you can go in and start raising the roof. (Wilson, June 25, 1999, p. A14)

As academic other, women who disrupt old norms do so at great risk to their careers, because they believe with good reason that their chances for acceptance correspond directly to their ability to imitate mainstream men. After the baby is born, the stakes remain high. The pattern of day-to-day responsibilities for women is reinforced by decade-by-decade expectations of men. Emily Toth offers this time line:

> For academia is still run according to unspoken male norms, according to the traditional clockwork of male careers. In his twenties, the academic male is supposed to be getting his degree; in his thirties, he gets tenure; in his forties he starts becoming distinguished in his field. Along the way, his time and energy go to research, while his wife deals with the everyday stuff, including children and home and food and clothing and keeping body and soul together (and never letting the children disturb Daddy's rest or writing). (1997, p. 119)

Several of the participants talked about their need to revise their tenure calendar to protect their chances of completing the tasks demanded of them. Rita, a Latina women who recently left her tenured position far from her home and partner to reestablish herself in a research institution near her partner, suggests, "There are people that move from administrative to full-time tenure track, or from teaching institutions to research institutions. You can't think of it as a six-year track; you have to think of it as a 10-year track."

Nora, a native Hawaiian, acknowledged that her geographic distance from family, while painful and isolating, had allowed her to move through her tenure process more quickly than she might have living near her family: "If I were in Hawaii, and I had an academic position, my family responsibilities would play a major role in everything I did. Because I was at home, I would have to deal with all the day-to-day kinds of things, every day of the week."

Irene, a Jewish Eastern European American, described the distance she now feels from her parents because of becoming an academic. "I am without question the most successful person in my family, and I think they're quite ambivalent about it. I'm a second-generation American—my parents were born in the U.S.—but there's such a heavy immigrant, working-class culture that comes with us. On the one hand, I was pushed to excel; on the other hand, they're very ambivalent about that and couldn't really guide me." Both Nora and Irene express the dilemma faced by many first-generation college-educated women—they risk membership in their family structure, even as they respond to the family's hopes and dreams for their success.

Linda, a European-American woman and director of theater with three young sons, described her experiences at theater conferences:

"When you see the women at the conferences who are doing all the papers and all the publishing and all the presentations, those are women without spouses, or their children are grown, or they've never been married and had children." All of these responses highlight the necessity for women academics to be cognizant of the patterns of the institution, which were created for a different gender and class, for a group of individuals who did not make decisions about professional commitments with a balanced life in mind.

According to Gregory (1995), Black women academics face similar challenges to establishing academic careers as other women, with some additional barriers. As racial and cultural minorities in primarily White institutions, they face additional layers of isolation. There is also the issue of greater minority status, because there is even less of a possibility to achieve a critical mass of Black women than of women in general. They must work outside the norms described above *and* cope with the isolation their race creates.

Deborah's experience as a junior faculty member in a private college affirms Gregory's (1995) perspective on the additional racial and cultural isolation faced by minority women. In recalling her academic socialization, she remarked, "People were not forthcoming to me about what it meant to be an academic. I don't remember having any mentoring conversations, whereas I knew that other new people were often invited out to dinner. I'm not sure exactly why, probably a combination of things. No one talked to me about tenure."

In her study of barriers to success and achievement in the academy, Gregory found that personal/family factors were a significant barrier. Specifically, her respondents rated four items: spouse's job mobility, spouse's negative views towards academic job/career, inability to accommodate family needs, and adequate support at home in the top 15 barriers, but of less importance than institutional factors. This portrayal of the spouse as a limitation for women's professional mobility, however, does not consider other cultural perspectives on family. Anna describes her role in her family this way: "There is a tradition for Indian women that there's a lot of strength in interdependence, in all of the traditions. There's no difficulty going on with your career, but the difficulty is that family comes first. Rather than not go on with your career, it's sort of a dual process. You cooperate with family. Your husband doesn't say what you can do, but there are responsibilities."

Women from indigenous cultures may have an advantage by not assuming that joining the Eurocentric mainstream is a positive move. Making recommendations for achieving success, however, Gregory focuses on mainstream values, draws on studies of Black management literature, and suggests a list of organizational behaviors and proactivity that is similar to the recommendations of Aisenberg and Harrington (1988). The tone of Gregory's work suggests that the usual advice pertains to Black women academics, only more so.

While the management literature can be a source of advice for academic women, much of it focuses on keeping both houses of work and family in order but doesn't encourage combining them. In the academy as in business, women are warned away from presenting a "family comes first" countenance. The advice women receive is often along the line of this witty, somewhat sarcastic quip from Toth's (1997) *Ms. Mentor's Impeccable Advice to Women in Academia*. She is responding to a junior woman faculty member who was discouraged from taking her young child to campus:

> You are in the immemorial bind between being a woman and— gasp—being a person in the eyes of your male academic colleagues. Having a baby, and showing the baby about, will not help you toward tenure, and may actively damage your chances. . . .
> Scarcely any family actually fits that model anymore, but men can still come much closer than women do. A man who is married is viewed as settled, an admirable adult; a woman who is married may be considered a hiring problem. But children, their care and feeding, are the great separator. People who are most often seen as mothers are not considered professional. (Toth 1997, p. 119)

Ironically, this view of family as unprofessional contradicts the expectation in smaller colleges that faculty "parent" paying students but not their own children. Linda outlined the long list of *in loco parentis* expectations of a faculty member who is a theater director and serves in a rural, residential private college: "All the evening work, where you do all the shows, weekend responsibilities, attend all the functions for prospective students, family weekends, and options, and all those kinds of extra things which count as faculty activity. Service to the college and the community. There was no consideration about my family. And if I were to raise them, then I'm risking my status as a full-fledged faculty member."

Adelle is a staunch advocate of bringing family into work and not allowing the academy to force women to deny their status as mothers. When her firstborn was just a baby, her department chair made a joke about the parallel between her and a mother from a T.V. show who left her baby in a dumpster. " I was livid! That's support for being a mom? He's a guy whose wife stayed home with his kids, so there was this huge amount of dig to it, and I was just so horrified that he was impugning my parenting, that I was at work because I had left my kid in a dumpster."

Adelle illuminated the double standard held for women and men with an example of how men who show family commitment are considered heroes. An up-and-coming male faculty member with a national reputation would say at a meeting, "'Oh I've got to leave at three. I've got to pick up the kids.' Everyone said, 'Oh how wonderful, an involved father. Isn't that great that this famous academic is going to pick up his children!' If a woman had said something like that, it would be, 'See, they're not committed. You can't really hire them. Their mind is always on their children.' The message was, 'You can be here. Just pretend you don't have any children.'"

Linda recalls learning about one of the letters in her tenure file: "In one of my supposedly supportive letters from a colleague in my own department, they questioned my commitment to the institution because I was married to an Australian!" The assumption here is that women follow their husbands and that they are a more risky hire for that reason.

In this next example, Rita has recently moved back to the same location as her partner, and they are finally able to begin their own family through adoption. "It's interesting because I just got a research leave for next spring, and the [adoption] placement will be right before that. So I'll probably let them know sometime in the fall. But I'm new there. They just gave me a research leave and a lot of money. Not that I really care what they think, but still!" Rita has the maturity and life experience to negotiate the tensions that will arise when she confronts the institutional norms by becoming a parent during an academic leave, but that doesn't make it easy. Like the others who tell their stories here, hers is one of making hard choices in an academic culture that has not valued commitment to family.

Deborah talked about her role as caretaker of her physically disabled partner: "Lorrie was very sick during that period. She was wheelchair bound, and so there was always this pull, and in fact she needed me there at the house. I needed to be at work, but I also needed to be at home." Even with two young adult sons mostly on their own, Deborah's family responsibilities created tremendous stress during her early years as an academic. Her health suffered, and she is only now regaining it.

These descriptions clearly indicate that academic women are constantly forced to choose family over work in a culture where only work is measured. While they have made hard choices and prevailed, the stress is evident in their reports.

## DEVELOPING AND MAINTAINING
## INTELLECTUAL INTEGRITY

There is a perennial debate in research circles about women's work, that is, the study of topics previously unstudied by an all white male research community. Women academics, and minority men for that matter, are counseled as graduate students and throughout their careers to avoid such scholarly ghettos for fear of risking their tenure and promotion. Much academic career literature describes this enculturation into the research community. Aisenburg and Harrington (1988) devote a chapter to women's work in *Women of Academe: Outsiders in the Sacred Grove*, spelling out in excruciating detail the power of the mainstream inhabitants to keep women from treading such paths. They capture the relationship of feminist work to the marriage plot in this description:

> What we are claiming about women's academic work, in the face of such variations, is that common patterns do appear, not as absolute qualities marking the work of all women, but as clusters of similarity, propensities to do similar kinds of work. And we see these commonalities as deriving from the common experience of women who set out on a quest for professional authority in a cultural climate still significantly defined by the marriage plot. This experience sets up perspectives and interests that unavoidably affect how women carry out their intellectual work—from the academic disciplines they enter, to the questions they ask and, often, to the values they apply in reaching answers to those questions. (pp. 85–86)

Because of their status as "other," women scholars often challenge the status quo; question the assumptions about scientific, literary, or social theory; and ask different questions than their predecessors. And they may choose to acknowledge their membership in their gender, ethnicity, race, or sexual orientation groups as central to their understanding of their research, rather than distancing themselves from their personal story.

Gloria Ladson-Billings (1997) describes her journey through graduate school and her struggle as a minority woman to reconcile her personal, public, and intellectual interests. She notes the complexity of these roles played by minority academic women in particular: "Rather, our position in the academy is typically the result of a collective struggle and support. Thus our understanding of our roles includes an intertwining of the personal and the public—the intellectual and the emotional—the scholarly and the political" (p. 59).

Ladson-Billings believes that minority women are frequently sensitive to their communities because they are the beneficiaries of the community's support and are often held up as tokens by which the other community members may be judged. Their intellectual quests often reflect this intertwining. Anna, an American Indian, talked about her role as the first in her family to become an academic. "Family is number one. The next is education. And that means the elder of the family setting that line for the rest of the family. It's a family value."

Nora advises junior faculty to hold steadfast to their own research agenda. Her focus on Hawaiian educational policy was considered risky in an institution with little history of research outside the mainstream. "Never give up on your integrity. I didn't do the kind of work people thought I should do. When I came up for reappointment, a senior faculty member said to me, 'You know we have some very serious concerns about your work.'" It was difficult for her to challenge traditional research agendas that were the norm. "That's the hardest thing to do, because you want to please, to fit in, to be accepted into the club."

Deborah, an African American, focused her early research on poor minority women, their disconnection with schools, and their children's experience in school. From her personal experiences, she's had to learn to stay true to herself. "My center is my personal integrity. I try to make sense of what's real and what's phony. I'm not going to collaborate in things I don't think are legitimate. I deliberately talk about my values."

## RECONCEPTUALIZING FAMILY AS INTEGRAL
## TO YOUR INTELLECTUAL JOURNEY

Although women and minorities are shaped by their academic enculturation, they have begun to influence their institutions as well. In addition to their choice of research topics, their day-to-day experiences as women, partners, mothers, and caretakers become integral to how they think about learning and teaching. Women whom I perceive as successful have reconceptualized the place of family in their intellectual development.

Penelope Peterson (1997) sketches her life history as a learner in a book she recently co-edited with Anna Neumann. Her tale of life informing learning includes a section on balancing work and family. She had begun to study feminism as an educational scholar but hadn't yet made meaning of the implications until faced with a real life decision to marry, parent, and remain a scholar:

> When I met another graduate student, Patrick Dickson, I began trying to ground the theoretical ideas of merging work and family in some everyday reality. We fell in love and quickly developed a wonderful relationship, except for one major stumbling block. Patrick loved children and wanted to have six. I, on the other hand, didn't think that I could have any if I also wanted to have a career as a professor of educational psychology. It was a difficult time for me as a young woman struggling to be a feminist and thinking about career and family. I tried to imagine how this would work and how we would create this new collaborative parenting relationship. Could Patrick and I learn flexibility in the ways that would be required to blend our lives

and balance home and work? Could I learn to parent along with Patrick while each of us was still learning to become a professor and an educational researcher? (pp. 217–18)

Later in the chapter, Peterson describes the learning journey of her son Andrew and how he offered her a case study of a toddler who didn't learn the way her empirical research indicated he should. Even in her compromise from six to only three children, she still gained many opportunities to study learning firsthand as her mothering informed her theorizing about educational psychology: "It's interesting that although what I learned at home prepared me well for school, it prepared me less well for motherhood. Having a baby when I was twenty-nine began the gradual change in the way I thought about the relationship between home and work. Even though I had taken multiple courses in developmental psychology, I hadn't learned how to be a real mother to a real baby. I wasn't prepared for Andrew" (p. 218).

Adelle enthusiastically described the influence of her parenting on her work: " I taught a course on working with parents of exceptional children before I had children, and now I look back on that and think, 'the nerve!' Of course, if anybody had said that to me, I would have been offended." As the proud owner of an Ed.D. and a specialist in the very subject, Adelle had no way of knowing how powerfully her children would shape a deepening understanding of her work. She expressed the potency of her children's stories about school and how their experiences have informed her teaching and writing.

Rita's research on the experiences of women undergraduates is informed by her work with them in student services. She looks at their lives and how they make meaning of their experiences much in the same way she reflects on her own journey. As an admissions person, her role in higher education was for many years student support, not classroom teaching. Mary Catherine Bateson (1989) portrays one of the participants in her book as a high-powered academic who made room for a different kind of life by letting go of an administrative position. "She increased her research and writing, picked up a number of consulting contracts, and has been increasingly involved in projects related to the homeless. The most important difference between her life then and now is that in escaping from a career track in which her rhythms were dictated from above, she has become able to orchestrate her own life" (Bateson, 1989, p. 175).

Bateson's work has been especially instructive for women who seek to balance academic and professional lives with personal goals. Her landmark perspective on the integration of life and work challenges many of the assumptions thrust upon women and minority faculty as the price for entering the academy.

## ENGAGING YOUR FAMILY IN
## PROBLEM SOLVING; SHARING YOUR JOURNEY

Many women describe the guilt and shame they feel when they make hard choices to attend a professional function and miss a family function or beg off a meeting to see a child's game. Yet recognizing they can't do it all, acknowledging their families as integral to their lives, and seeking support finally become a viable solution for some. The participants in this study identify their families as central to their success in the academy.

In this first example, a high school principal invites her family to join her in making her new position work. Women public school administrators, while not the focus of this study, face similar challenges as minorities in a White man's world. While many of the voices in the literature express the need to keep one's family a priority, this description is more proactive, showing us another way to engage family in composing a life:

> When I took the principalship, our children knew of the additional time I would spend away from home. Chores were assigned to each, with rewards at the end of the school year, such as a nice family vacation to spots where we would otherwise not be able to afford. Our children were always very helpful, so this arrangement was no problem. My husband was also very accommodating. He always encouraged me to achieve and work toward my goals. I think that his having to help with the cooking and other house chores during his college work while I provided really helped. (Gupton and Slick, 1996, p. 81)

Anna, an American Indian woman with responsibilities for a large extended family, felt torn about missing so many important family events during the years she completed graduate school and sought tenure: "But my family really rallied, all the good cooks in the family came to my house and they would cook. For years, I couldn't find all my pots and pans, because everyone was here cooking. And that's how I did it, because the rest of the family helped."

Linda and her husband agreed before their first child was born that he would stay home as primary caretaker, and she would stay in her current position. Colleagues and family members made it clear that he was as suspect as she for that decision to reverse traditional roles. "They would say something to the effect, 'What are you doing at work; you should be home.' And people would ask him at the grocery store, 'What are you, Mr. Mom for a day?' And he'd say, 'I'm Mr. Mom everyday!'" She names her husband, David, as her key support while she struggled to complete her dissertation and retain her position, insisting that she work on her writing while he cared for their young son.

Irene describes the place of her partner in her academic development as important to her peace of mind. "When I listen to other academics, particularly women whose partners are not academics, I often hear them say, 'He doesn't understand why I have to write! He thinks I'm neurotic, obsessive, a workaholic,' and so forth. In that way, I think I'm incredibly fortunate. We've helped each other a lot. Theresa was extremely instrumental in helping me learn how to teach." Rita admonishes junior faculty to resist the institution's efforts to shape one's sense of family or responsibilities toward family: "When people think of their families as being a hindrance in tenure, it's because other people see it that way. That's why a lot of women really form a callus that protects them from that kind of dichotomy, from that conceptualization of their lives. You can't allow the institution to make you think that way. . . . Tenure is great, but you can't cuddle up with it."

## CREATING A NETWORK FOR SUPPORT

The importance of creating a supportive network of friends, family, and colleagues cannot be overstated. The participants in this study talked animatedly about the critical role good colleagues played in their intellectual and personal development. As Anna points out in her recommendations for junior faculty, "Know that it's going to be difficult, and just know that it's tough. Use as much of a support system as you can."

Deborah found the SIG a safe place to initially present her research, which provided her with a network of like-minded researchers. "In fact, I started getting to know people there that I would see at other conferences, and so I started to make those kinds of friendships. Most of my support came from there."

Nora formed a writing group at her institution. "Have a network of women. I started a women's writing group. We call ourselves the Writer's Café. And there's about six or seven of us, all at different stages of our career. And we either talk about our writing, or we talk about the hellatious comments that are made. We have dinner together, we meet every week."

Many successful women credit their support groups for helping them get through tough professional twists and turns. But they caution the use of good judgment in the selection of those supporters. Adelle gives advice won through hard experience about choosing one's soulmates carefully:

> Find a support system with other women with children with whom you feel safe to have those conversations. And don't assume that it's safe to have them with everyone. . . . There are reasons why

it's better if your support system is not at your own institution. Use e-mail, phone calls, conferences. One of the roles that conferences have always served for me is support. Build a network. We need reassurance that the best thing you can give your child is a mother who is a fulfilled and satisfied person and doing important work in the world as a model.

## MINDING BODY AND SOUL

Many studies of faculty enculturation show the extreme measures to which new faculty go to obtain tenure. They often risk their mental and physical health as they follow in the footsteps of senior academics who make no attempt to modify the "paying your dues" culture that prevailed during their indoctrination. They go weeks and months without seeing much of family and friends, and they suffer from the constant grind of reaching for yet another brass ring. And many women feel that, as good scholars, they must do it all well. Linda talked about the notion of balance and stated, "You need to recognize that teeter-totter effect, that responsibility has to shift. It's never just equal, ever. Between work and school, and between the spouses. The whole idea of balance is just a joke I think. It's folly. I think it shifts all the time. And if you recognize that, personally, I think it makes life easier. Maybe a happy balance does occur, but it must be so quick that none of us recognize it!"

We receive messages about doing it all from pop psychologists (be a super mom turned academic), friends within and outside the academy, colleagues who figured they did it so you can too, and less-than-well-meaning foes. Irene addresses balance from a spiritual prospective: "The issue of balance is always present, of not getting completely consumed, of maintaining a healthy body, being aware of the aspects of my psyche that aren't necessarily developing or being exercised as much as I would like. I'm certainly aware, having just taken a sabbatical and learned how to just sit and be, of the need to develop friendships and relationships that aren't absolutely rooted in my academic work."

Rita advises new faculty to take care of themselves and avoid the crazy makers, those people who chat us up about the pressure they feel:

> Prioritize sleep in your life. I had to take care of my health, and no matter how hard I worked, I would always get seven or eight hours of sleep. And that had to do with how I structured my day and what I began to say no to and how I decided what not to do. I really encourage younger faculty to avoid getting into these conversations with other junior faculty about how long everybody worked, how much they were in on the weekends, how much they're doing. I think that there's this culture of one-upping.

Adelle concurs with the other participants in regard to striving for a healthy life. "Although I wasn't good at doing this myself, recognize that taking care of yourself is vital. I thought I should either be at work or with my children. It's not being selfish, it's in the best interest of both you and your family for you not to be insane."

The participants in this study cannot always claim success with living a balanced life, but to a woman they recommend making physical, mental, and spiritual health the highest priority. Risking life and metaphorical limb to obtain membership in a club that is built often by chewing up the inhabitants and spitting them out not only diminishes the individuals whose lives are damaged, but leaves little hope that the academy can be changed. The last section describes positive changes being wrought by women and minorities and gives us hope for a different future.

## COMPOSING A LIFE—BEYOND BALANCE

Voices from this study reflect recent literature challenging old enculturation models and practices and offer, instead, different ways of thinking about our lives. Like many feminist academics who have confronted the historic norms of the White male academy, Aisenberg and Harrington (1988) are proponents of transformation for women and advocate for changing what it means to be a professional:

> Combining new and old identities, women are trying to design a life that rejects the old conventional division of private and public identities. That is, women entering the professions seek a transformation of the self—the female self—as it has been defined restrictively for centuries, and they seek a greater integration between private and public selves. Further, they seek it through their efforts to reshape the norms and values that currently define professional life. Thus, as stated earlier, the entry of women into the professions in ever increasing numbers has truly revolutionary implications, because women seek not only to enter but also to change the nature of professional work. (p. 19)

Given the potency of the academic culture to socialize outsiders, and the marginalized status of women and minorities who seek membership in the academy, it is not easy to stay encouraged about the possibilities of us shaping it. Yet there is growing evidence that this sea change is underway. The change begins with each individual recognizing small steps along the path. Sue Middleton, an academic from New Zealand, expresses her appreciation of moving from the kitchen to authorship:

> I am privileged to be able to indulge in the luxury of writing. As Virginia Woolf (1978) explained, 'A woman must have money and a

room of her own if she is to write . . .' (p. 6). As a tenured academic, I can—with the mortgages, credit cards, and overdrafts extended to today's professional classes—purchase a computer and create study space. I gaze at the luminescent screen of my Macintosh, grateful for the clear black type that appears as I press the keys. Grateful for technology and tenure. Grateful for the salary that has brought release from the typewriter on the kitchen table, surrounded by scraps of food and children's comings and goings. (Middleton, 1993, p. 2)

Women must first find a room of their own and legitimize their place as intellectuals. With models like Virginia Woolf, we follow a courageous tradition. Once finding a voice, we become a force within departments and schools, and as newly tenured women begin to effect change in our workplaces. Anna named her department chair, an associate professor herself only recently tenured, as key to her survival through tenure. Now she herself is playing a similar role: "People that are going up for tenure can have someone as an advocate right on their committee. I've been chosen to be an advocate for two; one was successful, and one was not. But it was quite an honor because no one else had been chosen in two years."

Nora has taken on more influential faculty roles at her institution. "Now that I'm in sort of a senior role, my faculty has seen me as a senior faculty member for the last couple of years and have treated me that way. I've made a lot of decisions, made a lot of positive policies, made a lot of administrative decisions." Nora has already begun to see her influence on her department if not the greater division, and states this change in very pro-active terms.

Irene described her work this way: "All I can say is that my academic work has been so deeply satisfying for me in so many ways, all of the dimensions, teaching and research and administration. I've learned a lot from doing it, and I feel at home in this work in ways that I did not before." She is now serving in a leadership capacity in an institution not known for embracing values outside a very narrow mainstream.

On the policy level, there is work being conducted by organizations such as the American Association of Higher Education (AAHE) that will influence the way the academy treats faculty and their family. In a recent article, "Work, Family, and the Faculty Career," authors Grappa and MacDermid (1997) outline a series of recommendations for institutional leaders who are sincere about modifying a culture which has been unfriendly to families. In the section "New Ways of Thinking," they challenge institutional behavior to both genders when they state:

> Beliefs about gender roles also must change. Formal policies and informal practices still reinforce gender-based expectations and make it difficult for women and men to work as faculty while managing

dependent care responsibilities. Men generally hold the leadership positions—in colleges and universities as in industry. Most have benefitted from a different life history—support in their career endeavors by a wife primarily responsible for the family. Lacking personal experience in managing work-family conflicts, these leaders can be insensitive to the stereotypes and inequities currently faced by both genders. (p. 28)

Women must continue to educate their colleagues about the importance of recognizing complex lives beyond the academy. Sometimes, merely having a complex life is education enough. My story of a winding path without tenure continues. I went with great trepidation to my dean this winter to tell her we were expecting a second child in the summer (a lucky break, not planned!). Even knowing she was a professional who had herself stayed in the work force with young children, I was not comfortable making my family responsibilities public. And even though my husband is on the same faculty, I had concerns the new baby would be seen as a deterrent to my productivity rather than to his. Still, I must continue as if the academy accepts my choices and trust the individuals who are my friends to support me. I believe my age and maturity have been helpful in negotiating this stage of life, and I'm appreciative of other faculty on campus who have young children and make them a part of their academic lives.

I listen to the higher wisdom of my sisters as they speak from the heart about their experiences in the academy and revel in the knowledge that each of them is bringing that higher wisdom to their families, friends, and colleagues. The academy is a better place at the [beginning of the twenty-first century] because of the courage of these wise women. They are composing lives of wit and compassion, no longer attempting to be all things to all people, but being first true to themselves. As Bateson (1989) suggests, they have not only "recognize[d] the capacity for distraction, the divided will, as representing a higher wisdom"; they have invited a new generation of women colleagues to do the same.

## REFERENCES

Aisenberg, N., & Harrington, M. (1988). *Women of academe: Outsiders in the sacred grove*. Amherst: University of Massachusetts Press.

Bateson, M. C. (1989). *Composing a life*. New York: Penguin.

Caplan, P. J. 1993. *Lifting a ton of feathers: A women's guide to surviving in the academic world*. Toronto: Council of Ontario Universities.

Deneef, A. L., & Goodwin, C. D. (1995). *The academics handbook*. Durham & London: Duke University Press.

Grappa, J. M., & MacDermid, S. M. (1997). *Work, family, and the faculty career*. Inquiry no. 8. American Association for Higher Education, Washington, DC.

Gregory, S. T. (1995). *Black women in the academy*. Lantham, MD: University Press of America.

Gupton, S. L., & Slick, G. A. (1996). *Highly successful women administrators: The inside stories of how they got there*. Thousand Oaks, CA: Corwin.

Ladson-Billings, G. (1997). For colored girls who have considered suicide when the academy's not enough: Reflections of an African American woman scholar. In A. Neumann & P. Peterson (Eds.), *Learning from our lives: Women, research, and autobiography in education* (pp. 52–70). New York: Teachers College Press.

Middleton, S. (1993). *Educating feminists: Life history and pedagogy*. New York: Teachers College Press.

Peterson, P. (1997). Learning out of school and in: Self and experience at home, school, and work. In A. Neumann & P. Peterson (Eds.), *Learning from our lives: Women, research, and autobiography in education* (209–227). New York: Teachers College Press.

Toth, E. (1997). *Ms. Mentor's impeccable advice for women in academia*. Philadelphia: University of Pennsylvania Press.

Wilson, R. (June 25, 1999). Timing is everything: Academe's annual baby boom. *The Chronicle of Higher Education 45*, 42, A14–A15.

# CHAPTER 7

# Coping with
# Feelings of Fraudulence

## Janice Koch

The more hierarchical the activity or institution, and the higher up
we go in it, the greater our feelings of fraudulence are likely to be.
—Peggy McIntosh, 1985

The following personal story is an accounting of "feeling like a fraud"
when I set out to prepare my file on behalf of securing tenure at my university. I use the terms *fraud* or *fraudulence* to refer to a personal sense
of self-doubt that some people feel when they apply for advancement in
hierarchical systems. In the academy, preparing for the tenure process is
a lengthy and daunting procedure. In this chapter, I explore how personal feelings of self-doubt can express themselves during the application process for tenure. I make connections between personal feelings of
fraudulence and the absence of social entitlement to public sphere success. By social entitlement, I refer to early, consistent exposure to and
communication with people in positions of power who are like yourself.
Often, the absence of these role models coupled with low socioeconomic
status contribute to a lack of entitlement to "winning prizes" in the
academy. Feeling like a fraud, I argue, can also be an attribute as one
sets out to explore how systems of privilege suggest that people at the
"top" are somehow better than those "below." Understanding that all
individuals, at each level of the academy, may be well served by personal
critique, one can embrace feelings of fraudulence as being necessary to
encourage self-evaluation.

Because my research explores (1) issues of entitlement to science and
scientific careers and (2) inequities in precollege schooling with regard
to gender, this discussion contributes to the discourse on tenure in the

academy by exploring how one works outside of the hierarchy and uses that work to gain access to the same hierarchy. My story also illustrates the power of McIntosh's premise in her *Feeling like a Fraud* (1985), namely, that while access to privileged systems can promote feelings of personal fraudulence, those very feelings may "indicate an honest refusal to internalize the idea that having power or public exposure proves one's merit and/or authority" (p. 1).

In *Feeling like a Fraud: Part Two* (1989), Dr. McIntosh posits a baseline sense of authenticity, which gives one the ability to have feelings of fraudulence because it creates an awareness of the lack of fit between what one feels and what is said about one's virtue or competence or expected in public behavior (p. 1). I found this latter work on fraudulence to be helpful as I prepared my papers for tenure because the sense of authenticity McIntosh refers to was, for me, a home grounding that situated my work in the larger context of my life, of who I am and of how that differs from many of my peers. In that difference, I find both strength to pursue my work and feelings of fraudulence in contrast to others in my institution. Through my story, I hope to illustrate both the pain and the passion of being true to your beliefs, even when they appear to be serving opposing purposes.

## FEELINGS OF ENTITLEMENT

Coping with feelings of fraudulence is a phenomenon that affects individuals regardless of race, ethnicity, class, or gender. Feelings of "belonging" to hierarchies of power are often difficult to internalize. We know however that, while stories emerge of people who were unaccountably anxious when being praised or inexplicably nervous when receiving recognition, these feelings are much more prevalent among those individuals who did not grow up with a sense of entitlement to public sphere success.

Feeling entitled is often accompanied by being raised with social capital, a term I use to mean those taken-for-granted expectations of family and culture that would naturally presume public sphere success. For example, I raised my children in a neighborhood where all the children were expected to go to college and beyond, where education was valued and becoming productive members of society a given. Internalizing one's right to excel, young people worked toward personal success and were rewarded by the adults. Role models of successful professionals who looked and sounded like them abounded.

I often reflect upon my own childhood world, which held few expectations for public sphere success and even fewer role models. In the elementary and secondary schools I attended, neither women nor minorities occupied positions of educational leadership. Even now, women are clearly not represented in administration in equal proportions to their representation in teaching (Shakeshaft, 1998). Growing up in the East Bronx in New York City, the people in power in schools were White men. Being brought to the principal's office was a journey to a stern elderly man who doled out some sort of punishment. There were few women in positions of power or leadership when I was growing up.

Further, traditional American public education in the 1950s provided no historical role models. My friend, the late Cathy Nelson, often quoted one of her female high school students whom, when asked how she felt about history replied, "History is about dead white men and who cares?" (1998, p. 278). When I was becoming educated, women were absent from the curriculum, and no one noticed that they were missing. The historian Sara Evans (1983) said, "Having a history is a prerequisite to claiming a right to shape the future. That our power to shape the future comes in part because we know that we have shaped the past" (p. 231). Becoming an agent of one's own future is part of "feeling entitled."

Being socialized to feel that we do not belong in positions of power in institutions like the academy contributes to feelings of fraudulence. While there have been many interventions to assist women in feeling more entitled to their public sphere success (assertiveness training, public-speaking courses, etc.), the internalized feeling of "not belonging" often persists for women, particularly at times when publications are submitted and when promotion and tenure are the prize.

While I am writing this piece, I am wondering if readers will believe that this work is scholarly even though I use the first person and relate it to my own story. In this chapter, I argue that fraudulent feelings persist despite *and because of* our awareness of those very feelings. I am hoping that this chapter will help you to think through the down side *and the up side* of "feeling like a fraud" as you think about preparing your own tenure file.

## PREPARING THE TENURE FILE

I had submitted all my materials. Was it enough, I wondered? Do the binders look complete, professional? How about my personal statement? Was it too personal? Keeping a paper trail, neatly and well organized, was never my strength. The process of compiling the data and organizing my academic life into neat categories of university service, community service, school of education service, and department service was more than I could bear. Then the scholarly material had to be categorized: there were published papers, unpublished papers, chapters, books, journal articles, newsletter articles, and conference presentations. I had, over the years, tossed materials into a large cardboard box, and it took much longer to sort and organize than I had anticipated.

It was three days before my tenure file was due when I found myself in Minneapolis at the conference Research on Women and Education. I left the conference one day earlier than I had planned. This departure cost me dearly with the airline since I left before the mandatory Saturday night stay could guarantee my lower fare. With single-minded determination, I arrived home and collated, compiled, and bound all that was considered necessary for a respectable tenure file. How good it felt to have the tedium of the task behind and resume the teaching and research that had consumed the previous six years of my life. I was surprised by how little thought I had given to the tenure process until I was in the position of compiling my dossier. I wondered if I should have given more thought to this process, if, in fact, I had rushed through the mechanics of the process too hastily. I felt insecure and uneasy. My history at the institution was characterized by my being a doctoral student through the first half of my six years, and now that I had completed my doctoral degree, I thought that I was leaping through the next hoop in a hurried fashion.

Clearly, growing up poor in the east Bronx had taken its toll on my sense of entitlement to public sphere praise and prizes. The truck driver's little girl a tenured college professor? Surely not. But then, I argued with myself, You attended a specialized high school, available only to those who had passed a rigorous entrance exam. You won a research award for your dissertation from a prestigious university. Trying to internalize my own entitlement to the tenure prize was an ongoing struggle.

Lacking female role models, not having a familial history of academic success, and remembering how my mother died prematurely before I had reached my own adulthood made me feel lonely as I approached the tenure process. I felt like an outsider, an interloper, an immigrant, and a fraud. This is partly because, as I work to gain access to the hierarchy, I also work to undermine its hold on systems of learning. Consequently, I turned to my friend Peggy McIntosh and to her papers. She writes that when one feels like a fraud, such feelings of fraudulence are to be trusted (McIntosh, 1985). The struggle is to distinguish between the issue of my own personal entitlement and the larger issue of systems of privilege and power. While feeling like a fraud is often a painful reminder of the absence of feelings of personal entitlement in my own childhood, it is also a reminder of the ways in which hierarchical systems insist on absolute entitlement without permitting its members the reflective possibility of self-doubt and critique of the system. Because I seek not only to enter the world of the tenured professor but also to change the nature of the professional work (Aisenberg and Harrington, 1988), I am aware of the ambivalence I feel about the prize and my own right to claim it. McIntosh expresses these feelings in her Stone Center paper, *Feeling like a Fraud*: "While such feelings of fraudulence may be deplorable, especially if and when they trouble women more than men, these same feelings also may indicate a wise reluctance to believe in the accuracy of absolute ranking, and may point the way to a valid critique of hierarchical structures" (1985).

## THE SURPRISE

The academic year in which my materials were evaluated was an anxious time. Although there was no obvious reason to doubt that my credentials were excellent, I was looking forward to the end of the process and the final awarding of tenure designate. It was late spring when the provost asked me to his office. Why did he wish to see me? I had been at the university for almost six years and had never been called to his office. It had been a good year, I thought, except for one undergraduate section, which was struggling with feelings of inadequacy in their field assignments. Some were angry and frustrated; perhaps they had called the provost to complain that the class was not meeting their needs. "There goes tenure," I thought. I was acutely aware that this latter thought was irrational, and as I prepared for the meeting with the provost, I recognized that voice of personal self-doubt and tried to squelch it.

As I entered his office, the provost invited me to sit and explained that each year, the students in the graduating class voted for an outstanding professor in their years at the university; this year, he remarked, they voted for you. "Congratulations Janice; it is high praise and a distinctive honor," he said. After explaining the procedure for receiving the award at graduation, I left his office feeling proud and sad. I felt proud, for this was a student vote, and I love college teaching and respect my students. I felt sad for the frightened assistant professor who had struggled with the prospect of this meeting when I received the call to his office.

The tension between the joy of being accepted in the hierarchy and the personal doubt that I really deserve it never leaves. My work is to use those personal feelings of fraudulence to examine the system and contribute to it in ways that do not perpetuate the intimidating hierarchy.

## THE UP SIDE

My tenure has been decided upon, and I join the ranks of those minority of women who are tenured college professors (10–20 %). I was assisted in my efforts by my sisters, those women who came before me and mentored me and provided me with role models. I was assisted by my family, whose support reminded me of the power of unconditional love.

Do I join the ranks of those who would oppress, limit, and exert power over those who are untenured? Ah, that is where the real work lies, in the way we unravel, expose, and critique systems of oppression, and injustice that seek to limit the numbers of those who are unlike themselves in the public spheres of privileged systems.

That is the up side of the double vision of feeling like a fraud. It is a way of *valuing and welcoming* the feelings of inadequacy that deny internal entitlement. Once we feel entitled to using the language of power and to belonging to the ranks of the tenured professor, how do we hold on to feelings of fraudulence to critique the hierarchy and not buy in completely—to remain forever outside the system as a way to teach our students about how the system does not honor multiple voices and multiple visions for humanity, that, in its exclusivity, the process of belonging marginalizes the people who are not part of the hierarchy as *losers* and perpetuates what McIntosh (1983) calls the "win, lest you lose" mentality.

Knowing this helps you to honor your feelings of fraudulence and to hold on to those feelings in order to preserve your humanity. What is this system that causes me to feel other, lesser, or not good enough? How do I function in such a system and help it to become more inclusive, caring, responsive, and humane? Is it possible that the real frauds, as McIntosh claims are the ones who do not see the inherent fraudulence of seeing oneself as being the best and the brightest?

I encourage you to honor those feelings that place you outside of the sphere of entitlement to the academy. By doing so, you can critique the very system you are entering. This critique is essential if we are to authentically make a difference for students.

## A FEELING OF ENTITLEMENT

Coping with feelings of fraudulence makes it possible to acknowledge when those feelings are not operating. I am always aware of those moments when I am not fighting this "entitlement" struggle. As I reflect upon my work, I understand how my personal feelings of self-doubt have contributed to my own approach to science education with my college students.

I am a science teacher educator. I applied for tenure to continue to do what I deeply value, to work with students and share a vision of science and science education. I love to learn what the students' worlds have taught them about themselves, science, teachers, schools, and hierarchies. I am a role model for the students who never believed they could feel scientific about themselves. I am a woman in support of all students and especially aware of the students in my classes who have never known a scientific woman.

I tell many science stories. They are stories of teachers and children doing science together (Koch, 1999) as they struggle to make meaning of the natural worlds in which they live. My science stories describe teachers and children from all over the country. While my story telling is consistent with my research methodology as an ethnographer, it is also a way that I can engage my students in telling *their* stories. My authentic voice—that born of my experience in many classrooms—is an important reality for my teaching. I never have feelings of fraudulence in this conversational mode with my students. I am, as a teacher, sharing my stories in a way that invites others to join in. My style of teaching is a direct result of being raised outside of the sphere of entitlement. I associate my science stories with the stories my grandmother used to tell of arriving at Ellis Island at the end of the last century. The very cause of my feelings of fraudulence also forces me to seek ways of communicating that are more lateral, more conversational. In the end, the teaching award I received was a direct result of my inability to feel part of the system. It was related to my being "other," an outsider.

To some, it may seem "unscientific" to tell stories despite the rich history of ethnographic research in the social sciences. I risk that critique to invite into the conversation those who may be coping with feelings of fraudulence as they set out to be science teachers with very little background knowledge. How do I help them to gain new scientific knowledge and to be confident science learners?

I am most comfortable when I tell stories with my students. It is a stance as an educator that says, I have had these experiences and they have taught me much about the natural world. These experiences have propelled me forward as a science learner and a science teacher. That is very different from standing in front of the students and saying, "I am the expert and hence, you are not." When I am with my students, I have a large sense of entitlement and do not have feelings of fraudulence. When I am asked to stand at a podium, in front of audiences, to deliver a speech, I am often plagued with feelings of fraudulence. As McIntosh states, "The problem may not be that we can't stand at the podium, but that we can't stand the podium"

(1989, p. 3). Taking away the podiums has become a metaphor for myself as teacher and researcher.

When I tell my science stories, I have found an authentic voice that simultaneously invites students into the discourse and breaks down hierarchical divisions in the classroom. We are all storytellers, and I have much to learn from my students' stories. Feelings of fraudulence and my unease with being "all-knowing" or "the expert" consistently push me to find my authentic voice and share it with my students. McIntosh (1989) claims that these very feelings of authenticity give us the ability to recognize our feelings of fraudulence (p. 2).

Perhaps the real frauds are those who think they are the experts and never have feelings of fraudulence. If you experience feelings of fraudulence as you make your way in the academy toward tenure, it is useful to consider your own responses to these questions: Where do *my* feelings of fraudulence originate? Who are my mentors? What is the work I am most proud of? In what ways do hierarchies intimidate me, and what is the source of my fear? How does my work further the cause of social justice? What parts of the hierarchy do I wish I could change? How will gaining tenure further my own research agenda? Why should this institution support my continuing efforts?

As you explore your responses to these questions, remember that feeling like a fraud can be a "gift." Gift is a reference to the conscious awareness that the tenure prize is part of a larger system of privilege that, like all hierarchies, requires consistent critique. The gift of sometimes feeling like a fraud is to recognize that "winning the prize" is a step toward the freedom to do the work that is necessary to create just and caring learning environments where access to public sphere power means working toward positive social change.

## REFERENCES

Aisenberg, N., and Harrington. M. (1988). *Women of academe: Outsiders in the sacred grove.* Amherst: University of Massachusetts Press.

Evans, S. (1983). Toward a usable past: Feminism as history and politics. *Minnesota History* 48(6), 231–235.

Koch, J. (1999). *Science stories: Teachers and children as science learners.* Boston: Houghton Mifflin.

McIntosh, P. (1983). *Interactive phases of curricular re-vision: A feminist perspective.* Working paper no. 124, Wellesley, MA, Wellesley College Center for Research on Women.

McIntosh, P. (1985). *Feeling like a fraud.* Wellesley College: The Stone Center, Paper No. 18.

McIntosh, P. (1989). *Feeling like a fraud: Part two.* Wellesley College: The Stone Center, Paper No. 37.

Nelson, C. (1998). Teaching U.S. history: Room for imagination. In C. Nelson & K.Wilson (Eds.), *Seeding the process of multicultural education*. Minneapolis: Minnesota Inclusiveness Program.

Shakeshaft, C. (1998). Wild patience and bad fit: Assessing the impact of affirmative action on women in school administration. *Educational Researcher* 27(9), 10–12.

# CHAPTER 8

# The Caged Bird Sings: On Being Different and the Role of Advocacy

## Barbara K. Curry

The tenure and promotion experience in higher education is difficult at best.* It is particularly so for people who present the academy with their divergent backgrounds, research agendas, and scholarship interests. In institutions celebrated for their contributions to the betterment of society, women and minority faculty should not have to compartmentalize who they are in ways that are potentially destructive to their spirit and ultimately embattle their souls.

For example, as an African American I have found that our intellect has been problematized in much the same way that other aspects of our identity have been: our features, hair, dress, music, walk, and discourse. The national controversy over the texture of kinky hair is a vivid reminder of this. We have been conditioned to look at the natural state of our hair and see kinks rather than curls, and to desire the texture of other people's hair rather than our own. Our walk has been described as hip or vulgar instead of graceful. When we walk tall and proud, we are seen as haughty. Our lips for so long have been referred to in disparaging terms. Recently, they have been transformed through the media to represent sensual elements of our character. Our sexuality can not be private, will not be private. Through coaptation we have made

---

*The title of this discussion is borrowed from Maya Angelou's autobiography, *I Know Why the Caged Bird Sings*. The metaphor seemed appropriate here. The caged bird sings to live, to give testimony and affirm the value of its life. It must sing.

that part of our lives outrageously public. And, our discourse has become a characterization of people who have come in from the American bush to corrupt urbanity.

"We" African American women, like women in general, have become bitches and whores. As if by invitation, violence often becomes the thing we experience, replacing tenderness, compassion, and belovedness.

Our intellect, fully problematized, has been diagnosed as grossly inadequate to serve our country. Nor can it serve itself for that matter. However, it seems the African American intellect is stealthy even in its inadequacy. Despite our intellectual difficulties, we manage to plot ways to disentangle people from their appurtenances.

It seems that much of what we are as African Americans has been made perverse and something to be trained out of us. Yet as I observe popular American culture, I believe no single group of people has had more influence on defining it.

Who we are and what we stand for moderated by our connection to other people and our experiences makes up our identity. That identity is integral to the way we function in our personal lives, the way we interact with friends, family, and strangers alike. With regards to our careers, in particular, it guides our lives within the academy.

This discussion is based in the professorate and joins professional development and identity with career issues in the academy. The issues considered here include the construction of individual identity as researcher, scholar, and teacher. It will also consider the way meritocracy through promotion and tenure affirms or disaffirms identity, supports or inhibits creativity. The discussion is based on my perspective as an African American woman. It combines personal observation and impressions with the experiences of other faculty who have gone through the promotion and tenure process. It will conclude with some suggestions on self-advocacy for junior faculty.

## THE ACADEMY:
## AN IDEALIZED COMMUNITY OF SCHOLARS

The dominate American identity is imperious and institutionalized. It has normed an American way of being. It has defined beauty and the nuances of its exhibition. It defines who and what is valued and the ways in which aspects of an individual's identity are to be treated. Paradoxically and simultaneously it regulates. The dominate American identity covets and emulates exotic others, including their cultures. However, politization of race and ethnicity is insidious and in fundamental ways (ego development, strength, and maturity) influences the quality of our lives.

Politization of one's identity at the very least is experienced as unaffirming, requiring responses that explain and rationalize, identity, lifestyle, and culture. The intent of the requirement is not to gain understanding, rather to legitimizing a way of being under circumstances that favor the privileged. It is not surprising that the explanation does not result in entitlement.

The academy is not a decontextualized community, nor is it an unaffected social structure. The myth of the academy includes the development of the intellect so that it rejects what is not rational and is able to cure social pathologies. Through exposure to the intelligentsia, individuals are moved toward civility and tolerance and away from the need to belong to stratified communities.

Before coming to the academy, I believed it could be my refuge, a place to go to and hide away from the harshness of the world. I believed the intelligentsia would embrace and welcome me. As it turns out, although I would rather be an insider than an outsider to the academic community, the very same human condition—the need to judge, order and rank people—persists inside its barracks.

Separating reality from myth, I have found that minority faculty on campuses seem to be less valued than their colleagues. They continue to be marginalized and stereotyped by members of the academic community. Minority faculty are constrained and caged.

A new member of the faculty is required to explain, rationalize, and justify her standpoint as an African American. That demand ultimately puts her at risk for assignment to a status of lesser value than her colleagues. She remains at risk notwithstanding the development of a national identity that can be characterized as multiracial, multiethnic. The lens that comes with that standpoint provides a different take on issues that are folded into the postsecondary curriculum.

From my perspective, those issues necessarily include my Africanness and my Americanness. I have found that for colleagues and students the infusion of my relevance in this country is too arrogant, too deliberate, and unacceptable. However, they are eager to define me, explain my way of being, affirm or disaffirm my value. As a result, for colleagues and students, I have become an exception among my people.

To perceive of oneself as an exception, different, unique, extraordinary, is the beginning of one's participation in the process of coaptation. It is to suffer a loss of identity. It is a high price to pay for belonging.

For the novice or pioneer, survival in the academy has taken the form of disintegration of the self. Identity emerges forthrightly from the blending of interfamilial and extrafamilial experiences. This dialectical process serves as a source of continuity in construction of identity. Externally imposed adaptations, requiring denial or disintegration of aspects of one's identity, such as interfamilial organizing principles (what is right, what is wrong, treatment of others—codes of conduct including ways of being and caring) are an assault on the ego.

Becoming judgmental, detached, and impersonal are examples of adaptations that may conflict with personal codes of conduct. These kinds of adaptations are isolating. In addition, these adaptations may not be required of all new members of the academy. They may only be required of outsiders. To be otherwise (behaviors representing candidness and caring for example) may be construed as inappropriate behavior by colleagues and students. Consequently, the outsider is a poor choice for membership in the academy. Incompatibility can be addressed during procedures associated with meritocracy (promotion and tenure, contract renewal, interpretation of teaching evaluations).

Ultimately, the struggle in all of this is to become one's own person, individuated yet culturally grounded whether seated or unseated on the margin, adaptive and functioning well. A minority woman must find, in her construction of herself as a member of the professorate, the advocate who diligently, ploddingly strives to be authentic and integrated— a whole person.

## THE NEED FOR COMPATIBILITY OF IDENTITIES

The beginning of advocacy on behalf of one's self and the affirmation of one's identity as a member of a faculty is most significant during the promotion and tenure process. Within that process, as within the academy itself, we are required to negotiate between our public and private selves. This can be understood as mediating private and public self or ethnicity including multiracial identity and professional persona. Further, as a commentary on marginal ways of being, this should be reminiscent of the opening discussion on the requirement to explain, redefine, and reshape one's identity in order to find acceptances among one's colleagues.

There is vulnerability in the unauthentic persona. We are pressed to change by abandoning an essential part of ourselves in exchange for affiliation and conditional acceptance. However, conditional acceptance reduces the standing of the novice to something other than a peer and makes her transient in the academy.

Promotion and tenure represent a significant institutional long-term commitment. Faculties try to predict casualties of the process depending upon the number of candidates recommended in a given year and financial health, both present and future, of their institutions.

The judgment of an individual's value to the academy takes place within parameters set forth on institutional terms for meritocracy. In part, this is defined as the contribution to the profession based on the uniqueness of a body of work. Those qualifications are rigidly applied when differences are most apparent. Unfortunately, the academy is a place where the intelligentsia are not well trained in the aesthetics of differences.

At some point during development of most of our careers, we assume the role of self-advocate. In the academy, movement within the professorate or promotion and tenure is one of the most demanding of those occasions.

In many organizations, advocacy is seldom as public a matter as it is in the academy. In most organizations, perhaps with the exception of some firms and medical practices, work contracts are negotiated between individuals and their employer. It is not likely that that contract would be widely debated among the employee's peers in a public utility company, for example. There may be speculation on the value of an individual to the company, but hiring and promotion are not subject to open debate among peers.

The governing structure of the academy, with regards to academic personnel, is inclusive of its faculty members. This means that most members of the faculty are invited to enter into decision-making processes when the results directly influence academics. Consequently, the debate regarding one's professional life in the academy is almost always public. This is so notwithstanding that the work of faculty tends to be solitary with the exception of time spent in teaching and committee assignments. As a result, the forums and domains in which an individual works and is productive are also dramatically different from those in which the judgment of her value or work is made. The forums of her practice and production can conflict.

The judgment of an individual's value to her institution is a significant event in her professional life. The extent of that judgment's influence on defining the trajectory of her career is apparent when we look at the span of time leading to the assessment. The period of time from the contractual agreement to the promotion and tenure judgment can be a period of six to seven years depending upon institutional conventions.

The tension associated with the public nature of the process begins with tenure-track contractual arrangements. The value of the individual is measured against criteria governing professional activities in the areas of teaching, research and scholarship, and service. The influence of those years and criteria on faculty development is significant. A junior member of the faculty is hired based on his or her potential. However, what a faculty values as research and scholarship is central to those early years. Those values can and do preempt individual interests.

The advocate argues in favor of assignment of merit to a body of work. The individual seeking promotion and tenure must be her own advocate. Faculty within the candidate's department as well as those sitting on the committees may or may not serve as advocates in favor of granting promotion and tenure. There are of course individuals who argue against the candidate and who view themselves as advocates on principle and representatives of institutional interests. This is not to say that advocates in favor of the candidates do not view themselves similarly.

As stated earlier, within the procedural committees, people understand the role they play in the decision-making process based on their beliefs about the value and contribution an individual has made to her field and to her institution. Some faculty view their responsibilities as those of gate keepers. For them, the goal of the process is to find reasons not to award tenure. That goal is preserved often in the presence of support for tenure by external reviewers.

For some faculty, the goal is to find reasons to promote and award tenure. Prominence of these roles seems to depend upon the extent to which there is an affinity for the individual whose case is being reviewed. Consequently, the greater the perceived distance between the individual being assessed and those responsible for making judgments about the value of her work, the more likely a decision not to support promotion and tenure will result. By *distance*, I mean difference; diversity, including race, ethnicity, research, scholarship; and more global ways of being—professional persona.

If an individual is different, unless that difference is viewed as value added or trivial, she will be excluded. And if colleagues believe they understand a field, whether or not that belief is well founded, they will make judgments about the value of the candidate's work. Difficulties for candidates, as I see them, can be summarized as follows. It is impossible to approach the process objectively. It goes to the heart of who we think we are and the extent to which we are valued by others. Participants in the process view their jobs differently, and depending upon those views, a candidate has more or less advocacy to do on her own behalf. The more divergent the cultures of the candidate and committee members, the more difficult the process.

## MAKING THE CASE FOR COMPATIBILITY

How does an individual, serving as an advocate on her own behalf, approach these obstacles? At the beginning of our careers, we are most interested in paying the rent, putting food on the table, and paying our student loans. As a result we set aside the feelings that tell us the match we have just made when we agreed to an employment contract was not a good one. We place compatibility and congruence factors on the low end of the scale when they should be much higher. This kind of match gives us a lot of ground to cover in order to move further up that scale.

I suspect that the low match factor is often ignored by institutions as well. The stress experienced by an individual in this situation starts out high and continues to build. Incompatibility and incongruence can happen in each of the crucial areas in which the individual is judged by her peers. While the compatibility factor may be high for some members of a promotion and tenure committee, it may be low for other individuals. And it may be high or low for voting members of the academic unit. It is important to pay attention at the outset to the signals that seem to indicate the match between applicant and institution could be better.

Once a new faculty member is on campus, it is important that he or she not be anonymous. This is not a suggestion that junior faculty volunteer for service assignments that reduce the amount of time and energy they need to focus on continuing or building a research and publishing agenda. Rather, I am suggesting that a junior member of the faculty needs to be known by his area colleagues, by the department faculty, by faculty across campus, and by colleagues nationally who will be among those asked to advise his institution regarding the merit of his work.

Usually an individual does not check with campus advocacy groups until he is experiencing difficulty. Advocacy groups can be helpful. They provide workshops for faculty on professional development, including promotion and tenure. Those workshops offer valuable information about the process in general and about the process at the institution in particular. They also provide company for a journey that can be lonely and isolating. I believe it is helpful to attend workshops earlier in one's career on campus rather than later or during the year of candidacy.

The candidate should be familiar with promotion and tenure guidelines. Explanations of one's work should be aligned with these guidelines. Department guidelines tend to provide substantive directions for compiling a dossier and providing evidence supporting promotion. University or college guidelines tend to provide procedural information. Candidates should explain the body of his or her work with regards to national importance and contribution to his or her field. If there is a count or a specific number of journal articles, specifications for the kinds of journal that count, books, chapters, for example, candidates should provide that count and explain the significance of each of the journals. From the time a candidate is hired until she comes up for review, promotion and tenure documents should serve as product, procedural, and document guides.

Candidates should describe the body of their work within several subareas of research and scholarship. The subareas help provide coherency to a diverse publication portfolio. A candidate also should describe the relationship of those subareas to her overall body of work. This kind of information should also be presented at conferences when meeting peers who will be asked to judge an individual's work. The more candidates educate their peers regarding their work, the better able their peers will be to assess and fairly judge the work without giving mixed messages.

Candidates should find out who had difficulty going through the process and who went through it without a hitch. Both provide valuable information. "Smooth sailors" probably looked like everyone else. "Difficult timers" were probably somewhat unique, with research and publications that were not mainstream. As I stated earlier, both have insights into the process.

Dossier presentation is important. Faculty and committees are annoyed by sloppy, poorly presented work. The documents should be kept neat, nicely appointed, and convenient. Candidates should look at examples and stay within the conventions presented in promotion and tenure guidelines.

Candidates should stay on campus the year they apply for promotion, whether or not they are eligible for sabbatical. You cannot advocate for yourself if you are not on campus, and it is easier to say no to an individual who is not around to object. Even when a candidate's case for promotion is strong, it is best to anticipate that every quirky conceptualization will be applied to it by colleagues and committee members.

If a candidate has doubts, she should ask for advice from someone she trusts. That person should also be familiar with the process on campus. A candidate may want to defer applying for promotion until the following year if it is possible.

Deferment may not be an option. Sometimes those decisions are left to department chairs and deans. On some campuses, candidates are required to abide by those decisions, on others they may simply take it as friendly advice and apply notwithstanding. If a candidate has some doubts about the wisdom of applying, she should seek advice on how best to move forward when the decision is not hers to make.

Candidates may be able to withdraw at any point in the process. These are individual decisions based on individual circumstances and institutional conventions. Promotion and tenure guidelines should be uniformly applied. As suggested earlier, this does not preclude individual interpretations of those guidelines.

I believe mentoring through junior status in the academy is helpful provided that mentors match the needs of the individuals the arrangement is intended to benefit. This is not always the case. My advice regarding mentoring is to have as many as you can manage without allowing the diversity of opinions that come with them to be confusing and cloud your own judgment.

A single mentor may not be able to meet all of the needs of a candidate. Moreover, it is better to have the wisdom of several people rather than a single individual. As a new member of a faculty, a woman, and an African American, I found the process of promotion and tenure as well as the years leading to candidacy extremely stressful. I was trying to construct myself as a member of a faculty with little background experience of my own to bring to the enterprise. I also had the added tension of having to sort through the realities of an environment I idealized.

I was often lonely, afraid, angry, and unsure of myself. The culture of the academy was very strange to me. During that time, some of my mentors could deal with my emotions, while others could not. Some wanted to believe in me, but I suspect deeply seeded beliefs interfered with their ability to do so. I was often distressed by my own belief that I had made myself vulnerable by opening up to a mentor who was uncomfortable with the disclosure. My advice to junior faculty is to be wise and use good sense in determining how you will relate to mentors. I found my strongest support from a few colleagues scattered across my own and other college and university campuses and national women's groups associated with professional organizations.

This is probably a time that is best treated as a juncture in a promising career. It is a time when one can be prepared to stay or move on. As such, while candidates are coming up for promotion and tenure, they should consider receiving tenure as one of several possible outcomes. Candidates should consider others they feel are positive as well.

Promotion and tenure are critical in the adult identity development landscape. There are institutional issues of quality control that are difficult to separate from the human factor. I do not accept those issues as reasons not to take the process personally. I also believe that anyone who says they did not take it personally could either afford to minimize the process because of the support and affirmation they received from colleagues, or they are in denial about their experience. You cannot get more personal than assigning value to the body of an individual's life work, and based on that value tell her whether or not she must leave the institution she cares about.

I believe there is no such state as objectivity. And even when the promotion and tenure process proceeds without a hitch, a period of recovery follows. According to colleagues, the period could last for weeks, months, or years. The average from my discussion on the topic seems to be anywhere from one to two years. This is a period of getting over any hurt feelings sustained throughout the process; renewing research, scholarship, and teaching agendas; and simply enjoying having survived.

This is an ideal time to take a sabbatical. During the process, I felt that I needed to be in control constantly in order to meet any demands made by the committees. At the end of it, I was strained and tired. Taking a sabbatical helped me to regain perspective and to think about my future with an institution that was likely to be my home for at least a few more years. I also needed the distance to forgive the process. That may sound strange, but I really needed to forgive "it" and let go.

Our psyches work through issues that surface during this time in our lives. The promotion and tenure process is destabilizing; the recovery period involves restabilizing and consolidating changes. It is a period of healing and goal setting. And, if necessary, it is a time of reconciliation. As an African American on a majority campus, for me it was all of these.

# CHAPTER 9

# Resisting Common Injustice: Tenure Politics, Department Politics, Gay and Lesbian Politics

## Patricia M. McDonough

In this chapter, I focus on two issues related to the early careers and achievement of tenure for women; faculty of color; and gay, lesbian, and bisexual faculty: first, the role of department chairs in hiring and promotion processes and second, the special needs of gay, lesbian, and bisexual faculty. I will begin with an overview of the organizational terrain of the academy and a discussion of the role of the department chair. Then I will explore the special issues and concerns of lesbian, gay, and bisexual (LGB) people particularly through a selective telling of my own story. Finally, I will review the issues of department politics in tenure considerations, tenure criteria, and recommendations for strategic and successful partnerships between chairs and pretenure faculty.

Department chairs play important albeit ill-defined and ambiguous roles in the hiring, mentoring, and promotion of faculty (Creswell and Brown, 1992; Gmelch & Miskin, 1995; Tierney and Bensimon, 1996). The ambiguity comes from the fact that the role of department chairs can vary tremendously, depending on the nature of the particular postsecondary institution (research university, community college, liberal arts college, etc.), the size of the department or university, and the criteria and process of evaluating faculty for tenure, and so on. Another crucial factor is how a department chair interprets her role in nurturing and mentoring untenured faculty as well as whether and how to support faculty who are different.

A department chair's impact on an applicant begins with the transmission of information about that organization's culture in the job interview and orientation (Tierney & Bensimon, 1996). That culture is reinforced throughout the pretenure period through the presence or absence of mentoring, advocacy, encouragement, and enabling conditions (Creswell & Brown, 1992). Chairs can foster hostile and competitive or nurturing and cooperative departmental environments. Moreover, chairs make key policy decisions in determining faculty workloads, hiring and tenure review processes, and committee appointments.

Ultimately, achieving tenure is securing the right to become a permanent member of a particular community of scholars. A significant portion of the job of an assistant professor attempting to achieve tenure is building positive, productive relationships with her immediate colleagues in order to become a member of that community. Chairs can help in that process by structuring work opportunities (i.e., committee service, co-teaching, etc.) where assistant professors develop positive relationships with key colleagues and ward off potentially negative relationships.

However, a fundamental characteristic of organizations is that they structure routines for almost all tasks based on norms (Perrow, 1979), yet routines do not adequately serve anyone who is different from that norm. That can mean that in a department with all senior professors, there will likely be no established routines for socializing a new assistant professor. It can also mean that any other characteristic of difference—being a person of color, a woman, a gay, a lesbian, or a bisexual person—and individuals' reactions to that difference are potential inhibitors to building those collegial relationships.

## ISSUES FOR LESBIAN, GAY, AND BISEXUAL UNTENURED FACULTY

Gay, lesbian, and bisexual people face a unique set of concerns when contemplating academic careers, seeking faculty appointments, and working to achieve tenure. In most parts of the United States, it is still legal to discriminate against sexual minorities, and on many postsecondary campuses, nondiscrimination clauses do not include sexual orientation. Even putting aside legal discrimination, most gay, lesbian, and bisexual people are uncertain about colleagues' religious and personal beliefs and how they will be treated on a daily basis. For LGB people, the issue of whether and when to "come out" in graduate school, job searches, and pretenure years are all high-stakes decisions.

Also, LGB lives and issues in academe are staggeringly neglected (McNaron, 1997; Rhoads, 1994), and one task in creating paths to success in the sacred grove is to break through the silence engulfing gay academic lives (Mintz & Rothblum, 1997). Certainly, basic conditions of physical and public safety for LGB people, even on college campuses, must be dealt with before we can even begin to tackle issues of faculty development and the creation of organizational climates that are gay-affirming and support visibility.

Academic department chairs need to be an intellectual presence that ensures that community members discuss with each other their own personal experiences about the life of the community. Organizationally, universities privilege some voices while ideologically silencing others through the culture and power of the norm of heterosexuality, which not only has an oppressive hold on what is acceptable and deviant, but also enforces conformity rather than fostering empowerment.

A multitude of reports on gay, lesbian, and bisexual campus climates indicate that oppression and invisibility are virtually omnipresent (Tierney, 1993). Postsecondary institutions' cultures marginalize gay, lesbian, and bisexual peoples by the dualism inherent in private and public lives. When we assume that everyone is similar, then any difference disturbs the norm and reinforces a culture of silence for those organizational participants who are different. The culture of silencing is built by institutional policies, which claim to be universal statements of nondiscrimination but do not mention gay, lesbian, and bisexual people (about 90% of colleges do not recognize queers in their statements of nondiscrimination [National Gay and Lesbian Task Force, 1992]), as well as by institutional policies, which privilege heterosexual relationships, like benefits and housing policies. Anyone who is different is made invisible within these institutional norms.

For the untenured faculty member who is materially and symbolically viewed through the lens of being not fully authorized (i.e., untenured, not yet permanent) within the university community, being different is a liability, whether that comes from racial, ethnic, gender, or sexual difference from the norm. Moreover, having a research agenda focused on gay, lesbian, or bisexual issues necessitates a concern with the politics of researching topics seen as unsafe, sensitive, or political liabilities.

Using reflections on my own nine-year journey from lesbian job applicant facing these decisions to advisor of LGB students, to my current role as a department chair, I will develop each of these issues and then weave them together.

## MY PERSONAL JOURNEY

Eleven years ago, I applied for a tenure-track, faculty job at UCLA. I did so because my dissertation chair and other graduate school advisors repeatedly urged, and in fact insisted, that I do so. I was flattered, terrified, unprepared, and sure that my faculty candidacy would be very embarrassing and short-lived.

It literally had never occurred to me to aspire to such a job; I always assumed that faculty were other, smarter people. I started graduate school as a university employee taking classes, and there were other students who were acknowledged stars. Being a working-class lesbian in a big-name university was already an aspirational stretch, and I happily imagined that after graduate school I would go back to my previous work in university administration. Moreover, I was settled into my life. My partner and I were living in the San Francisco Bay area where we were out of the closet, safe, and settled into supportive and nurturing communities of friends and work. I certainly didn't want to move, and I certainly couldn't ask my partner to give up her job and community.

But my graduate school mentors advised me that I should at least apply and see how my academic credentials would be assessed, so I would know if I would be taken seriously if I ever did go after a faculty job. With that intent, I applied. The entire process was seductive, affirming, grueling, anxiety-producing, and overwhelming. The more I found out about being a faculty member, and the more I found out about this particular job, the more I wanted it. I applied. But I kept waiting for them to announce that I wasn't academically qualified and that they had made a terrible mistake.

My ambivalence about the job was actually and accidentally empowering. Because I couldn't imagine myself being a faculty member or moving, I wasn't invested in "having" to get the job; therefore, I was able to feel less pressure than normal and more myself throughout the application process. My empowerment and groundedness liberated me to think about how and when to come out as a lesbian.

Although I had been out to myself for 18 years and had been out in previous jobs, I had only officially been out to my advisor and the faculty in graduate school for less than a year. In fact, only after another graduate student had died suddenly of AIDS did any of the gay and lesbian students and one faculty member begin to mobilize and raise awareness around gay and lesbian issues. Also, the other gay faculty aspirants I knew were steadfastly closeted for fear of never getting hired. However, I didn't want to be in the closet anymore, and I wasn't afraid of losing a job I didn't really want. So I sought advice from a faculty member on campus who went through a prolonged tenure battle that centered on her being a feminist scholar and a lesbian. She advised me that I should wait until I had a firm job offer and then come out. If I waited till that point, she reasoned, and if UCLA tried to withdraw its offer, then I could have a legal case for discrimination—but more important, I could assess whether the campus and department climate would be hostile, neutral, or affirming on gay and lesbian issues. So I waited, and the surprise of surprises happened. UCLA offered me a faculty position.

I tried to determine how I would announce my lesbianism in order to assess the campus climate. I checked with professional colleagues to identify a "safe" UCLA colleague to first come out to and to find out what to expect from the department chair who was a white, heterosexual, older male. By now, I was terrified because I wanted the job even though I couldn't imagine how it would all work out. Also, it seemed an odd conversation to be having with a relative stranger who also happened to be offering me a great job.

Ultimately, I marshaled all my courage and called the department chair. I said that I had a life partner, that this was a decision we both would need to make, and that I wanted him to fly both of us to L.A. to check out housing and employment opportunities—I even asked him to set up appointments with the placement officer at the School of Social Work so that my partner could investigate jobs. He said, "OK, when do you both want to come down for a visit?" I nearly collapsed from all the imagined but unrealized homophobia.

I tell this story not to highlight how easy it is to come out, but to show the power of an affirming campus climate and department chair. That department chair really made a difference in welcoming me into the "sacred grove." He set up those appointments and validated my partner's role in my decision making, just as he would have for any heterosexual faculty candidate.

Having told my particular story, I need to go beyond the personal and report the evidence that many, if not most, gay, lesbian, and bisexual faculty have not shared my privilege but rather have daily faced persecution, discrimination, and hostility, as well as symbolic and material violence within college environments (McNaron, 1997; Mintz & Rothblum, 1997; Tierney, 1993). Since being gay and lesbian is not a visible characteristic like race or gender, coming out is both necessary and not something you do once. Gay, lesbian, and bisexual faculty constantly assess whether, when, how, and how often to come out of the closet. LGB faculty make daily coming out decisions in research and writing, teaching, and service. In my pretenure years, I often faced serious threats to my staying in the academy, some of them because I am a lesbian, but I also was supported by some acts of colleagues.

In my fourth year I decided I needed to contribute to the growing field of queer studies (albeit in a very minor way). When a journal in my field decided to do a special issue on LGB concerns, and a heterosexual colleague asked me to co-author a submission, I agreed. I felt that making a scholarly statement as a lesbian faculty member was important, although risky. I also knew that this was an important crucible for me personally. Moreover, I felt nurtured personally and professionally because my co-author was a powerful senior faculty member who made a commitment to me by inviting me to this co-authorship, as well as a commitment to the scholarship of lesbian, gay, and bisexual studies. I did fear that other senior colleagues might be uncomfortable with and unsupportive of LGB as a legitimate area of scholarship, and I might be viewed as being unfocused by adding a new area to my otherwise focused and unified research agenda. However, I needed to feel safe publishing on LGB topics in my pretenure years, in order to believe that tenure meant full acceptance if I were to attain it. We published that piece and, again, none of my imagined homophobia or negative consequences ever materialized or were made known to me.

As Tierney (1993) has shown us, the parameters of diversity are defined largely by how power is situated in institutions. On one occasion, my dean and school powerfully affirmed my lesbianism and created a positive work climate by providing a countermeasure to the larger institution's lack of domestic partner benefits. My partner had left her job (ironically, with an employer that offered domestic partner benefits) so that I could accept my assistant professorship, and privately paying for her health benefits was proving to be a financial burden for us. When I discussed the matter with my dean, he proposed a way to exercise organizational flexibility and use nonstate funds to pay for domestic partner benefits for all LGB staff and faculty. He made a proposal to the school's Executive Committee, who approved it as an issue of fundamental social justice. My school decided that even if the larger organization was to remain homophobic, they could create an affirming environment for LGB people until the larger corporate entity changed. Several years later the university finally authorized domestic partner benefits systemwide at the level of the regents. On that day, I finally felt equally treated as a member of the larger university community.

Interpersonally, I have always been out in departmental social gatherings, in my daily unofficial corridor conversations, and in public displays of my lesbianism in my office, where I have pictures of my partner, quotations up on the walls about the importance of being out, and a gay pride flag. However, although I am a faculty member in a university that is ostensibly committed to gay-affirming values through its nondiscrimination clause, gay, lesbian, and bisexual resource center and classes, there were times when my colleagues' real or potential homophobia, as well as their silence, created a hostile environment.

One example arose in the Executive Committee meeting in which the university approved my request for domestic partner benefits. Although the overwhelming majority of discussion, and, of course, the final outcome, were positive, the benefits were not approved before a homophobic complaint was raised. One senior member of the faculty spoke immediately after I made my request and said that she now felt that she was a member of the only category of employees still discriminated against—single people. She then asked shouldn't she be getting benefits for her pet. I was stunned and momentarily speechless, when one of my other colleagues chimed in and said that the comment was inappropriate and moved that we should approve my request.

I have never had difficulty raising LGB issues in the curriculum, and I support students who wanted to work on LGB research. However, at times I have found it much more difficult being out in the classroom because of feelings of personal vulnerability. As a new and untenured faculty member, I was once invited to speak about gay and lesbian issues in a class on multiculturalism and the university. In that class, I was confronted by a student who objected to homosexuality and gay curricular "agendas" on moral grounds. This student also sexualized his confrontation with me by stating that I hadn't yet met the right man! It's an understatement to say that I felt embarrassed, uncomfortable, and angry. The situation was made worse, though, by the fact that my colleague fell silent during the exchange. I was angry and felt unsupported by the colleague who had invited me in to speak. I began to think about how threatened and marginalized LGB students must feel, if I as a faculty member with ostensible power (although I wasn't gaining any benefit from it that moment) was feeling attacked and sexually harassed. I could only imagine the silencing power of discussions like these on students.

More than anything, I learned that I surely wasn't used to being the object of discussion in class, and that because of my personal pedagogical beliefs, I was a less effective teacher when I tackled gay and lesbian issues. In general when teaching, I believe that my role is to challenge students within an environment of safety, freedom, and empathy, so they can develop their thinking and their voices. I believe that as the teacher I not only must evidence genuine caring for all my students but also must sacrifice my own identity and personal needs to the students' needs (Silin, 1999). When I am confronted in a classroom with homophobia directed at me, I get angry and fear not being in control of my emotions, let alone the classroom. I have since learned that my task in dealing with LGB issues in class is to momentarily sacrifice my feelings—but not my politics. I now try to exercise discussion management when teaching about LGB issues so that all students can have voice and can work through the tough issues of homophobia.

For me at this stage of my career, I don't come out in the classroom as a confessional act of self-display but as a way to actualize gay-affirming campus climates in my classroom and department. Like Silin (1999),

I find that coming out in the classroom is a moral imperative, fraught with risks that come from being misunderstood and misrepresented. However, for the untenured LGB faculty member and students who are the potential future faculty, it can be perilous and threatening to their membership in the academy.

Lesbian, gay, and bisexual faculty members often experience *common injustices*, because it is legally, culturally, and religiously acceptable to be hostile, to insult, to discriminate, and to belittle our needs and us. Students, university presidents, and colleagues don't always feel the need to respect us or to treat us as full members of the academy and sometimes do us injustices through discriminatory action, sometimes by disrespectful behavior, and sometimes by silence and neglect (McNaron, 1997; Mintz & Rothblum, 1997; Tierney, 1993). Untenured LGB faculty need the institution to be mindful of their particular needs and for department chairs and other university faculty and leaders to create environments where LGB faculty will be supported and know that they will not be subjected to the common injustices that pervade contemporary life.

College climates can be made more inclusive through the following policies that acknowledge a diversity of sexual identities, such as protective clauses related to sexual orientation; safe spaces, resources, and trained, sensitized staff to help queer faculty deal with their unique issues; and conditions that support research and teaching on gay, lesbian, and bisexual lives. It is important to make clear the task of full empowerment of gay, lesbian, and bisexual untenured faculty. Tierney (1993) calls for changes in the enduring college cultures that foster dialogues of support and understanding across differences and the creation of university climates that are safe, affirm individual differences, and draw individuals into dialogues about norms, silencing, and otherness.

## DEPARTMENT CHAIRS

I now am chair of a department of approximately fifty tenure-track faculty. A main source of tension stems from balancing the inevitable role of being the "guardian at the gate" of academic personnel actions and wanting to be the facilitator at the gate and make that role proactively supportive of untenured faculty. My first strategy in being a proactive department chair was to reflect on my own and colleagues' experiences as untenured faculty members and ask the following questions: What made us feel empowered? What helped to socialize us? What made us feel a part of a community? What can I do now as department chair?

Academic department chairs can improve the quality of untenured professors' worklives by ensuring full participation in all departmental decision making and meetings. Whenever and wherever policies are being made, untenured faculty should be present so that they can learn those aspects of faculty work and so that they and their tenured colleagues symbolically recognize the necessity of their full participation. The most essential decisions and committee opportunities for untenured faculty are on departmental personnel appointments and reviews. Although untenured faculty at almost every institution cannot take part in tenure decisions, many institutions provide valuable learning opportunities for pretenure faculty on search committees where candidate credentials are assessed; in routine merit reviews of faculty at all ranks; and at meetings where faculty governance by-laws are established or changed.

Chairs often have significant discretion in determining individual faculty courseloads, can sometimes establish departmental policy for course buyout rates, and have valuable experience to transmit about ways to manipulate the intensity of teaching preparation. For example, all academic departments have expectations for the average number of courses taught per year per faculty member, and a common practice when hiring new faculty is to offer a one-to-two course reduction for the first year or two. However, what most new faculty don't understand is that there are other ways to manipulate the meeting of that average teaching load.

For example, if a faculty member teaches in a research university with lower average courseloads (i.e., four courses a year), and the university is on a quarter system, a faculty member could, over two academic years, protect up to nine consecutive months for research if she teaches two courses each in the fall and winter quarters of the first year and then teaches two courses each in the winter and spring quarters of the next year. Another example might be where a department chair protects a new faculty member's time by assigning her to teach smaller seminars instead of large lecture classes or assigns new faculty to courses where the students are less demanding (e.g., nonmajors versus majors, or part-time students versus full-time students). Moreover, if the department has course buyout rates for faculty who secure external funding for research or other activities, chairs can sometimes set lower rates for untenured faculty than for senior faculty, which could preserve more of a grant's resources for research assistants.

Academic department chairs can also protect faculty from themselves and others. Many untenured faculty suffer from being overburdened with significant program responsibility. Chairs can establish departmental policies that prohibit their colleagues from saddling pretenure faculty with too much administrative responsibility in order to protect untenured faculty's time to do the teaching and research that will be key to gaining tenure. Also, department chairs can offer untenured faculty protection to say no to the many requests of students, faculty, and other administrators. In particular, women and LGB faculty as well as faculty of color are likely to face significant pressure to "give" to their communities as advisors to student groups, serving on committees, and so on.

A crucial role for academic department chairs in supporting the work of untenured faculty is mentoring. Mentors can ensure that pretenure faculty receive structured, systematic feedback on all aspects of their performance, specifically areas needing improvements (Tierney & Bensimon, 1996). Mentoring programs for pretenure faculty can be structured in many ways: committees can be established for all pretenure faculty or can be individually tailored per faculty member, individual mentors can be assigned to faculty, or individual pretenure faculty can ask senior colleagues to serve as mentors.

However, mentoring itself is a delicate balancing act. Mentors want to be supportive and to create safe spaces for raising difficult issues, and they want to provide symbolic and material mentoring supports (i.e., decoding what journals the department would most value, the relative assessment of teaching versus research in tenure decisions, etc.). Institutionally sponsored mentorship programs also exist to help the untenured faculty member understand the department's expectations and normative pathways to success. However, given that all mentors eventually serve as part of the peer group that votes on tenure decisions, many assistant professors find it virtually impossible to separate mentoring from monitoring.

Aside from being clear about tenure expectations, academic department chairs can also intervene at key monetary and professional development points. New faculty often have come from graduate school and lives of near poverty, and if a faculty member doesn't have external grants for her own research, she will be more likely to accept any summer work, even if it distracts her from her own research agenda. Department chairs could help by finding summer salary and other important salary supplements. Having faculty development sessions to help untenured faculty learn how to secure research funding is also important, as is having senior colleagues introduce pretenure faculty to major players in the field who can eventually write external review letters. Other faculty development sessions that department chairs could sponsor are peer discussions of writing, impediments to writing, and successful strategies for dealing with revising and resubmitting manuscripts.

Academic department chairs also can support new faculty by helping them improve their use of time, clarifying their needs and expectations, identifying and rewarding successes, and encouraging the development of productive collaborations (Boice, 1992). Finally, chairs can help pretenure faculty by talking about their accomplishments to other colleagues and deans, by providing opportunities for visibility, by befriending pretenure faculty and informally acknowledging excellent performance (Creswell & Brown, 1992).

## IF TENURE IS MERIT BASED,
## WHY CARE ABOUT DEPARTMENT POLITICS?

The ultimate yardstick for every tenure decision is a locally defined, merit-based mix of productivity in teaching, research, and service. The specific standards and means of assessing achievement in each of these domains, however, will vary over time, context, and place. Some institutions value teaching and will weight teaching loads, student evaluations, and pedagogical techniques more heavily than research in its tenure process. In other institutions, reasonable teaching abilities will be necessary, but the real focus in the tenure decision will be on research productivity. Within some fields, only peer-reviewed journals will "count," while for other disciplines, only books published by scholarly presses will be valued. Having a tenurable record is very often hard to specify and almost always not clear-cut.

Very few faculty come to the tenure decision point with a case that would be uniformly judged as either tenurable or completely untenurable (Whicker, Kronenfeld, & Strickland, 1993). Thus, tenure decisions, along with every codified and uncodified expectation of the achievement needed in order to secure tenure, are inevitably coupled with the highly complex social and political processes of tenure. These processes revolve around issues of specialization, peer review, departmental politics, secrecy, and unfortunately, personality. Also, sometimes tenure processes reflect the larger politics of race, gender, and sexual orientation.

Most academics are hired to be specialists, and with the proliferation of knowledge and subfields, it is increasingly difficult for colleagues to know each others' specialized domains well enough to judge journal quality, the impact of an individual faculty member's contribution to the field, and so on. Thus tenure processes can be favorably or unfavorably impacted by who constitutes your review committee and how well they interpret your work and assess its impact on the field. Other interpreters of faculty work are the external reviewers whose letters frame the context for assessing a tenure candidate's contribution to the field; thus the selection of these individuals is crucial.

Also, most tenure decisions are an evaluation by your peers, not a single "boss." Therefore, successful faculty need to rely not on single administrators but must have a wide base of support in the faculty. Moreover, cross-campus tenure decision makers usually take into account the size of the support or dissenting opinion; that is, unanimous or strong positive votes are usually "worth more" than mixed votes (Whicker, Kronenfeld, & Strickland, 1993).

Right or wrong, your tenure decision not only impacts your life but also could be perceived to have a significant impact on future allocations of faculty billets within the department, assessments of the department's reputation or prestige, or the balance of power between coalitions within the department. Also, because they are made by secret ballot, tenure decisions are subject to the vagaries of all voting processes where people can vote the merits of a case, their conscience, or on the basis of grudges (Whicker, Kronenfeld, & Strickland, 1993).

Finally, your faculty peers are people, and human tendencies are such that personality issues sometimes come into play. If you are seen as a team player or a good citizen, people may consciously or unconsciously weigh your qualifications more positively. Any powerful difference—being lesbian, gay, or bisexual; being a person of color; or being a woman—could affect the assessment of your suitability for tenure. Again, this is a place where a department chair could actively work to ensure that these issues do not come into play in tenure decision making.

Finally, I offer four principles for success in the tenure process: knowing yourself and your rhythms; identifying successful organizational strategies and identifying where the flexibility and discretion is in your institution's operations; building a tenurable record; and understanding the membership processes of your academic community.

## Knowing Yourself and Your Rhythms

New faculty are always multitasking and have multiple learning curves that they need to be attentive to in the early years. Although they may have taught before, they are most likely learning to teach more, in new areas, or in new ways at the same time as they are ratcheting up their writing productivity, learning how to deal with reviewers and journal editors, learning a new community, and responding to student needs. It is important that new faculty know their own rhythms: Do you write best in the morning or in large uninterrupted blocks? Do you put so much time into teaching that you can't write during the same terms as when you teach? The more new faculty are reflective about their own practice and honest about their abilities to juggle tasks, the more they will be able to develop successful time and task management strategies. An interesting footnote to this principle is that research on faculty and productivity has provided two insights: first, most new faculty spend too much time on class preparation, and second, the most productive faculty are those who allocate similar amounts of time to both writing and teaching on a regular basis (Boice, 1992).

## Identifying Organizational Flexibility and Discretion

What are your department's expectations for individual faculty courseloads? Can untenured faculty rearrange their teaching schedules to accommodate their needs for data collection or for large writing projects? Have faculty sometimes been allowed to teach "lighter" workload courses? Will the department allow you to use external funding to buy yourself out of teaching for a term? Can your mentor(s) agree to run interference with other faculty, students, and administrators who want you to serve on committees, and so on? Asking your colleagues, particularly your newly tenured colleagues, what tips and techniques they used or have heard of being used to boost productivity is also a good way to expand your toolkit of tacit organizational knowledge.

## Building a Tenurable Record

Obviously, nothing will substitute for getting a clear understanding of what your institution and department's expectations for tenure are. How many publications do faculty who successfully achieve tenure at your institution tend to have? Are they books or articles, and if so, in what kinds of journals? What is the department's norm for teaching? What kinds of service expectations do your colleagues have? You will need to develop a plan for how you will build that package of achievements. Keeping track on an everyday basis of accomplishments, that is, updating your curriculum vitae as you accomplish a task, is a good building block. Setting specific goals, mobilizing institutional resources, and maximizing and balancing your efforts will also be key to success.

## Understanding Membership in Your Academic Community

Academics often use phrases such as *good citizenship* and *collegiality* to describe the values and benefits of involvement and participation in the life of the community. What this means is that aside from tasks of individual teaching and research responsibilities, departments and schools are communities where other work needs to be done. All faculty want their colleagues to share the load and contribute fairly to teaching, committee assignments, admissions processes, and so on. Decisions about tenure invariably involve assessments of how much an individual will be a contributing member of the departmental community and can be counted on.

Proactive chairs can structure mentoring experiences that help untenured faculty attend to their own rhythms and can help them to know what the research base tells us about productive faculty. Chairs can also strategize with untenured faculty to manipulate workloads or can sponsor informal sharing sessions between newly tenured faculty and pretenure faculty focusing on specific information, such as what is a successful package of achievements.

Chairs need to help pretenure faculty become members of their academic communities, particularly when that faculty member is a person of color; a woman; or a gay, lesbian, or bisexual person. Chairs will or should know their tenured colleagues' beliefs and values and should interrupt codes of silence and help untenured and tenured faculty build the necessary collegial relationships.

Finally, department chairs can provide many forms of valuable assistance to pretenure faculty, most of which untenured faculty might not even know to ask about. Thus, department chairs need to actively help untenured faculty understand the role of chairs and the kinds of support they can provide.

I would like to conclude this section on being a proactive department chair with a few suggestions on how to empower junior faculty and students, foster support across differences, and create climates that are safe, affirm individual differences and build dialogues about norms, silences, and otherness.

This past year, two other senior lesbians and I strategized on how to break the silence on LGB issues in our department. At the school's beginning-of-the-year faculty retreat, I announced our plans as part of my department chair's report. I stated that the silence surrounding LGB issues was deafening and that we had received reports from students that it was a very chilly climate. I further announced that we would be initiating LB gatherings at an off-campus location (to protect those LGB individuals who didn't feel safe coming out on campus) to talk about issues and needs. We initiated dinner gatherings during the fall quarter for LGB people and discussed whatever issues people brought forward. Collectively, we developed a plan for LGB support needs and for educating our department.

At an early January retreat on diversity issues that the Dean sponsored for the school's faculty (our department and one other department), the Dean asked for a report from one of my fellow faculty on LGB issues. (The symbolism of the Dean including LGB issues in a diversity discussion was a first and elevated the issue to the School's policy agenda.) My colleague did a fabulous job of describing the absolute silence that exists in our curricular, research, and programmatic initiatives and its impact. She then announced three activities that we subsequently carried out over the winter and spring quarters.

First, we continued the LGB social gatherings for support and community building. Second, we instituted a monthly reading group for LGB and heterosexual people on LGB topics that would promote visibility, learning, and bridge building between LGB and non-LGB people. Third, we instituted a "Safe Zones" series of workshops. These workshops have been instituted at many campuses across the country, but had just begun at UCLA. The Safe Zone program has three components:

1. a training workshop on how to make your piece of the campus an environment that is understanding of the needs of lesbian, gay, bisexual, and transgendered people on campus
2. a literature packet including information and resources on sexual orientation issues and
3. a Safe Zone sticker that symbolizes a visible commitment to making our workplaces safe and welcoming for all UCLA community members, especially LGB people

These initiatives haven't changed the world or UCLA, but they have made our department climate better, have broken through the silence, and have established an agenda for us to keep working on. Any individual or group could implement these initiatives on any campus; however the addition of the symbolism of senior faculty leadership and the chair's endorsement and leadership did confer institutional legitimacy to these efforts.

## CONCLUSION

Although the achievement of tenure for women; faculty of color; and gay, lesbian, and bisexual faculty can be quite difficult, there are opportunities for assistant professors to help themselves and ways for department chairs to be proactive. Department chairs can significantly assist pretenure faculty by

- making favorable policies for workloads, course buyout, and hiring and tenure review;
- ensuring full participation in all departmental decision making;
- protecting untenured faculty's time for research from too much teaching or administrative responsibility;

142 McDONOUGH

- providing mentoring—structured, systematic feedback on all aspects of faculty performance;
- helping with key monetary and professional development assistance;
- providing visibility and acknowledging excellent performance;
- helping faculty develop a wide base of departmental support and a national network of colleagues who might be able to provide external review letters; and
- creating supportive environments where common injustices are not allowed.

Regardless of what department chairs do, pretenure faculty can become empowered and maximize their opportunities for successfully achieving tenure by knowing themselves, their work styles, and their time needs; identifying locally successful strategies and organizational flexibility; understanding the locally defined criteria for tenure and building a tenurable record; and understanding what their colleagues expect of them as members of an academic community. Finally, college campuses must be made more gay affirming through policies that acknowledge and protect LGB students, staff, and faculty, as well as campus climates that support research and teaching on gay, lesbian, and bisexual lives. Every faculty member, administrator, and student needs to work toward campus environments where LGB people are supported and not subjected to the common injustices that pervade contemporary life.

## REFERENCES

Boice, R. (1992). *The new faculty member*. San Francisco: Jossey-Bass.
Creswell, J. W., & Brown, M. (1992). How chairpersons enhance faculty research: A grounded study. *Review of Higher Education* 16: 41–62.
Gmelch, G. H., & Miskin, V. D. (1995). *Chairing an academic department*. Thousand Oaks, CA: Sage.
Mintz, B., & Rothblum, E. (1997). *Lesbians in academia: Degrees of freedom*. NY: Routledge.
McNaron, T. A. H. (1997). *Poisoned ivy: Lesbian and gay academics confronting homophobia*. Philadelphia: Temple University Press.
National Gay and Lesbian Task Force. (1992). *Partial list of colleges and universities with non-discrimination policies which include sexual orientation*. Washington, DC: NGTLF Policy Institute.
Perrow, C. (1979). *Complex organizations: A critical essay*. Chicago: Scott Foresman.
Rhoads, R. A. (1994). *Coming out in college: The struggle for a queer identity*. Westport, CT: Bergin and Garvey.

Silin, J. (1999). Teaching as a gay man: Pedagogical resistance or public spectacle? *Gay and Lesbian Quarterly* (5):95–106.

Tierney, W. G. (1993). *Building communities of difference: Higher education in the 21st century.*

Tierney, W. G., & Bensimon, E. M. (1996). *Promotion and tenure: Community and socialization in academe.* Albany: State University of New York Press.

Whicker, M. L., Kronenfeld, J. J., & Strickland, R. A. (1993). *Getting tenure.* Newbury Park: Sage.

# PART III

# *The Process of Getting Tenure: Advice along the Way*

Completing the triad of adult learning theory (Merriam and Cafferella, 1999), which includes context, learner, and process, this section focuses on the process of getting tenure. Here chapter authors provide concrete advice about the tasks of writing and publishing, teaching effectively, the scholarship of outreach, and using a journal to steer a successful course through often rough tenure waters.

In chapter 10, Sandra Hollingsworth leads the reader to becoming a better writer. In chapter eleven, Joanne E. Cooper and Sheryl E. Nojima describe the problems and possibilities for self-exploration available to faculty through the teaching role. They also discuss the current move toward the scholarship of teaching. Following the seminal work of Boyer (1990), in chapter 12, Pennie G. Foster-Fishman and Dannelle D. Stevens describe the rationale and the process of reframing and redefining traditional "service" in a broader, not-so-traditional way, as scholarship. Chapter 13, by Dannelle D. Stevens and Joanne E. Cooper, illustrates a method for documenting and reflecting on the tenure journey through journal keeping. Finally, Joanne E. Cooper and Dannelle D. Stevens close the book with a discussion of composing an academic life, summarizing the issues and strategies that have been previously shared.

## REFERENCES

Boyer, E. L. (1990). *Scholarship reconsidered: Priorities of the professoriate.* Princeton, NJ: Carnegie Foundation of the Advancement of Teaching.

Merriam, S., & Cafferella, R. (1999). *Learning in adulthood: A comprehensive guide.* San Francisco: Jossey-Bass.

# CHAPTER 10

# Writing and Publishing

## Sandra Hollingsworth

### INTRODUCTION

I learned how to write five times. The first time was at home before I began school in central Texas—writing stories and songs for my friends and family in a rather loose, phrase-not-sentence, chatty style with "invented spelling." The second time was in Mrs. Johnson's first-grade classroom. Mrs. Johnson told me that what I'd learned about writing at home was "wrong." So, being a good girl, I abandoned my story-telling style for properly punctuated complete sentences in stick-and-ball printing.

The third time I learned to write, I was in the midst of the chemical explosion of mind and body called "adolescence." "School" writing couldn't express my emotions, my longings, my new insights into the writings of ee cummings, Ayn Rand, and Betty Friedan. So I jumped back to my story-telling style, with a little more structure this time, and wrote well enough to earn me a position as editor of our high school newspaper—and 11th prize in a regional creative writing contest!

The fourth time I learned to write was in graduate school. Mrs. Johnson–trained professors met me there and retaught me to strangle the feeling out of my words, stuff them into APA style, and "say something significant, or don't say anything at all." It was only after I was safely graduated and into my life as an untenured professor that I learned to write for the fifth and last time. Oh yes, I was advised to stick to my "graduate school" writing as I advanced toward tenure. I tried that advice. But writing without passion didn't get me published.

This chapter is organized in four parts: (1) learning how to write—for real, (2) finding something worth writing about, (3) putting it down on paper, and (4) getting published.

## LEARNING HOW TO WRITE—FOR REAL

"I know now that for me as for many women, learning to write as a strong-voiced, confident individual uncomfortably jolts one's sense of self and one's female stereotype; it involves more than simply learning writing skills." (Goulston, 1987). Wendy Goulston's words evoke both the difficulty and the freedom that accompany learning to write for real—not for school. In other words, learning to write for real involves learning the lovely and hard things about *ourselves* that we eventually express in writing about others.

When I teach classes in writing, I tell students they have to begin by writing something—one phrase or one sentence or one paragraph—they really like—and, eventually, to write something they like that also reveals something about themselves. Then I ask them to write, and write and write. In the process, they discover many interesting and courageous things about themselves and begin to really feel confident in their abilities to write for real.

After adopting the habit of these practice sessions, the students begin to feel so confident in themselves as ordinary heroes in their own lives, in fact, that they don't die when something they write is rejected for publication. They just keep on writing. Eventually, they write something that someone else feels confident about, and they get published.

What happens next is that a few people reading the students' publications also like the real writing and initiate lifelong relationships—relationships that give the students even more pleasure than publishing. Along the way, of course, a few other people hate what they write and/or are jealous of their published accomplishments, but such "grand rejections" only keep the students humble and help improve their writing. So now I'll teach you how to write for real.

*Step 1. Develop the Habit of Writing Practice*

Buy a copy of Natalie Goldberg, *Writing Down the Bones: Freeing the Writer Within*, Boston: Shambhala, 1986. ISBN 0–87773–375–9. It'll set you back about $10.00. Open it to page 8. Read the rules for "First Thoughts." The basic unit of writing practice is the timed exercise. You may time yourself for 10 minutes, 20 minutes, or 1 hour. It's up to you. What does matter is that whatever amount of time you choose for that session, you must commit yourself to it and for that full period.

1. *Keep your hand moving.* (Don't pause to reread the line you have just written. That's stalling and trying to get control of what you're saying.)

2. *Don't cross out.* (That is editing as you write. Even if you write something you didn't mean to write, leave it.)

3. *Don't worry about spelling, punctuation, grammar.* (Don't even care about staying within the margins and lines on the page.)

4. *Lose control.*

5. *Don't think. Don't get logical.*

6. *Go for the jugular.* (If something comes up in your writing that is scary or naked, dive right into it. It probably has lots of energy.)

Practice sustained writing every day. *Every day.* What you do is put your pen to paper and write. Write at least for 10 minutes without stopping. Write about what's in front of you—exactly what you see. That practice will lead you to write without outlining, thinking, planning. Eventually, you'll learn to write for real—and you'll learn a lot about who you are and what's important to you and save yourself thousands of dollars in therapy. I name that kind of writing "writing below thought." Here's my example, composed right now as you read this:

> *I am sitting in front of this Macintosh PowerBook G3 on a table-which-converts-into-a-bed in our cab-over camper. We are parked in a roadside campground on the Columbia River in Umatailla, Oregon. It is mid-June. I can see a portion of the screen-saver of a California Poppy behind the computer-window on which I 'm writing. I can also see the sun dappling through the east-side camper windows—reflecting the cottonwood trees in brisk wind. My partner sits across the table from me in a salmon-colored shirt (a good color on her) holding a blue pen we got from the Far Horizon 's 49er Village Campground, searching (her right hand holding up her forehead and the pen) the map for the next part of our journey. I also notice peripherally a cup of coffee (I have the Bullwinkle cup this morning) to my right. In our camper oven are cinnamon rolls warming, steaming, and enticing me to stop writing I glance at the Taiwanese watch on my left wrist. I 've only been writingfor 3 minutes. I have to keep going. What else?*
>
> *The morning wind is suddenly stronger, blowing our new apple-print vinyl table cloth off the picnic table on the left side of our camper. I remember an old wind. a cold wind. ratting the poorly-housed window panes of a rented two-room apartment in Tillamook, Oregon. I was all of 19 then, married for two years with an almost one-year-old baby boy. We were flat-out poor. The apartment cost us $57.00 a month, and our total income was about $281. My well-intentioned husband bought us a new car—a 1965 yellow Mustang—and our payments were $129.00 a month. We felt like as wealthy as our parents when we drove the car, but the payments left us very little for food, gasoline to get to work diapers, or doctor visits.*

*Once the diapers were bought and washed, drying them on a clothes-line outside of the apartment was out of the question. I tried to dry them by the single wall heater, listening for the steam from the drying to overpower the sound of the baby 's labored breathing and coughing, and the windows rattling in the wind, but the diapers just quietly mildewed. My next act was to weep for a more secure life as a daughter and student without my own family responsibilities. Then I remembered the silver dollar collection, hidden in a shoe box in the closet.*

*If my quick calculations are correct, I had 171 silver dollars in that shoe box. What that meant to a new, poor mother-of-a-baby in rainy Oregon was that now my son could have warm, dry diapers every week for a long, long time. It wasn't enough to keep the windows from rattling in the rainy wind and sleet, nor the baby from eventually developing, and surviving, pneumonia, but it was just enough.*

*Twelve minutes. I can stop my writing practice. If my teacher were to ask me to read the portion of the writing practice I really liked, I would read the third paragraph.*

Now you try the same exercise. And this time, really go buy the book.

### Step 2. Put Aside the APA Manual

I can hear your complaints. "But we have to write—for real." Writing for scholarly publication—or putting it down on paper—will come in the third section. Here's another exercise:

Take a piece of your data that is particularly intriguing. Tell a story about it. Use the sustained writing practice technique to "write below thought." Really write about it for 10–20–30 minutes—depending on how much you've practiced step 1 (the more you practice writing, the longer you can really write).

### Step 3: Find Your Own Voice by Reading
### Other Women Who Have Found Their Own Voices

Be careful here! You'll find emotions that will awaken many of your own. Read autobiographical works: Sara Lawrence Lightfoot, *Balm in Gilead: Journey of a Healer*, Addison Wesley, 1988. bell hooks, *Talking Back: Thinking Feminist, Thinking Black*, South End Press, 1989, p. 75: "No wonder our working-class parents from poor backgrounds feared our entry into such a world, intuiting perhaps that we might learn to be ashamed of where we had come from, that we might never return home, or come back only to lord it over them."

Gloria Anzaldua, *Borderlands: La Frontera: The New Mestiza*, Aunt Lute Books, San Francisco, 1987, p. 73: "When I write it feels like I'm carving bone. It feels like I'm creating my own face, my own heart—

a Nahuatl concept. My soul makes itself through the creative act. It is constantly remaking and giving birth to itself through my body. It is this learning to live with *la Coatlicue* that transforms living in the Borderlands from a nightmare into a numinous experience. It is always a path/state to something else."

Mary Catherine Bateson, *Composing a Life*, Atlantic Monthly Press, 1989.

Mary Catherine Bateson, *Peripheral Visions: Learning along the Way*, HarperCollins, 1994, p. 9: "Many [educational] proposals have too narrow a focus, are directed at local problems when the entire concept of education needs to be rethought. . . . Ambiguity is the warp of life, not something to be eliminated. Learning to savor the vertigo of doing without answers or making shift and making do with fragmentary ones opens up the pleasures of recognizing and playing with pattern, finding coherence within complexity, sharing within multiplicity."

Patricia Bell-Scott, Life Notes: *Personal Writings by Contemporary Black Women*, Norton, 1994.

Carolyn G. Hilbrun, *Writing a Woman 's Life*, Ballantine Books, 1988.

If one is not permitted to express anger or even to recognize it within oneself, one is, by simple extension, refused both power and control. Virginia Woolf's *Three Guineas* (1938) is an example of a feminist essay that was universally condemned at its publication because of its anger, its terrible "tone."

Virginia Woolfe, *A Room of One 's Own*, Harcourt-Brace, 1929.

Eudora Welty, *One Writer's Beginnings*, Warner Books, 1983.

Reading "Death of a Salesman" opened my eyes. And I had received the shock of having read poetry: Marilyn Sewell, *Cries of the Spirit: A Celebration of Women 's Spirituality*, Beacon, 1991; Marge Piercy, *The Moon Is Always Female*, NY: Knopf, 1977; Marge Piercy, *Circles on the Water*, NY: Knopf, 1982.

And listen to music: Gloria Estefan, "Close my Eyes."

Add your own music that helps clarify what you want to say. Now go back to *Step 1: Practice Writing for Real*. If you want more, buy Natalie Goldberg's second book, *Wild Mind: Living the Writer 's Life*, New York: Bantam Books, 1990. ISBN 0–553347756–6. Open it to page 73:

> You know it, but you don't know how to break through. A helpful technique: right in the middle of saying nothing, right in the middle of the sentence, put a dash and write: "What I really want to say is . . ." and go on writing. It allows you to drop to a deeper level or to make a one-hundred-and-eighty-degree turn in what you were writing. It's a device to help you connect with what is going on inside.
>
> I got up and meditated this morning and then I ran. I came to the Galisteo Newsstand and had a grapefruit sparkler, then I—what I

really want to say is I had a miserable dream last night. Something about Nazis and I can't remember it. Before I went to sleep, I stuck my bubble gum on the nightstand and I don't know how many more nights I can go without making love. It was a blue Sunday and I pretended I was happy watering my vegetable garden. I'm not happy. I'm lonely. Loneliness is a dog that has followed me for years. It's a black dog and I have no peace.

## FINDING SOMETHING WORTH WRITING ABOUT

How do you find something worth writing about? I thought you'd never ask.

### Step 1. Follow Your Passion

Forget trying to study something your graduate advisor studied or even something you did for your dissertation. Now is the time to discover what you really get excited about. What real questions do you have about your field? What brought you here in the first place? Find something that you don't have the answers for—some really interesting puzzles with zing. Remember, you'll need to hang on to the romance of studying the area you select for years and years—past the initial highs of discovery. So look deeply and choose wisely.

### Step 2. Develop a Line of Research

A line of research is something you find through your passion and is of deep interest to you (and hopefully of significant value to the field at the time you are interested in it) that is also part of your work and your life. Maxine Greene, quoting Jean-Paul Sartre, calls this kind of work a "life project" (Greene, 1979). How do you find yours? Begin by reading women-who-have-developed-a-line-of-research:

- Patricia Hill Collins, *Black Feminist Thought: Knowledge, Consciousness and the Politics of Empowerment*, Routledge, 1990.

- Jane Gaskell, *Women and Education*, Detselig Enterprises, Calgary, Alberta, 1991.

- Susan E. Noffke, *Educational Action Research: Becoming Practically Critical*, Teachers College Press, 1995.

- or me, Sandra Hollingsworth, *Teacher Research and Urban Literacy Education: Conversations and Lessons in a Feminist Key*, Teachers College Press, 1994.

Since I know how my line of research developed better than the others I've suggested, I'll tell you the story of how I did it.

When I was in graduate school, I worked with professors who studied reading acquisition, or how children acquired the ability to read proficiently. That meant that those professors (and I) spent lots of time in classrooms and laboratory settings observing and testing different ways different children learned to read through different theoretical approaches to reading expressed in basal texts and to make some sense of the different patterns across them. Then the professors (and I) would go back to the university and try to teach new teachers to teach children to read through our own classes—the best way we could justify through our own favorite theoretical approaches.

As I studied these phenomena, it occurred to me over and over again that it was not one particular theory-turned-basal strategy that worked in learning to read (such as the top-down approach/ "whole language method" or the bottom-up approach/ "decoding method"), but it was the cleverness of the teacher.

So in developing my line of research, I followed my passion, my real questions. For example, how do we improve the lives of children by teaching them to read? How does a really powerful teacher figure out what to do for different children? I focused that passion by studying the teachers that my colleagues and I taught—that is, I began to study how teachers I taught learned to teach reading. Now my focus incorporated my passionate research interest, my professional responsibilities or academic life, and (since I also had a son who did not learn to read in school) my personal life. I learned that to tell the story of learning to teach best, I would need to collaborate with the teachers from whom I learned.

I learned, from listening, that it was their own inquiry, their group-supported investigations or action research, that made a difference in their abilities to teach reading. It was our group's common passion that all students in urban schools would learn to read no matter what and learn to "read the world" as well as the "word" (see Freire & Macedo, 1987) that kept us exploring this line of work together long enough so I could really discover something worth writing about.

Over the years, we wrote a series of studies about learning to teach literacy in urban classrooms that eventually led to a book. And, of course, we're not finished. We've all gone on to other areas of interest in our lives which led to outer circles around the core of learning to teach—politics, leadership, resources, politics. And we hope to have a book about those different paths near the end of our careers.

*Step 3. Schedule Your Writing Time First*

I was fortunate to begin my university career at a research university. As I'm now employed at a university that emphasizes teaching (and heavy course loads) over research, I realize just how important the habits established at my first university were. At U.C. Berkeley, the faculty tradition was to reserve every Friday as a research and writing day. That day was "scheduled for writing," just like other days were scheduled for teaching and committee work. That habit allowed me the space to devote to my writing.

It's not always Friday now, nor necessarily the same day each week, but my writing days go on my calendar each month and are guarded as carefully as any other professional obligation.

*Step 4. Develop Resources:*
*Grants, Graduate Students, Networks, Friends*

While you're developing your line of research, also develop your resources for writing. Turn your technical writing skills toward the gaining of grants to support your line of research, to buy you released time for writing, and to employ graduate students to assist you with your research projects.

Three resources for this kind of writing are Arthur Asa Berger, *Improving Writing Skills: Memos, Letters, Reports, and Proposals,* Sage, 1993; Soraya M. Coley and Cynthia A. Swcheinberg, *Proposal Writing,* Sage, 1990, and Lawrence F. Locke, Waneen Wyrick Spirduso, and Stephen J. Silvervan, *Proposals That Work,* 3rd edition, Sage, 1993. Particularly helpful in the Locke and colleagues volume are the annotated proposal examples. A qualitative example on pages 212–48 illustrates the kind of language that would be necessary to explain qualitative research to proposal readers who may be unfamiliar with it. Good stuff.

*Step 5. Other Things to Do While Developing a Line of Research*

If you wait until the exact right line of research appears before you begin to write anything, you may be retired, voluntarily or involuntarily. So along the way, do some writing that will get you in print, but not necessarily with the reputation of your evolving line of research that will earn you tenure.

Do quick studies. While you're reading other people's lines of research, and something clicks with some data you've already collected, write up an article over a weekend or two. Polish it (using details presented in the following part of this chapter) and then send it off. Volunteer to read manuscripts for journals and proposals for conferences.

Do this kind of work throughout your career. Do as careful a job of reviewing a proposal as you would writing an article, send back comments in a thoughtful, timely way, and you'll find a way of keeping current in your field throughout your entire career and make some good contacts for yourself when your line of research comes together. Write book reviews. While you're reading to find your line of research, write book reviews and send them in to journals. Write them cleverly and kindly. You'll earn publications for your CV and become very familiar with the literature and various kinds of journals.

## PUTTING IT DOWN ON PAPER

OK. You've followed your passion, found something worth studying and writing about, maybe even are beginning a budding line of research. Now you have to write and rewrite and write again. Don't give up. Need help? Did you think I'd get you this far in the chapter and not give you the steps to putting your work on paper?

### Step 1. Find Good Methods of Data Collection and Analysis

Maybe what you learned in graduate school will support the line of research you want to develop. If so, you are lucky. Just go ahead. However, if you are like me, and the experimental design approach does not get at the questions and passions you hold about your area of interest, then you'll have to explore alternative methods of gathering and analyzing data.

What I discovered is that learning to teach urban kids to read and critique the world was not a question that could be answered within the research paradigm I had learned from studying cognitive psychology in graduate school. I also discovered that some of the limitations on teachers' learning came because they were "perceived" as less knowledgeable than they could be. That is, because they taught in what is problematically defined as a "woman's profession" (see Laird, 1988), teachers were given prescriptions for "what works," and they were kept from discovering what really worked for them. Telling them how they were to be studied wouldn't work either.

To make a long story short (there is a page limit to this chapter), I had to discover alternative ways of collecting and analyzing data on learning to teach before I could get the full story of what I was learning down on paper. Below are some of the sources I used. You may find these useful, or you may have to keep looking. There are many, many different ways of finding the method that will be true to your passion, your way of interpreting the world. and your line of research.

Mary Maynard and June Purvis, *Researching Women 's Lives from a Feminist Perspective,* Taylor and Francis, 1994.

Liz Stanley, *Feminist Praxis: Research, Theory and Epistemology in Feminist Sociology,* Routledge, 1990.

Shulamit Reinharz, *Feminist Methods in Social Research,* Oxford University Press, 1992.

Catherine Kohler Riessman, *Narrative Analysis,* Sage, 1993.

*Step 2. Tell the Story in Your Own Voice:*
*Quiet Your Mind and Take Risks*

After you have your data, your "ahas," and are ready to put what you've learned down on paper, you'll want to do it in your own style. You'll need to "find your voice." But you don't have to struggle. Learn how by reading authors who write about writing. The following are examples:

Anne Lamott, *Bird by Bird: Some Instructions on Writing and Life,* Pantheon, 1994, page 117: "The best way to get quiet, other than the combination of extensive therapy, Prozac, and a lobotomy, is to first notice that the station is on. KFKD is on every single morning when I sit down at my desk. So I sit for a moment and—say a small prayer—please help me get out of the way so I can write what wants to be written."

Anne Dillard, *The Writing Life,* Harper and Row, 1989.

William Zinsser, *On Writing Well,* HarperCollins, 1991.

Peter Elbow, *Writing with Power: Techniques for Mastering the Writing Process,* Oxford University Press, 1981, page 312:

> Look for real voice and realize it is there in everything to be used. Yet remember, too, that you are looking for something mysterious and hidden. There are no outward linguistic characteristics to point to in writing with real voice. Resonance or impact on readers is all there is. . . . The best clue I know is that as you begin to develop real voice, your whirring will probably cause more comment from readers than before (though not necessarily more favorable comment).

*Writing Down the Bones,* page 17:

> When you begin to write this way—right out of your own mind—you might have to be willing to write junk for five years, because we have accumulated it over many more than that and have been gladly avoiding it in ourselves. We have to look at our own inertia, insecurities, self-hate, fear that, in truth, we have nothing valuable to say. It is true that when we began anything new, resistances fly in our face. Now you have the opportunity to not run or be tossed away, but to look at them black and white on paper and see what their silly voices say. When your writing blooms out of the back of this garbage and compost, it is very stable. You are not running from anything. You can have a sense of artistic security.

A book I just located that I like a lot for my students who are much more orderly about their writing than I am (she recommends outlining!) is Anne Sigismund Huff, *Writing for Scholarly Publication*, Sage, 1999. I received this book as compensation for a book review I did for a publisher. It didn't cost me a thing. It will cost you something, however; and if you like a more logical approach than the one I've offered so far in this chapter but still holds true to a similar philosophy, it's worth the cost. For example, on page 38 Huff suggests that you follow your passion but gives a caveat that makes a lot of sense: "Do what really interests you—within reason. Projects that codify or test what my mother already knows (and my mother knows a lot) are problematic. Life is short. Outcomes, including fame, are very difficult to predict. It therefore makes a lot of sense to me that each scholar should try to answer questions that genuinely perplex him or her." Here is another example from page 3: "Scholarship is Conversation. . . . Scholarly work is rooted in the lively exchange of ideas—conversation at its best." And one from page 9: "You should anticipate making an impact on the scholarly conversation of your field, from the very beginning of your career. The critical questions to answer are these:

- Which conversations should I participate in?
- Who are the important 'conversants'?
- What are the scholars talking about now?"

What are the most interesting things I can add to the conversation?

If you become interested in too many conversations, find the focus of your writing project by committing to a few (e.g., three) different conversations or literatures and choose a small part which forms the intersection of the three. (I haven't paraphrased this excellent idea adequately; you'll just have to read pages 17–20, entitled "Managing Scholarship" for yourself.)

Here's another great idea from page 35: Establish a "bottom drawer" to file project possibilities. The bottom drawer of your desk has several attractive features as a research tool. First, you can and should keep the drawer shut most of the time, opening it only long enough to throw in your latest ideas. Think about making this drawer a permanent part of your work environment. Not that I frequently have ideas for new projects throughout the research and writing process. They are not just research and writing ideas, but teaching and other possibilities as well. Unfortunately, they often distract me from the work at hand. I take advantage of the intrinsic generative nature of scholarship by writing a brief description of each possibility as it intrudes upon me. Then I file it in my bottom drawer for later consideration.

I don't literally use a "bottom drawer" in my desk, but I do use two computer files I call "papers in thought" (new ideas) and the slightly more developed "papers in progress" (the beginnings of a new article).

Huff also describes the pros and cons of writing collaboratively. Now I've already told you that I really get a lot of ideas, inspiration, and plain hard work from writing collaboratively with teachers. She gives you another angle on page 21: "Co-authorship is especially tempting because it seems that sharing the load will allow you to participate in more research and writing projects than you could carry out alone."

Although this is certainly true, collaboration takes time, Furthermore, in my experience, it is easy to overcommit. Many jointly conceived projects are never published because they die at the back of a co-author's crowded desk. If you know my work with Margie Gallego, you'll realize much more than publications through a long-term collaborative partnership. Huff recommends a reasonable balance to your writing program. Here I'm quoting from page 41:

- Keep the pipeline full by considering the time requirements of different projects.
- Mix coauthored projects with projects done alone.
- Mix projects of great personal but low field appeal with "sure hit" projects.

Finally, here's one last good idea that I'm going to cite from Huff (the rest you'll have to read for yourselves). This one comes from page 55: Use exemplars.

> An exemplar is a document already in the literature that accomplishes the kind of task you are trying to accomplish in an effective way. It does not have to address the subject that interests you. . . . Exemplars of scholarly writing provide ideas for approaching unfamiliar communication tasks. . . . [Exemplars can]
>
> - Help authors define their purpose more clearly
> - Can be used to structure and solve problems in writing
> - Are a springboard for innovating beyond the structures used by others.

### Step 3. Now Go Back and Edit

And edit. And edit. Edit alone, with a friend, with a group. But keep the story in mind. Pay attention to the story first, the technicalities last. Get every word to convey the realness of your story, the honesty in your data, the significance of your story. Finally, check out the details with the American Psychological Association (APA) style manual or any other you choose.

*Step. 4. Check the Publication Requirements*
*of the Journal to Which You're Submitting*

Now is the time to follow the rules.

## GETTING PUBLISHED

If you've "gotten" the ideas in the beginning of this chapter, this last section is a piece of cake almost. Here are some final steps.

### Step 1. Call the Editor before You Submit

Don't be afraid. Editors are just people like you and me (in fact, I am one). If you're afraid, rehearse all the possibilities before you call. Your phone rehearsal might go something like this:

> "Hello, Dr. Famous, it's me, lowly assistant professor." (Start over!)
>
> "Hello, Dr. Keeper-of-the-Key to the Kingdom, it's me, Dying-to-be-Published."
>
> No.
>
> "Dr. Hollingsworth. I'm so and so from such and such university. I have an article ready for publication that I think might fit well in your journal. Here's the gist of it———(Keep it brief). What do you think?"

Now Dr. Hollingsworth will either tell you that your work won't fit in this journal (and suggest another one for submission), or she'll ask you to submit the article for blind review, which you could do without ever telephoning, but now she'll remember who you were and maybe even be intrigued enough with the prior knowledge of your topic to send it to reviewers who are in the same conversation (and who might review it favorably).

### Step 2. Submit before the Text Is "Perfect"

Anne Sigismund Huff would disagree with me, but, from my point of view, no text is ready for publication, so you might as well send in your best shot and then be ready to revise. My first publication was co-authored with my dissertation chair, John Sheffelbine. After we'd worked some months on the text, John still thought it needed more revision before sending it out. My take was that it wasn't perfect but that it was close enough to warrant acceptance with revisions. (Besides, I was just tired of revising! ) So I sent it out, and it was accepted without revisions. Maybe reading it today, John and I would see many things I still would change (see Sheffelbine & Hollingsworth, *Journal of Teacher Education*, 1987), but it got us into the conversation on learning to teach and earned me a job at U.C. Berkeley.

*Step 3. Celebrate the Mailing of an Article*

Have an ice cream cone. Walk in the woods. Sleep late the next morning. Soak in a warm tub. Whatever happens next, you deserve to celebrate now.

*Step 4. Call the Editor If You Get a Rejection*

Ask why you were rejected. Ask what you could do to make the text more acceptable to the journal, to other journals. Ask for other advice on your line of research. Open *Writing Down the Bones* to page 17 again: "If you are not afraid of the voices inside you, you will not fear the critics outside you. "

*Step 5. Rewrite and Send Out Again—Soon*

Be open to criticism, be willing to rewrite, and send the article to another journal. Don't let it die.

*Step 6. Relax*

Trust yourself. Read Anne Lamott, page 180:

> I went through a real crisis of faith about two-thirds of the way through my last novel. The thing is that I had gotten twenty-seven bad reviews in a row on my previous novel, and I was feeling just the merest bit unsure about my skills and the joys of publication. But during that crisis of faith, I made a commitment to the characters in the new novel, instead of to the book itself. So I spent a little time at my desk every day, just writing down memories of my family, my youth. I went for walks and saw lots of matinees—I read. I spent as much time as I could outdoors while I waited for my unconscious to open a door and beckon.

*Step 7. Present Your Work at Conferences*

Talk about what you're writing (and either publishing or not yet publishing). Networking will help you become invited by others in similar conversations as you to submit chapters to their books. Those articles that don't make it into journal publications may even do better as book chapters. Other important things to do at conferences: talk with someone whose work you like (make a specific appointment before the conference begins) or join a special interest group (SIG) for support.

*Step 8. Keep Writing!*

Keep believing in yourself and your passions, and keep practicing writing for real.

REFERENCES

Freire, P., & Macedo, D. (1987). *Literacy: Reading the word and the world.* New York: Bergin & Garvey.

Goulston, W. (1987). Women writing. In C. L. Caywood and G. R. Overing (Eds.), *Teaching writing: Pedagogy, gender, and equity* (pp. 4–18). Albany: State University of New York Press.

Greene, M. (1979). Teaching as personal reality. In A. Liebermann and L. Miller (Eds.), *New perspectives for staff development.* New York: Teachers College Press.

Wolfe, V. (1938). *Three guineas.* New York: Harcourt, Brace & World.

# CHAPTER 11

# *Teaching:*
# *Academic Whitewater Rafting*

## Joanne E. Cooper
## and Sheryl E. Nojima

College teaching has been called the "educational equivalent of white-water rafting" (Brookfield, 1990, p. 2). One minute you are high on the success of a recent class in which students were energized and excited about the day's topic. The next minute you are "capsizing," your "self-confidence shaken," feeling "awash in self-doubt." Junior faculty are often scrambling to prepare syllabi and lectures, to understand the culture of their new institution and its norms around teaching and grading, and to respond to students of varying ethnicities and abilities. Some students won't talk. Some won't stop talking. Some fall asleep. Some insult their neighbors. Yet their evaluations may be crucial to the tenure and promotion process.

Teaching is the arena in which all of a faculty member's self-doubts can be played out, resulting in conflicts between the need to maintain authority in the classroom and the desire to win the affection of students (Tompkins, 1996). This chapter begins with a discussion of views on teaching in academe and how this process is influenced by culture and the faculty reward structure. We then present the challenges faced by new faculty as they negotiate the shoals and rough waters of teaching, while juggling the multiple demands of teaching, research, and service. Finally, we offer new faculty advice on how best to meet those challenges, while attempting to maintain a sense of their own integrity and identity (Palmer, 1998).

In their first years new faculty must address the basics of teaching: learning to establish classroom comfort and rapport, balancing their time between teaching and other academic activities, and moderating teaching preparation so that it does not undermine the enjoyment of teaching itself (Boice, 1992). This chapter is aimed at helping new faculty tackle these basics. We present sound suggestions that will help new faculty to begin to think critically about their own teaching, to find both comfort and rewards in the teaching process, to learn how to recover quickly from both frustrations and disappointments, and to learn the tacit knowledge about teaching that may be hidden from their immediate view (Brookfield, 1995; Boice, 1992). When faculty are able to take these steps, they gain entrance to a place where generations of students' lives can be transformed by their professors' invitations to discover, explore, and inhabit "the most truthful places in the landscape of self and world" (Palmer, 1998). This ability is most crucial for women and minority faculty who have a groundbreaking opportunity to serve as powerful mentors and role models for higher education's increasingly diverse student populations, those who may become tomorrow's future faculty.

## VIEWS ON TEACHING IN THE ACADEMY

By and large, the views of teaching in academe are shaped by a dynamic interplay between institutional mission and reward structure, which exists within the context of organizational culture. This ever-changing relationship may be attributed to the evolving roles of both institutions of higher learning in society and faculty in the academy. Institutions of higher education have focused on various aspects of the trilogy of teaching, research, and service throughout the nation's history. The original priority of the professoriate in colonial times was on teaching. Later, service was emphasized, and finally, the challenges of research became the central focus as the conviction that knowledge was advanced through research and experimentation grew. The emphasis on research is still a recent phenomenon, having been introduced to American higher education in 1906 (Boyer, 1990). However, its importance is fairly undisputed today. As Boyer (1990, p. 15) states, "Today, when we speak of being 'scholarly,' it usually means having academic rank in a college or university and being engaged in research and publication." True scholars, by current standards, are those "who conduct research, publish, and then perhaps convey their knowledge to students" (Boyer, 1990, p. 15). Yet Boyer adds that "teaching at its best, shapes both research and practice" (1990, p. 16).

Although faculty are often perceived as autonomous individuals, they are nevertheless members of academic disciplines, departments, and institutions, each with its own culture or set of shared values, beliefs, and assumptions. The elements contributing to an institutional culture that relate to the teaching-research balance include the institution's mission, organizational structure, physical environment, and student and faculty characteristics (Austin, 1996). Situated at the intersection between disciplinary and institutional culture, faculty in some departments may be torn by conflicting views about what constitutes an acceptable balance of teaching and research in the work of faculty (Austin, 1996).

Regardless of its importance, teaching is but one facet of faculty work in most colleges and universities today. The essential activities of faculty work are often predicated by an institutional mission statement (Austin, 1996; Gray and Diamond, 1994). Such mission statements will vary among types of institutions with respect to differences in size and identities but will generally include the triumvirate of teaching, research, and service. Community colleges, liberal arts colleges, and comprehensive colleges have traditionally emphasized teaching as the primary role of the faculty member, while doctorate-granting and research universities expect faculty to publish scholarly work and receive grants to conduct their research. Austin (1996) contends that this teaching-research balance is of particular significance in the socialization of faculty.

New faculty receive mixed messages about the importance of teaching. In a study of faculty from different disciplines at twelve institutions across the United States, Tierney and Bensimon (1996, p. 65) identified the fundamental lesson learned by junior faculty was that "teaching is not that important; if it were, there would be more discussions about what constitutes good teaching." In addition, new faculty in Boice's (1992) study of four cohorts at two campuses, one research and one comprehensive, were distressed over their senior colleagues' negativism toward students and their displeasure toward teaching. Despite this neglect, teaching evaluations by students are often afforded much credence by department chairs and senior faculty serving on tenure review committees (Tierney & Bensimon, 1996; Boice, 1992). New faculty must sort through these mixed messages, always remaining aware of the gravity teaching evaluations may have on tenure and promotion decisions.

While attending to the department's stated criteria for tenure and promotion, new faculty members must structure their work and allocate their time in congruence with the reward structure of their institution. They must arrange their activities in the interests of efficiency in order to achieve the most productive use of their time. The old adage "publish or perish" continues to bridge rhetoric and reality at many institutions, including colleges that claim to underscore teaching (Tierney & Bensimon, 1996, p. 67). Faculty must deal with the demands on their time and energy, ascertaining where to place their efforts in order to succeed. New faculty who are constantly overwhelmed may manage to publish but perhaps compromise quality in other areas of their work, jeopardizing their tenure review, and thus perishing in the end.

Moreover, teaching scores may be so high that departments believe new faculty are spending too much time on teaching. In their longitudinal study of pretenure faculty, Olsen and Sorcinelli (1992, p. 17) reported that faculty felt that it was "dangerous" to feel more committed to teaching because one could "drop dead trying to be a good teacher and not be recognized." Thus, new faculty are often advised against being *great* teachers; instead, being *good* is good enough (Tierney & Bensimon, 1996).

One persistent myth in the academy has been that one must be a good researcher in order to be a good teacher (Terenzini & Pascarella, 1994). Some have argued that good researchers are on the cutting edge of their fields and ignite enthusiasm for learning in their students (Terenzini & Pascarella, 1994). They claim that faculty will bring their research findings into the classroom and that this is intellectually stimulating to students. However, while the research acknowledges the existence of such extraordinary faculty, Terenzini & Pascarella (1994) note a poor correlation between undergraduate instruction and scholarly productivity. There is currently little evidence that good researchers automatically make good teachers, and the benefits of scholarly research have not materialized in the form of more effective undergraduate instruction (Terenzini & Pascarella, 1994).

In sum, teaching has not received the prestige and rewards of other areas of faculty work, namely, research and scholarly productivity. While the importance of teaching to pretenure faculty depends somewhat on the type of institution they are situated in and the culture of that institution, most junior faculty face the reality that teaching is not as valued as research in the teaching, research, service balance. Yet teaching is still viewed as an important faculty role, one that holds many rewards over a lifetime in the academy. First, teaching evaluations are taken seriously in the tenure and promotion process. Tierney & Bensimon (1996, p. 63) state that "student evaluations were given much credence in every institution we visited." Second, teaching takes time and effort. In can be an exhausting process that eats up much of a new faculty member's time. In his study of new faculty, Boice (1992) found that inexperienced faculty who failed to make adjustments to the job frequently continued to teach defensively, trying to avoid punishment, especially in the form of student complaints to campus administrators. In short, these faculty members failed to find ways to moderate the amount of time spent on teaching and to feeling more comfortable in the classroom. The next section takes a closer look at the challenges new faculty face and the ways in which they might successfully meet these challenges.

## CHALLENGES OF TEACHING

There is a vast array of complex dilemmas facing new faculty as they develop into teachers. The challenges of teaching are many, and they come in a variety of forms. The underlying concern common to all new faculty is the fear of not getting tenure due to the contradiction between teaching demands and institutional rewards for research (Tierney & Bensimon, 1996; Whitt, 1991). This section discusses four major issues that challenge new faculty in their transformation from graduate student to professor in the academy.

### Unrealistic Expectations

As a new faculty member fresh out of graduate school, the single most powerful impulse is to teach as you were taught. In other words, you simply pour on the material and lecture yourself into an exhausted state, making sure the students get the point that you know a lot to help you cover up the agonizing doubts that you know nothing or at least not enough to ever be a professor (Tompkins, 1996).

Unfortunately, most new Ph.D.s today still start their new faculty positions with little or no training in how to teach. Jane Tompkins, in *A Life in School* (1996), accurately describes this predicament: "In the early to mid-sixties, graduate schools didn't train people to teach—most of them still don't, really—the presumption being that you would walk into a classroom and do more or less what had been done to you. At least that's what I guessed the presumption was; the matter never came up" (p. 85).

The underlying assumption today in academe is that new hires bring with them the skills and knowledge they need to succeed (Whitt, 1991). In fact, it is presumed that once graduate students become faculty members, they already know how to teach or can readily figure it out on their own (Boice, 1992). Moreover, faculty get little help in learning how to teach; most institutions that provide instructional development at all provide it for teaching assistants. In reality, faculty are taught about the subject they are to teach but are seldom taught how to teach it (Kugel, 1993). They receive little or no training in teaching, learning, and pedagogical methods (Stark & Lattuca, 1997) and will tend to teach how they were taught, modeling instruction they once received as students (Chickering & Reisser, 1993; Kugel, 1993). How can all faculty be expected to be good teachers when they are not even taught skills they are expected to perform? Is this a realistic goal? How attainable is this goal?

Joanne discovered, when she took her first tenure-track position at a research university that she had learned to teach during the ten years she spent teaching in a community college. There the primary emphasis was on teaching, not research, and much more attention was spent on the needs of adult learners. The focus of community colleges is frequently on current innovations to working with those who are there because they've had trouble learning in a traditional educational setting or have simply been out of school so long their learning skills are very rusty. More and more frequently, universities too are encountering adult learners returning to school or those in need of remedial work before they can begin the business of college-level instruction. Thus, the new faculty member in a college or university faces these dilemmas, but without the supporting organizational culture that values teaching or the attention to how to approach the task of college teaching.

*Anxiety and Time Pressure*

Sorcinelli (1992) reported an increase in the proportion of new faculty who characterize their work lives as "very stressful" from 33% in 1986 to 71% in 1990. With unclear or unstated goals (Whitt, 1991), it is not uncommon for new faculty to not know how much is enough (Tierney & Bensimon, 1996). They will describe their life as a "triathalon" of "never-ending work" at a "relentless pace" (Tierney & Bensimon, 1996, p. 61). Whitt (1991) adds that there is no start-up time for new faculty. In fact, they are expected to "hit the ground running" from the very first day on the job (Whitt, 1991, p. 185).

No wonder new faculty are anxious about the teaching part of their job. As Boice (1992) indicates, this is the portion of the job that provides the more immediate feedback than responses to publishing efforts. New faculty would know right away if they are totally bombing out in the classroom. If they are so terrified and numb that they don't notice, they find out at the end of the term when they read their course evaluations. Many new faculty then spend most of their time on reading material, preparing lectures, and generally trying to figure out how to manage the hapless souls that have been placed in their cognitive care. Jane Tompkins (1996, p. 88) describes her approach as "like a horse with a bit in its teeth. I ran and ran, leaping ditches and fences, getting mud splashed, stumbling occasionally, but always regaining my stride, plunging ahead, unconscious of everything except the perilousness of the task and my own expenditure of effort."

*Isolation and the Lack of Collegial Relationships*

In her study of a school of education, Whitt (1991) reported that new faculty members conveyed high expectations for collegial relationships characterized by sharing of ideas and values with likeminded individuals. Instead, new faculty found that they were wandering in a fragmented community with rare opportunities for interconnection among colleagues (Whitt, 1991). Boice (1992) described feelings of loneliness and isolation experienced by new faculty. This was accompanied by their senior colleagues' inattention to teaching and low levels of social support for teaching.

Many new faculty also reported a painful transition from graduate school to the professoriate, because as graduate students there was frequent communication and interaction with fellow graduate students and dissertation committee members (Boice, 1992). It takes getting used to feelings of loneliness. A new faculty member in Whitt's (1991, p. 183) study acknowledged, "Full professors provide little contact and little support for new faculty." Another spoke of the expectation of "others to come to me because I'm new here," but instead, this new faculty member was the one to initiate interaction with senior colleagues (Whitt, 1991, p. 183).

Because new faculty are on display and because they want so badly to prove that they know enough to be part of the esteemed company of "fellows" known as the faculty, the bumps in the road can be especially painful. This role may be doubly painful for women and minorities because they frequently do not have powerful role models that assure them that they are up to the job. The word *professor* immediately conjures up an image of someone with a beard, smoking a pipe, who has leather patches on the elbows of his wool tweed sports coat. Woman obviously do not and cannot ever fit this image. Faculty of color have similar trouble seeing themselves in their white, male colleagues. Thus, women and faculty of color must forge their own images of their professional selves, and this new identity is often forced. As Jane Tompkins (1996, p. 90) states,

> If nothing else, I wish I had been warned about what an ego-battering enterprise teaching can be. Teaching, by its very nature, exposes the self to myriad forms of criticism and rejection, as well as to emulation and flattery and love. Day after day, teachers are up there, on display; no matter how good they are, it's impossible not to get shot down. If only I'd known, if only someone I respected had talked to me honestly about teaching, I might have been saved from a lot of pain.

How one responds to this pain, which comes to *all* faculty at *every* stage in their career, is key.

*Comfort and Confidence in the Classroom*

All fine scholars have at some time suffered from the feeling that they've somehow failed their students, not connected with them, or ended up looking like a fool (Brookfield, 1990; Carse, 1994; hooks, 1994; Palmer, 1998). Parker Palmer (1998, p. 36) describes the fear that can be a constant companion to the teaching enterprise:

> After thirty years of teaching, my own fear remains close at hand. It is there when I enter a classroom and feel the undertow into which I have jumped. It is there when I ask a question—and my students keep a silence as stony as if I had asked them to betray their friends. It is there whenever it feels as if I have lost control: a mind-boggling question is asked, an irrational conflict emerges, or students get lost in my lecture because I myself am lost. When a class that has gone badly comes to a merciful end, I am fearful long after it is over—fearful that I am not just a bad teacher, but a bad person, so closely is my sense of self tied to the work I do.

The uppermost question in the minds of new faculty is, Will I survive? Many are not confident about their teaching (Boice, 1992) and feel extremely vulnerable in front of the class for the first time (Kugel, 1993). Their greatest fear is making fools out of themselves in their first public appearance (Kugel, 1993; Boice, 1992). Although newly minted Ph.D.s are thought to know their research very well, as new faculty, they often do not necessarily understand their course material very well. Consequently, their presentations are unclear and disorganized (Kugel, 1993). It is no wonder that they will and do make fools out of themselves. But Kugel (1993) insists that new faculty will learn better the more they teach. As a result teaching improves, and new faculty are able to manage more comfortably as they acquire confidence in the classroom.

## SUGGESTIONS

Despite the many challenges of teaching for new faculty, the unrealistic expectations, the anxiety, the isolation, and the lack of confidence many feel, there are concrete steps that junior faculty can take in their efforts to meet these challenges. There are ways to transform one's fears into excitement about the possibilities teaching affords. One of the greatest possibilities, as Parker Palmer states, is to learn to know the self better. There are opportunities to question, probe, to reach new understandings, and of course, the satisfaction of watching your students learn and grow. Below is a list of ways to meet the challenges of teaching in the academy gleaned from the experiences of veterans, those whose own lives have been dedicated to this task.

*Transform Fear into Excitement*

One of the keys is to remember that your students, too, are afraid, afraid of not understanding, afraid of looking foolish in front of their peers, afraid of failing. Yet all this fear need not lead to educational paralysis. From there new faculty must work toward the reduction of fear, their own and that of their students. They must think back to their own experiences in the classroom as students. Focusing on beloved teachers, classrooms filled with laughter and the excitement of learning, the thrill of new insights, of working through a fog to new understandings, will help new faculty to recreate those events in their own classrooms. What sparked that energy? What helped keep the students alive and engaged?

Joanne adheres to the premise that she must be having fun. She states,

> If I'm not having fun, how can I expect anyone else to? Secondly, you gotta laugh (or otherwise you might cry?). I always tell jokes and stories. If nothing else, they help *me* get through the class, especially when what I do falls flat. Third, the students need a chance to speak in a safe atmosphere. This means giving them lots of opportunities to talk to each other. Students can learn a lot from each other, and they need a chance to try to articulate their new thoughts in their own words. Everyone whose mouth is moving has the potential to be learning something new, so the more mouths that are moving at the same time, the better off things are.

Finally, admit you are human. Joanne remembers one class where she was explaining to the students on the first night of class that she was not a quantifier (hence don't ask her how many pages your paper should be because she will tell you "enough to cover the subject, and so on). One student raised her hand and asked if that was why the assignments on the course outline were numbered one, two, four. Joanne states:

> I laughed and laughed. That wasn't the reason (I'd omitted three and forgot to change the numbers), but it was a beautiful illustration! When I got the evaluations back from that first night (see Stephen Brookfield's 1995 Critical Incident Questionnaire—it's wonderful!), one student wrote that the action she found most helpful in class had been when I laughed at my own mistake. It was a powerful reminder that students are so afraid to make a mistake in class, because we do not give them permission. We leave them with the impression that everything they say and everything *we* say must be brilliant. This is not human. Don't buy into it.

*Always Seek New Possibilities*

Joyful, exciting, and engaging encounters in the classroom always remain a possibility for new faculty in their work as teachers. Of course the work will not always be joyful. As Stephen Brookfield (1990, p. 5) reminds us, "Some days you eat the bear, some days the bear eats you." But as bell hooks (1994, p. 207) asserts, "The classroom, with all its limitations, remains a location of possibility. We must remember not to allow the limitations of others to become ours. In that field of possibility we have the opportunity to labor for freedom, to demand of ourselves and our comrades, an openness of mind and heart that allows us to face reality even as we collectively imagine ways to move beyond boundaries, to transgress."

For women and faculty of color, the possibilities are even greater, to move beyond the images of the professor as a bearded, white, middle-class male smoking his pipe, to new possibilities for both teacher and learner. With new images of teachers and learners come new possibilities for ideas in the classroom, ideas that can ignite a sense of connection and possibility for the entire academy.

This sense of possibility, this place of fertile ground for new ideas, the classroom, is often what keeps faculty members going. As bell hooks (1994, p. 205) states, "Most of us are not inclined to see discussion of pedagogy as central to our academic work and intellectual growth, or the practice of teaching as work that enhances and enriches scholarship. Yet it has been the mutual interplay of thinking, writing, and sharing ideas as an intellectual and teacher that creates whatever insights are in my work. My devotion to that interplay keeps me teaching in academic settings, despite their difficulty."

Parker Palmer (1998) too, senses the wealth of possibility in the teaching enterprise. The greatest possibility, as he sees it, is to learn to know the self better. He lists three important sources to the "tangles of teaching" (p. 2), "First, the subjects we teach are as large and complex as life itself, so our knowledge of them is always flawed and partial. . . . Second, the students we teach are larger than life and even more complex. To see them clearly and see them whole, and respond to them wisely in the moment, requires a fusion of Freud and Solomon that few of us achieve," and third, "we teach who we are." "As I teach," Parker states, "I project the condition of my soul onto my students, my subject, and our way of being together. The entanglements I experience in the classroom are often no more or less than the convolutions of my inner life. Viewed from this angle, teaching holds a mirror to the soul. If I am willing to look in that mirror and not run from what I see, I have a chance to gain self-knowledge—and knowing myself is as crucial to good teaching as knowing my students and my subject."

*Develop a Critically Reflective Practice*

Brookfield (1995, p. xiii) defines a critically reflective practice as one in which "teachers discover and examine their values, beliefs, and assumptions . . . in a spirit full of hope for the future." Critical reflection happens when we not only identify but also scrutinize the taken-for-granted beliefs and assumptions that bring meaning to who we are and the way we go about our work. This process gives rise to a critical rationale for a more informed practice guided by a "vision of where you are going and why you are going there" (Brookfield, 1990, p. 15). Brookfield (1990) contends that as novice teachers, we are surrounded with ambiguity and humiliation. Our survival is profoundly dependent on a well-conceived, clear set of aims and purposes. A critical rationale enables us to navigate through the rapids and storms, because we are emotionally grounded. Moreover, if we start to communicate our rationale to our students, we also begin to cultivate a democratic trust, which will enliven our classroom (Brookfield, 1995).

To unearth our beliefs and assumptions about teaching, Brookfield (1995) suggests viewing what we do through four distinct but interconnected lenses: (1) our autobiographies as teachers and learners, (2) our students' eyes, (3) our colleagues' experiences, and (4) the theoretical literature. First, analyzing our own deep experiences helps us to realize some of the long-lasting memories as learners that guide our teaching or explain why we gravitate toward certain practices, especially in times of crises and ambiguity. Second, seeing through the eyes of our students illuminates how they experience our teaching and their learning. Knowing what is difficult, threatening, simple, or comfortable allows us to teach more responsively to meet their needs. Third, experiences and perceptions of our colleagues offer a view as seen by others who work in situations comparable to ours. Engaging in conversations with our colleagues assures us that we are not suffering alone and broadens our likelihood of discovering an explanation to interpret our particular setting. Fourth, theoretical literature may further inform our practice through alternative perspectives. Brookfield (1990, 1995) suggests a variety of techniques that may be used in combination to exercise a critically reflective practice: teaching logs, teacher learning audits, peer observations, student learning journals, and periodic critical incident questionnaires.

## THE SCHOLARSHIP OF TEACHING

Much of what Brookfield suggests falls under the category of the scholarship of teaching. First credited with coining the phrase, Ernest Boyer (1990, p. 23) describes teaching as a "dynamic endeavor" that aims to connect the teacher's knowledge and the student's learning. The scholarship of teaching, in essence, refers to the teacher as a role model of lifelong learning by becoming a learner among students, advancing his or her own understanding of the subject. Faculty facilitate the learning process through activities such as classroom discussion in which questions are posed by students driving faculty into uncharted territories of knowledge. Boyer (1990, p. 24) contends that "inspired teaching keeps the flame of scholarship alive." Without the vision of scholarship in teaching, "the continuity of knowledge will be broken" as "teaching both educates and entices future scholars" (Boyer, 1990, pp. 23–24).

Boyer suggested four mutually dependent and overlapping forms of inquiry focused on learning: the arts of discovery, application, integration, and teaching. Eugene Rice (1994) has expanded on Boyer's conception of scholarships, emphasizing the idea of the university as a community of inquiry, one in which faculty are engaged "in what Gerhard Caspar has called the defining activity of research and teaching: the search to know" (Bender & Gray, 1999). A spirit of inquiry or the search to know is certainly evident in Brookfield's four functions, the search to know through autobiographical exploration, through the viewpoints of others (both students and colleagues) and through an exploration of the theoretical literature.

Three additional central features of the scholarship of teaching that Hutchings and Shulman (1999) have added are that the inquiry be public, open to critique or evaluation, and in a form that others can build on. They underscore the importance of inquiry that goes beyond the improvement of individual classroom practices by aiming to advance practice throughout the profession. The scholarship of teaching must be "the mechanism through which the profession of teaching advances itself" so that it "has the potential to serve all teachers . . . and students" (Hutchings & Shulman, 1999, p. 14).

Current challenges to the scholarship of teaching movement include an exploration of credible methods of inquiry, the need to keep scholarship open to a wider set of inquiries, questions about the most appropriate forms or media for making results available to the field, and the need for a culture and infrastructure that will sustain these forms of inquiry over the long haul. A variety of innovative forms of dissemination are currently emerging, including books, colloquia, course portfolios, and online resources exchanges (for example, see the Carnegie Web site: www.carnegiefoundation.org). As these new forms of inquiry and the dissemination of such efforts emerge, larger questions about how institutions might support and sustain this work appear. Hutchings and Shulman (1999, p. 15) suggest that "campuses should think about redefining the work of their institutional research offices." Here institutional researchers might ask "much tougher, more central questions" such as, What are our students really learning? What do they understand deeply? What kinds of human beings are they becoming—intellectually, morally, in terms of civic responsibility? How does our teaching affect that learning, and how might it do so more effectively?

For the untenured individual scholar, these questions offer exciting forms of inquiry that may prove new routes to tenure while enhancing the collective work of colleges and universities toward assessing their impact on students as a whole.

## SUMMARY

The scholarship of teaching underscores a central point made in this chapter, that teaching must be approached fearlessly and with a genuine openness to the possibilities of learning through the teaching process. One of our role models here is James P. Carse of New York University. Although an award-winning teacher, he, like many, suffers from self-doubt. After some moments of despair in a lecture he was giving, he describes how he was suddenly able to go on (Carse, 1994, p. 70): "Then I began to be confident my teaching was making a difference, that maybe the world can be made to notice." As he wandered around the classroom, still intent on his subject matter, he looked down at a student's open notebook: "The pages contained nothing but neat columns of numbers from one to seventy-five. Instead of taking notes, he was staring intently at the second hand on his watch, not aware that I was only inches away. The numbers from seventy-five to forty-five were already crossed off. He X-ed out another as I watched. Forty-four minutes to go" (p. 71).

The point here is that although it matters what you ask, it matters more that you ask. As long as new faculty are not saying, "This is too hard, I give up," and asking which window they should walk out of, they are on the right track. Their ceaseless questions will lead somewhere, and that somewhere will teach them something about themselves and the condition of the human race. Who, after all, could ask for more than this?

College teaching is by no means an easy task. It is as complex as our students and as challenging as learning to know the self better. In addition, it may not be valued by your colleagues, although in the end, if you are a poor teacher, it will matter to them and to tenure and promotion committees. More to the point, it will matter to you. As Palmer (1998) has stated, college teachers project the condition of their souls onto their students. When the entanglements you experience in the classroom mimic the tangles of your inner life, the challenges to sort out that inner life are great. Thus, teaching affords each of us the opportunity to facilitate the growth and learning of others, while it simultaneously offers us the opportunity to learn and grow ourselves. It may be the single most important thing we do as faculty members, and the outcomes are crucial to our own growth and development, as well as that of our students and the institutions we live and work in.

## REFERENCES

Austin, A. E. (1996). Institutional and departmental cultures: The relationship between teaching and research. In J. M. Braxton (Ed.), *New Directions for Institutional Research*, No. 90. San Francisco: Jossey-Bass.

Bender, E., & Gray, D. (April, 1999). The scholarship of teaching. *Research and Creative Activity*. Indiana University, vol. XXII, No. 1, 1–3.

Boice, R. (1992). *The new faculty member: Supporting and fostering professional development*. San Francisco: Jossey-Bass.

Boyer, E. L. (1990). *Scholarship reconsidered: Priorities of the professoriate*. San Francisco: Jossey-Bass.

Brookfield, S. D. (1990). *The skillful teacher*. San Francisco: Jossey-Bass.

Brookfield, S. D. (1995). *Becoming a critically reflective teacher*. San Francisco: Jossey-Bass.

Carse, J. (1994). *Breakfast at the victory: The mysticism of ordinary experience*. San Francisco: Harper.

Chickering, A. W., and Reisser, L. (1993). *Education and identity*. San Francisco: Jossey-Bass.

Gray, P. J., and Diamond, R. M. (1994). Defining faculty work: Providing useful information for deans and department chairs. In M. K. Kinnick (Ed.), *New Directions for Institutional Research*, No. 84. San Francisco: Jossey-Bass.

hooks, b. (1994). *Teaching to transgress: Education as the practice of freedom*. New York: Routledge.

Hutchings, P., & Shulman, L. S. (September/October, 1999). The scholarship of teaching: New elaborations, new developments. *Change*, 11–15.

Kagan, D. M. (1992). Professional growth among preservice and beginning teachers. *Review of Educational Research* 62(2), 129–169.

Knowles, J. G. (Ed.) (1992). Models for understanding pre-service and beginning teachers' biographies: Illustrations from case studies. In *Studying teachers' lives*. New York: Routledge.

Kugel, P. (1993). How professors develop as teachers. *Studies in higher education* (18) 3, 31–328.

Olsen, D., & Sorcinelli, M. (1992). The Pretenure Years: a longitudinal perspective. In M. D. Sorcinelli and A. E. Austin (Eds.), *Developing new and junior faculty*. New Directions for Teaching and Learning, no. 50. San Francisco: Jossey-Bass.

Palmer, P. J. (1998). *The courage to teach: Exploring the inner landscape of a teacher's life*. San Francisco, Jossey-Bass.

Rice, E. (1991). The new American scholar: Scholarship and the purposes of the university (Spring, 1991). *Metropolitan Universities* 1:4, 7–18.

Schon, D. (1987). *Educating the Reflective Practitioner.* San Francisco: Jossey-Bass.

Soper, J., Matson, J., and Burton, L. (1996). *Methods in engineering leadership development: The Penn State experience.* Accreditatiion Board for Engineering and Technology(ABET) Annual Meeting.

Sorcinelli, M. D. (1992). New and junior faculty stress: Research and responses. In M. D. Sorcinelli & A. E. Austin (Eds.), *Developing new and junior faculty.* New Directions for Teaching and Learning, no. 50. San Francisco: Jossey-Bass.

Stark, J. S., & Lattuca, L. R. (1997). *Shaping the college curriculum: Academic plans in action.* Needham, MA: Allyn & Bacon.

Terenzini, P. T., & Pascarella, E. T. (January-February, 1994). Living with myths: Undergraduate education in America. *Change: The Magazine of Higher Learning* 26(1), 28–32.

Tierney, W. G., & Bensimon, E. M. (1996). *Promotion and tenure: Community and socialization in academe.* Albany: State University of New York Press.

Tompkins, J. (1996). *A life in school: What the teacher learned.* New York: Addison-Wesley.

Whitt, E. J. (1991). Hit the ground running: Experiences of new faculty in a school of education. *Review of Higher Education* 14(2), 177–197.

CHAPTER 12

# Outreach in a New Light: Documenting the Scholarship of Application

## Pennie G. Foster-Fishman
## and Dannelle D. Stevens

Entering the academy as a new nontenured faculty member can often seem like an adventure in wonderland for women and minority faculty.[1] With little mentoring and direction from others, you, as a new faculty member, must determine the activities in which to engage to succeed as a scholar. For the first time since graduate school, you seem to have more freedom to choose when, where, and how to spend your time and yet more pressures to perform. In addition to building your own research agenda, you may be expected to design classes you never taught before, provide a variety of services to the academic and larger community, and advise/mentor others for the first time. Ultimately, you must decide how to balance these competing demands while still building a vitae that will eventually lead to tenure. Most new faculty who find this balance do so with little guidance and with great difficulty (Boice, 1992; Tierney & Bensimon, 1996).

If advice is given on how to allocate your time and make effective use of your talents, the message is often to focus on publications and grant writing and to minimize time spent on other activities. This advice is certainly well founded. While most academic institutions may expect new faculty members to engage in a variety of activities, often only the scholarship produced from and for research (e.g., publications, grants) counts toward tenure. Overall, this reality often causes many new faculty to question the feasibility of pursuing their own interests and values when such activity detracts from the "publish or perish" mentality. This tension is particularly present for new faculty women and minorities whose passions and interests often involve extensive time working in the community and mentoring students. Eventually, for many women and minority faculty, the question becomes, How can I remain true to myself, pursue my interests and passions, and still be a successful scholar who receives tenure?

The purpose of this chapter is to provide you, new women and minority faculty, with one potential venue for addressing the above tension. We will acquaint you with a broader definition of scholarship, one that includes the community-based outreach work[2] that women and minority faculty typically pursue with passion and commitment. We will share a model for documenting the scholarship in outreach work, with the hope that such evidence can foster the inclusion of this work in your tenure and promotion materials. The source of the thinking of these projects was a Kellogg-Foundation project (Driscoll & Lynton, 1999) in which both authors participated. All 16 Kellogg participants were doing extensive outreach in their communities. The authors of this chapter, Pennie, an assistant professor of psychology from Michigan State University, and Dannelle, a school-university partnerships coordinator from Portland State University, both worked over 2 years with the 14 other Kellogg faculty members from across the United States on this project.

The Kellogg project challenge was to extract and define the scholarship embedded in our community work and to create portfolios that described and documented our outreach scholarship. Ultimately, the purpose of the Kellogg project was to create a means for faculty to capture and validate outreach scholarship for consideration during promotion and tenure reviews. By sharing our experiences—particularly what we learned about the new models of scholarship and how to document outreach scholarship—we hope that we will empower other women and minority faculty to define, capture, and validate outreach as scholarship. To do this, we will first define outreach scholarship and put it into the context of other forms of scholarship. Second, we describe how to "make the case" for outreach scholarship by applying the framework designed by the Kellogg project participants to our own efforts. Finally, we discuss the benefits and dilemmas associated with the documentation of outreach scholarship.

## A MORE INCLUSIVE DEFINITION OF SCHOLARSHIP

The traditional understanding of faculty roles and responsibilities does not adequately support some essential faculty activities, for example, curricular reform or direct involvement in proposing and implementing solutions to society's pressing problems. We must recognize that faculty attention to such issues can be a legitimate expression of scholarship and can be evaluated and rewarded as such.

—Johnson and Wamser, 1997, p. 44

Higher education is currently experiencing a paradigm shift around the definition of scholarship (Boyer, 1990; Schon, 1995; Johnson and Wamser, 1997). *Scholarship* has historically referred to the process of learning and building knowledge (Johnson & Wamser, 1997), and as a term, has been solely used to describe activities that demonstrate the discovery and generation of knowledge (e.g., grants, research, peer-reviewed journal articles) (Boyer, 1990). Not surprisingly, higher education institutions—particularly those that have increasingly valued and supported the process of scholarship—have created a reward structure that supports this restricted definition. Only those efforts that have led to or reflected knowledge generation—research and publications—have been rewarded and valued within the academy. This narrow emphasis has created a significant dissonance for faculty who have found these reward structures incongruent with the range of teaching, outreach, and other research activities they pursue and with the passions and interests they hold. In other words, while university settings have expected faculty to be excellent teachers, good citizens, *and* nationally recognized researchers, often only the latter has been considered the work of scholars and has been truly valued and rewarded.

This restricted notion of scholarship has created numerous tensions within and problems for the academy. This restricted, shall we say "classical view," of scholarship has ignored the diverse roles and responsibilities pursued by most faculty and has ignored the diverse faculty talents found within most academic institutions (Johnson & Wamser, 1997). It has inadvertently penalized many women and minority faculty members who often conduct more of the "unrecognized" work of the academy (advising, teaching, and serving students and communities) than their male colleagues (Parks, 1996). It has ignored the critical educational and societal obligations of academic institutions, obligations that need immediate attention, given the widening "gap between values in the academy and the needs of the larger world" (Boyer, 1990, p. 22; Lynton, 1995). And this restricted notion of scholarship has misrepresented the very process of knowledge construction and learning, suggesting incorrectly that knowledge emerges solely from our own research pursuits and ignoring the important role community partners play in knowledge construction (Boyer, 1990).

In an attempt to promote a definition of scholarship that more fully encompasses the diversity in university mission and legitimizes the full range of faculty roles and responsibilities, Boyer (1990) published *Scholarship Reconsidered: Priorities of the Professoriate*. In this landmark publication, Boyer challenged members of the academy to embrace a more inclusive definition of scholarship, one that would recognize the full range of faculty roles and responsibilities and the university's teaching and civic responsibilities. He argued that scholarship in the academy actually takes on four different yet interdependent forms: the scholarship of discovery, the scholarship of integration, the scholarship of application (outreach or engagement), and the scholarship of teaching. He challenged the academy to reformulate its mission and its standards for evaluation to better reflect this diversity.

The *scholarship of discovery* refers to the familiar and traditional world of research and supports the pursuit of knowledge for its own sake. The *scholarship of integration* recognizes the need for integrative, interpretive, and multidisciplinary work that finds linkages across disciplines and studies. The *scholarship of teaching* refers to the process of disseminating and transforming knowledge for both the audience and the instructor. Finally, the *scholarship of application*—the focus of this chapter—refers to the process of applying knowledge toward the resolution of real societal problems and involves the inclusion of our community partners in knowledge generation. Encompassed within the scholarship of application is the outreach work many faculty, especially women and minority faculty, pursue.

Boyer's publication (1990) has had a significant impact on higher education, causing many to recognize that scholarship comes in multiple forms. In fact, in their 1994 survey on faculty roles and rewards, the Carnegie Foundation found that 78% of all universities and colleges were broadening their definitions of scholarship to include the full range of activities in which faculty are engaged (Glassick, Huber, & Maeroff, 1997). The majority of these institutions were also in the process of redefining faculty roles (86%) and realigning institutional mission and faculty rewards (66%). These changes are well reflected in the efforts of several institutions, including Portland State University, Michigan State University, University of Wisconsin, Oregon State University, and University of Illinois. These institutions are developing and implementing promotion and tenure review processes to reflect the range of faculty roles. For faculty engaged in outreach work, Boyer's work is especially promising in that he demonstrates that *outreach is a part of the work of scholars and a valued part of the academic mission.*[3]

The broadening of our notions of scholarship and the development of acceptable methods of capturing and evaluating this work have particular importance for women and minority faculty. Boyer's more inclusive definition better reflects the range of scholarly activities and, perhaps more important, provides for a reward structure more likely to acknowledge outreach work (Johnson & Wamser, 1997). Since women and minority faculty are often interested in working in the field and addressing critical social problems, (Parks, 1996; Antonio, 1998), their work creates valuable outcomes beyond typical research publications. In the traditional framework of scholarship, these additional outcomes, such as creating effective interventions, building community capacity, promoting community change, using community expertise, and designing community space or useful products, are ignored and perhaps even devalued. Boyer's approach to the scholarship of application values this work and provides a framework for demonstrating the scholarship in these endeavors. In addition, given that minorities and women often have difficulty in the academy, particularly proceeding up the academic ranks (Parks, 1996; Glazer-Raymo, 1999; Turner & Myers, 2000), it seems particularly important to consider venues for capturing the diversity of the scholarship associated with their varied pursuits.

While Boyer's challenge has been heralded as launching an important paradigm shift (Schon, 1995; Glassick, Huber, & Maeroff, 1997), the question remains how to implement this broader notion of scholarship within faculty reward systems. The Kellogg project was assigned the task of demonstrating that the scholarship in application, that is, in outreach work, could be documented, subjected to peer review, and assessed by a set of consistent standards. Ultimately, it was hoped that this documentation could be used for promotion and tenure purposes. During the Kellogg project we developed ways to conceptualize, document, and submit for external review the scholarship in our own outreach endeavors. We now turn to discussing these.

## MAKING THE CASE FOR THE SCHOLARSHIP IN OUTREACH

What does scholarship mean in your outreach activities, and how do you "capture" it in ways that are meaningful and useful for the faculty review process? In order to convince others of the scholarship in your outreach endeavors, you need to "make your case" by demonstrating the quality, value, and impact of the work you conduct (Lynton, 1995). In outreach work, this is often a daunting task given that quantifiable and sometimes even written products like publications are not typical outcomes. Other, more flexible venues for capturing the complexity of scholarship within outreach work are needed. Some have suggested that portfolios, files that present "rich and varied" materials as evidence of scholarship (Glassick, Huber, & Maeroff,

## TABLE 12.1
### Structuring and Documenting the Scholarship of Outreach:
### Kellogg Project, Michigan State University and Portland State University

| Kellogg Project: | Michigan State University: "Points of Distinction" | Portland State University: Promotion & Tenure Guidelines |
|---|---|---|
| *Key Portfolio Elements* | | |
| I. Narrative<br>A. Guiding Framework<br>  1.Purpose<br>  2.Process<br>  3.Outcomes<br>B. Reflection | Significance (A1, A3, B)*<br>Context (A1, A2, A3)*<br>Scholarship (A2, A3, B)*<br>Impact (A3, B)* | Goals (A1)*<br>Methods (A2)*<br>Communication<br>  (A1, A2, A3)*<br>Significance (A3, B)*<br>Ethical Behavior (B)* |
| II. Documentation of Outreach Scholarship<br>Evidence used:<br>• Archival data<br>• Written, verbal products<br>• Visual displays<br>• Changes in policy<br>• New methods developed<br>• Teaching byproducts<br>• Letters of support | Evidence used by Pennie at Michigan State:<br>• Conceptual model for evaluation used by partner<br>• Feedback reports to community and state<br>• Meeting minutes showing relevancy & impact on partners<br>• Practitioner publication<br>• Letters of support | Evidence used by Dannelle at Portland State:<br>• Partnership newsletter<br>• Conference brochures<br>• Faculty forum presentation schedule<br>• Grants written with partner<br>• Survey and evaluation report summaries<br>• Meeting minutes showing impact on partners<br>• Letters of support |

* The letters and numbers (A1, A2, A3, and B) show how the MSU and PSU elements relate to the Kellogg Project Key Portfolio Elements.

1997), could be used to document this form of scholarship (Edgerton, Hutchings, & Quinlan, 1991; Froh, Gray, & Lambert, 1993). Portfolios have become popular vehicles for documenting the scholarship of teaching (Stetson, 1991; Seldin, 1997) and are emerging as a recognized vehicle for documenting the scholarship of outreach.

The big question is, however, what do you include in the outreach portfolio, and how do you arrange it for presentation? Several factors have to be considered when deciding on the content and organization of the portfolio. In the Kellogg project, we decided that two key elements needed to be in every portfolio: a *narrative* describing the project and *evidence* documenting the project's impact. Within the narrative, a guiding framework that includes a statement of purpose, a description of the process and outcomes, and critical reflection should be included. Table 12.1, column 1 illustrates these elements. Table 12.2 elaborates the guiding framework with a description of the key elements in the statement of purpose, process, and outcomes.

Even though all 16 of the Kellogg participants felt that these elements were central to "making the case" for the scholarship of outreach, we also knew that the portfolio itself would take a different shape depending on the kind of project you are involved in, the discipline you represent, and the institution in which you are working. After all, the 16 faculty involved in the Kellogg project represented 13 disciplines, ranging

TABLE 12.2
Driscoll and Lynton's (1999) Framework
for Documenting Outreach Scholarship

| *Purpose* | *Process* | *Outcomes* |
|---|---|---|
| ✔ Needs & priorities of external partner | Attainable goals | Benefits to external partner |
| ✔ Institutional mission & priorities | Appropriate method | Benefits to faculty |
| ✔ Existing & potential resources | Ongoing adaptation | Benefits to students |
| ✔ External partner expertise & experience | Continuous reflections | Benefits to institution & unit |
| ✔ Individual expertise & experience | | Benefits to discipline |
| ✔ Situation-specific aspects of purpose | | |
| ✔ Individual development aspects of purpose | | |

from art to veterinary medicine to engineering and represented four different institutions. Therefore, each portfolio was shaped by the nature of the outreach project, institutional priorities, and the faculty member involved. Driscoll and Lynton (1999) have assembled the Kellogg faculty portfolios in a volume designed to guide the development of an outreach portfolio.

Certainly the university and departmental context in which you are working play a key role in determining the value and support for outreach scholarship. We do not pretend that all academic institutions in the United States value outreach scholarship and will count it for promotion and tenure. Even though you can make the case for your work, institutions are at different developmental points in their ability to honor and reward outreach scholarship. It is best to "test the waters" before putting an extraordinary amount of effort into this type of portfolio. How do you test the waters, that is, decide if it is worth the effort to use outreach scholarship as part of your scholarly agenda? There are several proactive steps you can take to make this decision. Talk to your department chair and the chair of the promotion and tenure committee about outreach scholarship and its historical and current role in promotion and tenure. Read your promotion and tenure guidelines carefully and discuss any unclear points with your supervisors and peers. Find faculty who are engaged in outreach in order to learn about how they used these activities in their promotion and tenure cases. If you have a faculty development office, contact the director for another viewpoint. Continually ask questions and seek clarifications of policies and procedures. Document meetings with supervisors about their responses to your queries. In this book, chapter 3 by Phyllis Bronstein and Judith Ramaley describes additional steps to take to find out about your institutional climate. In chapter 9 Patricia McDonough, as a current department chair, writes about how to work with your department chair.

Pennie and Dannelle were working at two different institutions, respectively, a Research I institution, Michigan State University (MSU), and a Research II institution, Portland State University (PSU). Following Boyer's guidelines in the last three years, both institutions had developed new policies to reward outreach, as well as teaching scholarship. If you compare columns 2 and 3 in table 12.1, MSU and PSU appear to have had different categories for documenting outreach. Yet, upon further analysis, both MSU and PSU outreach criteria included all of the key elements we developed in the Kellogg project for documentation and evaluation of outreach. In particular, a faculty committee at MSU developed their "Points of Distinction" (table 12.3). Pennie used her outreach work as a part of her promotion and tenure case and shaped her portfolio to fit within MSU's "Points of Distinction" framework. A PSU committee developed a promotion and tenure framework, evaluated by criteria that embraced Boyer's definition of scholarship across community outreach, service, and research (table 12.4). Using this framework and considering these criteria, Dannelle developed her narrative to support an allocation

TABLE 12.3
Glassick, Huber & Maeroff's (1997)
Standards for Evaluating Outreach Scholarship

✔ Clear goals
✔ Adequate preparation
✔ Appropriate methods
✔ Significant results
✔ Reflective critique

TABLE 12.4
Michigan State University's Criteria for
Evaluating Quality Outreach Scholarship

| | |
|---|---|
| ✔ Significance | • To what extent does the outreach initiative address issues that are important to the public, specific stakeholders, and the scholarly community? |
| ✔ Context | • To what extent is the outreach initiative shaped by knowledge that is current, cross-disciplinary, and appropriate to the issue? |
| ✔ | • To what extent does the work promote the generation, transmission, application, and utilization of knowledge? |
| ✔ Scholarship | • To what extent is the outreach initiative shaped by knowledge that is current, cross-disciplinary, and appropriate to the issue?<br>• To what extent does the work promote the generation, transmission, application, and utilization of knowledge? |
| ✔ Impact (external & (internal) | • To what extent does the outreach effort benefit and affect the issue, community, or individuals (e.g., by meeting the project's goals, satisfying the stakeholders, developing mechanisms for sustainability), and the university (e.g., by leading to innovations in curriculum, offering possibilities for student learning, identifying new research opportunities)? |

of 50% of her faculty work as outreach. She was successful in her bid for tenure and promotion.

In the Kellogg project, we all developed portfolios to make the case for scholarship in our outreach projects. Before we describe the organization and content of our portfolios, we first describe the specific projects we targeted in the Kellogg project. This context-setting information is provided to help you better understand the documentation information we provide below, to show you how the project itself interacts with the type of documentation, and to also illustrate that outreach scholarship occurs in a variety of contexts and projects.

## Two Examples of Outreach Scholarship

Pennie is an assistant professor in the Department of Psychology at Michigan State University. As a community psychologist, all of her research involves extensive work in the community. The project she documented involved her multiple-year involvement with one county that was attempting to implement several human service delivery reforms (e.g., shifting service delivery away from a medical-model orientation and toward a more client-empowerment mode). She was brought into the community to help them design and implement an evaluation of these service reform efforts. Her portfolio focuses on the processes she used to create a partnership with this community, create evaluation questions that met community needs while also building upon the relevant scientific literature, and build community capacity in this area. She also describes the impact of this evaluation on the community, herself, and her students.

Dannelle, an associate professor in the Curriculum and Instruction Department in the Graduate School of Education at Portland State University, was hired to fill a tenure-track position as school-university partnerships coordinator. All of her teaching, research, and outreach was influenced by her work of bridging institutional boundaries. The project she documented was the development of Professional Development Schools in her graduate school. These are school-university partnerships designed to foster the professional development of practicing teachers, the education of preservice teachers, and collaborative research in the university and the schools. Her portfolio focuses on the processes she used to create partnerships that contributed to her teaching, research, and outreach capacity. She also documents the impact on the community partners with whom she interacts.

## The Organization and Content of an Outreach Portfolio

Through our efforts and those of the other 14 faculty participants in the Kellogg project, and with the guidance of the project leaders Ernest Lynton and Amy Driscoll, as noted above, we realized that to capture the scholarship in outreach we needed to include (1) a narrative that includes a guiding framework and a personal reflection on critical decisions and events; and (2) documentation that includes evidence of the methods used and outcomes achieved (tables 12.1 and 12.2) (Driscoll & Lynton, 1999). We describe these in more detail below.

**The Narrative**    The narrative is a highly reflective, personal document that records the scholar's thinking about the purpose, actions, and outcomes of her work, including her critiques of these endeavors. Because the scholarship of application occurs in the purpose, processes, *and* outcomes of a service project, particular attention is given to how a project is carried out, how these methods promoted the scholarship of the endeavor, and what benefits accrued to the multiple audiences.

Overall, these narratives must include evidence of good scholarship, convince the reviewers that such scholarship has occurred, and be organized in a manner that effectively presents this evidence (Glassick, Huber, & Maeroff, 1997). Several different frameworks currently exist for guiding faculty in creating these narratives ( Michigan State University, 1996; Portland State University, 1996; Glassick, Huber, & Maeroff, 1997; Driscoll & Lynton, 1999) (see tables 12.2–12.4). Overall, these frameworks have much in common, in that they all suggest that scholars provide rich details about the significance, process, and outcomes of their work and include critical reflections about the lesson learned. However, as Driscoll and Lynton (1999) note, any portfolio framework should only be viewed as a guide. Faculty should adapt existing frameworks and/or create new ones that allow them to meet the unique needs of their institutions and disciplines. In our own documentation efforts, we each uniquely combined suggestions from different frameworks, creating templates that met the unique needs of our specific projects and the demands of our campus units and universities. We describe below our two frameworks for documenting the scholarship of application.

**A Guiding Framework**    One guiding framework that was particularly helpful to us was Driscoll and Lynton's (1999) suggestion that we include in our narrative the project's purpose, process, and outcomes. Pennie used this framework as the organizational structure for her portfolio (first purpose, then process, then outcomes), while Dannelle used the key elements in the framework but placed them in a different order. Contentwise, both Pennie and Dannelle included the critical content suggested by Driscoll and Lynton (1999), Glassick, Huber, & Maeroff (1997), and their own university's standards for outreach scholarship. Michigan State University's *Points of Distinction* provided specific criteria to be used for evaluating the scholarship in outreach. Pennie attempted to describe how she met each of these criteria in her document. Dannelle followed the criteria in the framework in the PSU "Promotion and Tenure (P and T) Guidelines" (Portland State University, 1996). PSU's "P and T Guidelines" gave direction for documenting scholarship in teaching, outreach, and traditional research. In the end, Pennie and Dannelle's portfolios varied greatly in their structure and in how they demonstrated the scholarship in their outreach. This difference was the result of the inherent outreach project differences and their institutional expectations but also of their disciplinary differences (psychology and education) and differences in their individual writing styles. Below we describe in more detail the key elements included in the narrative and illustrate how both Pennie and Dannelle included this information in their portfolios.

**Project Purpose**    Often inserted at the beginning of the narrative, this section should provide a rich description of the project's purpose and how this purpose *met the needs* of the targeted community setting, the faculty's member's professional interests and expertise, and institutional and departmental goals (what MSU refers to as the project's "significance"). Critical to this section is a *clear description of the project's purpose and objectives* (Glassick, Huber, & Maeroff, 1997; Driscoll & Lynton, 1999). This section should also demonstrate that *project objectives were realistic and achievable*, and that the *project addressed important questions and issues for both the community and the faculty member's discipline* (Glassick, Huber, & Maeroff, 1997). This last point is particularly important to demonstrate and is at the crux of evaluating the scholarship in outreach endeavors. Outreach projects, like other more traditional venues of scholarship, must contribute to knowledge. Therefore, it is important to describe the knowledge needed by both the community context and the faculty member's discipline and how this project created the context for such learning and knowledge application. Often, not unlike traditional research projects, this means *identifying the critical, underlying intellectual question* in your work and describing how this project pursued this question.

To address the above, Pennie included the following sections in the purpose section of her narrative:

- *The context:* A description of the larger social/political issues leading to the need for this project. This also included a description of the need for this knowledge within her discipline.
- *The setting:* A description of the targeted community context and its specific needs and how this context provided an excellent setting to examine the larger issues.

- *The project:* A description of how this project got initiated, players involved, and the project's overall purpose.

- *Scientific significance:* A description of how this project linked to her research and of the specific research questions examined. The larger, scientific body of knowledge relevant to this project was highlighted here.

- *Resource availablity:* A description of the resources (e.g., grants, in-kind) available for this endeavor.

- *Link to institutional mission and priorities:* A description of how this endeavor supported her university's mission and the purpose of her department.

To address the purpose section of her portfolio, Dannelle included the following information:

- *Link to job description:* The advertised job description that Dannelle responded to when seeking the school-university partnership coordinator position at Portland State in order to demonstrate how she is fulfilling the expectations of that position.

- *The context:* A description of the institutional and school needs that this partnership addressed.

- *The setting:* A description of the schools and school districts in which the work took place.

- *The project:* A description of the project goals, participants involved, and activities, all collaboratively designed.

- *Link to institutional priorities:* A description of how this work met the long-term goals of this urban institution whose mission is to make an impact on local schools through university partnerships.

**The Process**  After documenting the purpose, you will need to document the process in your outreach endeavors. This is central to making the case for the scholarship of application. An effective and collaborative process, including how you design and carry out your work in the community, distinguishes faculty work that can be defended and supported as scholarship from faculty work that meets the traditional service expectation of the academy. When discussing the process in your work, it is important to demonstrate that you have *adequately prepared for this endeavor*, that your *methods are appropriate*, and that your *goals are attainable* (Glassick, Huber, & Maeroff, 1997; Driscoll & Lynton, 1999). Often, this includes describing the processes you used to assess the community's needs, to involve the community collaboratively in this effort, and to fit the emerging intellectual question into its relevant literature base. Perhaps more important, you need to demonstrate that you have *continuously reflected about the project and its process*, and when necessary, *appropriately adapted your methods* (Glassick, Huber, & Maeroff, 1997; Driscoll & Lynton, 1999). You need to describe what insights you have gleaned about the process as the project unfolded and then how you integrated these insights into your future work. Below is an outline describing how Pennie addressed the process components in her portfolio.

- *Developing a strong community/university partnership:* A description of the efforts taken to actively involve the community in all stages of the evaluation effort.
- *Linking theory with practice:* A description of the steps taken to develop evaluation questions and methods that addressed community needs while building upon existing literature bases.
- *Evaluation methodology:* A description of the evaluation methods used.

Dannelle's portfolio included several examples of processes she used to develop as well as assess her school-university partnership project:

- *Identifying partners' needs:* A description of meetings, agendas, and outcomes, showed how partners collaborated on identifying needs and continually adjusting projects to meet these needs.
- *Sustaining communication throughout the partnership:* A description of the sustaining activities (e.g., meetings, newsletters, conferences) that were organized to foster networking and communication.
- *Analyzing journal entries:* A description of the use of journal entries for analysis and reflection on effective and ineffective steps taken to foster the partnership across the institutional boundaries.

**The Outcomes**    After making sure that your portfolio attends to the purpose and the process involved in your outreach efforts, portfolios must also demonstrate that an outreach project achieved significant results and benefits for its multiple stakeholders (Glassick, Huber, & Maeroff, 1997; Driscoll & Lynton, 1999). This section is critical because it demonstrates the value-added nature of the endeavor. It answers the question: What happened for the community, my students, my institution, my discipline, and my own professional and personal development as a result of my involvement in this endeavor? While this may include a description of traditional academic outcomes, such as conference presentations and publications, the primary purpose here is to demonstrate the typically excluded but quite valuable outcomes often achieved in outreach work. Through Driscoll and Lynton (1999), the Kellogg participants suggest that such benefits could include (1) benefits for external partners, such as meeting immediate needs, enhancing local capacity, creating new resources, and promoting sustainability of efforts; (2) benefits for the faculty member, such as enhanced professional skills and capacity, enhanced teaching, and new research questions and methods; (3) benefits for students, such as enhanced learning opportunities, personal and professional networks, personal development, and community involvement; (4) benefits to the profession, such as additions to the knowledge base, improved methodology, and effective dissemination; and (5) benefits to the institution/unit, such as support of the university mission, strengthening external ties, and promoting the reputation in the community. Below is a description of what Pennie included about outcomes in her portfolio:

- *Impacting local policy and practice:* A description of how evaluation findings were disseminated to community members and how these findings were used by the community to change local policy and practices.

- *Impacting statewide policy and practice:* A description of how evaluation findings were disseminated statewide to leaders, service providers, and policy makers and how these findings were used to examine other policies and practices.

- *Contributing to a knowledge base:* A description of how the evaluation findings advanced science and the efforts made to disseminate this information to the academic community through publications and conference presentations.

- *Enhancing local capacity:* A description of how this project built community capacity to conduct evaluations and to implement service delivery reforms.

- *Strengthening my capacity:* A description of how her involvement in this project enhanced Pennie's technical skills as an evaluator and researcher, her reputation statewide, her program of research, and the benefits for the students with whom she was involved in this effort.

Dannelle documented the outcomes of her project in a variety of ways.

- *Impacting school/university relations:* A description of the formation of an active advisory board.

- *Contributing to knowledge base about partnerships:* A description of the processes used to develop the partnerships was disseminated by both school-based and university partners at local, regional, and national conferences and through refereed publications (Stevens & Everhart, 2000).

- *Impacting statewide policy and practice:* A description of statewide planning committees in which she participated that supported a regional conference and impacted school-university involvement in action research projects.

- *Enhancing local capacity:* A description of teacher-generated action research projects presented at a regional conference attended by faculty and teachers from 15 school districts.

- *Strengthening my capacity:* A description of how the project enhanced her understanding of how action research works with teachers and schools and how a university would get involved in helping teachers with these projects.

**Critical Reflection**    Scholarship involves active reflection, including critiquing your methods and processes, assessing the value of the outcomes, and adapting your work in response to such reflection. Such reflection is particularly important in outreach endeavors, given the complexity of working in the community and the importance of modifying your techniques to develop locally relevant theories and solutions (Bartunek & Louis, 1996). The documentation of such reflection is a critical component of demonstrating the scholarship in your outreach (Driscoll & Lynton, 1999; Glassick, Huber, & Maeroff, 1997). By describing your insights about the local context, the interaction between the university and the community, the lessons learned in implementation, and how you correspondingly responded to and adapted your methods, you as a faculty member can demonstrate the knowledge-building processes embedded in your efforts. This reflection can be included throughout the narrative and/or in a distinct section in the document. Some examples of the issues we reflected upon are given below.

Pennie's Reflective Content: (1) reflection on the community leader's mixed response to our evaluation, what this response meant, and what I could have done differently to improve their reaction; (2) reflection on the complexity of the methodology we used, how we could have simplified it, and what resources would be needed in the future; (3) reflection on how the evaluation team became embedded within the local ecology and part of the community dynamics and the impact of this on the evaluation.

Dannelle's Reflective Content: (1) reflection on written feedback from conference participants; (2) reflection on the complexity of bringing university and school cultures together to accomplish common goals; (3) reflection on how to integrate the knowledge generated about action research into university action research classes; (4) reflection on how to assist a school district administration in making action research part of teachers' ongoing professional development.

**Evidence of the Methods Used and Outcomes Achieved**    In addition to the narrative described above, portfolios must also include evidence of your work, including materials that illustrate your methods and outcomes. Evidence comes in a variety of forms, including (a) *archival data,* which describes your involvement in or impact on the community (e.g., meeting minutes, newspaper clippings, advertisements); (b) *written, verbal, or visual products* produced for the project, including feedback reports, media products, graphic designs, training materials, workshop materials; (c) *documented changes in policy or practices,* such as stated organizational or community policies or community shifts in practices; (d) *methods developed,* including measurement scales developed, evaluation and implementation plans, community partnership-building meeting minutes; (e) *teaching byproducts,* including abstracts from relevant students' written work, curriculum changes, course syllabus; and (f) *letters of support from community partners.* While this evidence is easiest to collect during the project, it can also be collected retrospectively, as was the case in both of our portfolios. Below is a brief description of the evidence included in our two portfolios.

Pennie's Evidence: (1) conceptual model for the evaluation; (2) multiple feedback reports provided to the community and state; (3) countywide planning board meeting minutes discussing relevancy and impact of evaluation; (4) practitioner publication; (5) letter of support from community partners.

Dannelle's Evidence: (1) faculty forum presentations; (2) format for action research school district staff development program; (3) sample grants written with school districts; (4) school—university partnership action research conference programs; (5) network newsletters; (6) results of surveys used to evaluate the project; (7) sample minutes of meetings; (8) newsletter describing collaborative projects; (9) letters of support from state office of education.

**Benefits of Documentation**    In our opinion and personal experience, the documentation of the scholarship in your outreach endeavors has numerous benefits. By providing a legitimate venue for "making the case" about the scholarship in your outreach, it broadens the scope of work that can be considered in promotion and tenure review processes.

For women and minority faculty readers, such documentation may ultimately lead to the valuing of the work that often draws you to the academy and that you, alone, often pursue within your roles (Parks, 1996). Documentation also enhances your visibility within the academy, providing colleagues with a rich description of your efforts and the outcomes accomplished. Because outreach occurs outside of the academy and involves processes and impacts typically not considered within the review process, much of the labor and most of the rewards have remained misunderstood and ignored by the institution. Pennie found that her portfolio elicited a real understanding of and appreciation for her outreach work by many of her colleagues and several university administrators. As one administrator commented after reviewing Pennie's portfolio: "I had no idea our faculty were engaged in such great work. What can we do to continue to support such efforts?" Dannelle participated in several faculty development workshops and described her portfolio to others. As a result, the faculty development director placed Dannelle's promotion and tenure narrative on the university website as a model for other faculty who wished to use outreach as part of their case for promotion and tenure.

Documentation also provides a valuable opportunity for personal and professional development. Faculty—and we include ourselves in this claim—rarely take the time to reflect upon and document the quality of the processes and outcomes of their work. The documentation process requires this reflection, and both of us found that such reflection provided us with rich opportunities for personal and professional growth. For example, both of us have used the lessons we learned in this reflection about ourselves and the work we do to enhance the quality of other outreach pursuits.

Documentation also promotes the development of "standards of excellence" for outreach work that future scholars can use to guide their work in the community. While these standards should not be viewed as absolute measures of quality outreach, they could be used to promote discussion around the planning and design of outreach work. Certainly, all outreach projects need to be designed to meet the unique needs of the targeted context and the specific nature of the endeavor. However, across all contexts, issues of significance, contextual relevance, and impact are important to consider. The criteria listed in tables 12.1–12.5 provide an excellent starting point for this discussion.

**Difficulties with the Documentation Process**    As minorities and women, you often enter the academy with a stronger commitment to social justice than the white, male majority (Parks, 1996; Antonio, 1998). This professional and personal commitment is demonstrated in your work in the community. For minorities in particular, community members expect you to be involved in their activities and advocate for their interests. However, community work takes time and requires a different kind of documentation than typical faculty work. The time it takes to drive back and forth, attend meetings, return phone calls, and be accessible to the community to meet its expectations eats into the other demands on your time such as teaching and traditional research. It is not always evident in community outreach just what needs to be documented and how you are going to gather the evidence to support your claim. To document this very important outreach work as scholarship requires systematic attention and effort. That means that you have to take time to document your efforts. See chapter 13 (Stevens & Cooper) for a way to make the documentation process a bit simpler through keeping a professional journal.

Furthermore, part of our case for the scholarship of outreach lies in documenting the process by which certain outcomes were obtained. That means you have to note the processes, including the collaborations, the letters, the phone calls, the memos, and the organizational structures and then you have to eventually evaluate how all of these processes (methods) contributed or did not contribute to the outcomes you achieved. Sometimes you may not know ahead of time which process contributed to your success. Through reflection and analysis, you can pull out the significant factors. Unlike traditional scholarship where the processes are usually standard "treatments," outreach processes may be unique and unusual for the academy. Thus, another difficulty is to make sure you identify the processes that contributed to the desired outcomes and make the case for their impact on the project.

An additional complication is the need for you to document your singular contribution to this collaborative effort. For us this is one of the most difficult parts of documenting the scholarship of outreach. You know you would not have achieved these significant outcomes without your community partners. Yet you must extract your contribution to the project. You will have to examine what you have done to contribute to the collaborative purpose, process, and outcomes. This may feel like a violation of the spirit of the work. After all, you may have gotten into outreach work to serve your community, not "toot your own horn," so to speak. Yet to document outreach scholarship, you must identify your unique contribution. You must ask others to acknowledge your contribution to the development of the project, to write about your leadership, and to show how the project achieved the specific outcomes because of your expertise, your knowledge, and your collaborative skills. Then you must summarize these "glowing" accounts in your narrative.

TABLE 12.5

Portland State University's Promotion and Tenure Guidelines for
Evaluating the Quality and Significance of Scholarly Accomplishments

| Criteria for Scholarship | Criteria Applied to Community Outreach | Criteria Applied to Teaching | Criteria Applied to Research |
|---|---|---|---|
| ✔ Goals: Clarity & relevance of goals | • Has clear objectives <br> • Addresses substantive intellectual problems or issues | • Has learning objectives appropriate to curriculum & current state of knowledge in the field | • Has clear inquiry objectives <br> • Addresses substantive intellectual goals |
| ✔ Knowledge: Masters of existing knowledge | • Provides high quality assistance which depends on mastering existing knowledge | • Educates others well which depends on mastering existing knowledge | • Conducts meaningful research which depends on mastering existing knowledge |
| ✔ Methods: Appropriate use of methodology & resources | • Uses well-constructed methods to evaluate effects of the method on community problems | • Uses appropriate pedagogy & instructional techniques to maximize student learning <br> • Uses appropriate methodology to evaluate the effectiveness of curricular activities | • Uses rigorous research methods that require well-constructed instruments to evaluate the effectiveness of tested hypotheses |

*(continued on next page)*

TABLE 12.5 (continued)

| Criteria for Scholarship | Criteria Applied to Community Outreach | Criteria Applied to Teaching | Criteria Applied to Research |
|---|---|---|---|
| ✔ Communication: Effectiveness of communication | • Makes formal, oral presentations that meet professional standards for audience | • Communicates in ways that build positive student rapport<br>• Communicates to clarify knowledge<br>• Disseminates results of curricular innovations to teaching peers | • Makes formal, oral presentations that meet professional standards of audience |
| ✔ Results: Significance of results | • Makes a difference in communities & beyond<br>• Defines or resolves relevant social problems<br>• Improves existing practices<br>• Widely disseminates knowledge gained from project to those not directly benefitting from project | • Raises student motivation to learn<br>• Develops students' lifelong learning skills<br>• Contributes to students' knowledge, skills & abilities<br>• Communicates pedagogical innovations to peers who adopt approaches | • Widely disseminates work to invite scrutiny & to measure varying degrees of critical acclaim<br>• Considers more than the direct user satisfaction to evaluate quality & significance of an intellectual contribution |
| ✔ Ethics: Consistently ethical behavior | • Fosters a respectful relationship with community participants | • Fosters a respectful relationship with students & teaching peers | • Fosters a respectful relationship with peers<br>• Properly credits sources of information in writing, reports, articles & books<br>• Follows human subject review process |

Finally, as indicated above, doing outreach scholarship is not just a matter of attending a series of meetings or serving on several advisory boards. Outreach scholarship requires the identification of outcomes valued both by the faculty member and by the community partner. These outcomes emerge as the result of your efforts (and talents) as a faculty member and the efforts of your community partners. It is important to remember that the project's outcomes may not look like traditional academic outcomes, such as student achievement or a number of articles published in scholarly journals. For example, outreach outcomes may be the creation of a community counseling center that serves a low-income neighborhood. Other outcomes might be a newsletter that shares knowledge across the community or a conference that facilitates knowledge dissemination across various community partners. Mere letters of support may be suspect by promotion and tenure committees. Genuine, unsolicited responses of community partners can be more persuasive. For outreach scholarship, you will have to find evidence of your contribution to these outcomes. Often that evidence is not immediately obvious.

## CONCLUSION

In many ways, the academy itself has entered a kind of wonderland in its exploration of how to value, reward, and support this new, expanded view of scholarship. With few existing models for how to document and evaluate the scholarship within the varied roles and responsibilities of faculty, many institutions are grappling with how to successfully institutionalize and implement this broader notion of scholarship, the scholarship of application. In our experience, the creation of a portfolio that describes the scholarship within our outreach endeavors and provides evidence for such scholarship can be an effective venue for such documentation. If faculty involvement in such documentation is coupled with institutional support for and recognition of such scholarship, the academy could be well on its way toward developing a reward system that actually reflects its teaching, research, and service mission.

## NOTES

1. Acknowledgements: We would like to thank Amy Driscoll and Ernest Lynton for their wonderful leadership on this national effort to document the scholarship in our outreach. We thank them and the other fourteen faculty members involved in the Kellogg Foundation project Documenting the Scholarship in Professional Service and Outreach for all of their insights and wisdom

around defining and documenting outreach scholarship. These contributors were: IUPUI—Michael R. Cohen, C. Roger Jarjoura, Florence Juillerat, and Sandy Purgener; Michigan State University—Pennie G. Foster-Fishman, James W. Lloyd, Warren J. Rauhe, and Cheryl Rosaen; Portland State University—Susan Agre-Kippenhan, Franz Rad, Particia A. Schechter, and Dannelle D. Stevens; and University of Memphis—David N. Cox, Stan Hyland, Ben L. Kedia, and Steven M. Ross.

2. We use the term *outreach* in this chapter to refer to the community-based activities faculty engage in that require the faculty member's expertise and that contribute to the identification and/or resolution of community-based problems (Johnson and Wamser, 1997). The terms *community outreach, scholarship of engagement, scholarship of application,* and *professional service* are often used interchangeably by higher education institutions.

3. Others have discussed the impact of Boyer's work on the scholarship of teaching. See Seldin (1997) and Stetson (1991) for a discussion of the development and documentation of scholarship in our teaching endeavors.

## REFERENCES

Antonio, A. L. (1998, Oct). *Faculty of color reconsidered: Retaining scholars for the future.* Paper presented at the conference, Keeping Our Faculties: Addressing the Recruitment and Retention of Faculty of Color in Higher Education, Minneapolis, MN.

Bartunek, J. M., & Louis, M. R. (1996). *Insider outsider team research.* Thousand Oaks, CA: Sage.

Boice, R. (1992). *The new faculty member: Supporting and fostering professional development.* San Francisco: Jossey-Bass.

Boyer, E. L. (1990). *Scholarship reconsidered: Priorities of the professoriate.* Princeton, NJ: Carnegie Foundation for the Advancement of Teaching.

Driscoll, A., & Lynton, E. (Eds.) (1999). *Making outreach visible: A guide to documenting professional service and outreach.* Washington, DC: American Association for Higher Education.

Edgerton, R., Hutchings, P., & Quinlan, K. (1991). *The teaching portfolio: Capturing the scholarship in teaching.* Washington, DC: American Association of Higher Education.

Froh, R. C., Gray, P. J., & Lambert, L. M. (1993). Representing faculty work: The professional portfolio. In R. Diamon & R. E. Adam (Eds.), *Recognizing faculty work: Reward systems for the year 2000.* San Francisco: Jossey Bass.

Glassick, C. E., Huber, M. T., & Maeroff, G. I. (1997). *Scholarship Assessed: Evaluation of the Professoriate* (Chapters 1, 2, & 4). San Francisco: Jossey Bass.

Glazer-Raymo, J. (1999). *Shattering the myths: Women in academe.* Baltimore: John Hopkins University Press.

Johnson, R. N., & Wamser, C. C. (1997). Respective diverse scholarly work: The key to advancing the multiple missions of the urban university. *Metropolitan Universities* 7(4), 43–59.

Lynton, E. A. (1995). *Making the case for professional service.* Washington, DC: American Association for Higher Education.

Michigan State University (1996). *Points of distinction: A guidebook for planning and evaluating quality outreach.* East Lansing: Michigan State University.

Parks, S. M. (1996). Research, teaching, and service: Why shouldn't women's work count? *Journal of Higher Education* 67(1), 46–84.

Portland State University (1996). Guidelines for promotion and tenure. Portland: Portland State University.

Schon, D. A. (November/December 1995). Knowing in action: The new scholarship requires a new epistemology. *Change,* 27–34.

Seldin, P. (1997). *The teaching portfolio: A practical guide to improved performance and promotion/tenure decisions.* Bolton: Anker Publishing.

Stetson, N. E. (1991). Implementing and maintaining a classroom research program for faculty. In T. A. Angelo (Ed.), *Classroom research: Early lessons from success.* New Directions for teaching and learning, No. 46. San Francisco: Jossey-Bass.

Stevens, D. D., & Everhart, R. E. (2000). Designing and tailoring school/university partnerships: A straightjacket, security blanket or just a loose coat? *The Professional Educator* 22 (2), 39–49.

Tierney, W. G., & Bensimon, E. M. (1996). *Promotion and tenure: Community and socialization in academe.* New York: State University of New York Press.

Turner, C. S., & Myers, S. L. (2000). *Faculty of color in academe: Bittersweet success.* Boston: Allyn & Bacon.

# CHAPTER 13

# *Reflecting on Your Journey: How to Keep a Professional/Personal Journal*

## Dannelle D. Stevens
## and Joanne E. Cooper

No time. Absolutely no time to write in a journal. Just barely
enough time to prepare for classes, attend meetings, start my
research, and get on with the job of being a new tenure-track faculty member. Having to write in a journal with all the other
expectations, feeling the pressure to keep a journal—well, that is
just one more way to feel guilty . . . not needed. No way.

Similar to the above frustrated and harried faculty member, you may
also feel that journal keeping is not for you. You have heard of the
value of reflection but believe there is just no time to reflect in the way
you should. You may reject the notion of journal keeping because, as
students in our classes have said, "journals are just for emotional
release. How could they be helpful in my academic career?" The purpose of this chapter is to discuss the potential value of keeping a pro-
fessional-personal journal for you, as new faculty members. The
authors are veteran journal keepers who have taught classes on journal
keeping for several years. Based on this experience and the wealth of literature on the value of reflection, we will introduce you to many ways
of keeping a journal that meet some of the unique and demanding
expectations of our profession.

From our experience and that of many others, we believe that keeping a journal is time well spent. Keeping a journal is a powerful practice

that can lead to a healthier and even a more organized life. Osterman and Kottkamp (1993, p. 73) state, "The act of writing one's thoughts seems to have a substantially different and greater impact" than oral statements. Naming our reality in written form allows us to "pause, cycle back, reread, and rethink the very descriptions and ideas we are formulating, and we capture our thought processes in a product to which we may return to reassess, search for options, and plan for the future" (p. 88). Others note that cognitive activities are stimulated by journal keeping; these include observation, speculation, doubt, questioning, self-awareness, problem stating, problem solving, emoting, and idea generation (Holt, 1994). According to Schneider (1994 in Kerka, 1996), reflective journal writing in particular is "closest to natural speech, and writing can flow without self-consciousness or inhibition. It reveals thought processes and mental habits, it aids memory and it provides a context for healing and growth. Journals are a safe place to practice writing daily without the restrictions of form, audience and evaluation" (p. 2).

Just what is a journal? Is it a diary? Is it a collection of entries in your pocket calendar? Is it a log of your activities in your "day timer"? At the very least, the entries in every journal are dated. That is the minimal definition of a journal. However, the entries, what goes on those pages, is up to you. Typically, you write in a diary every day. However, in the models of journals we present, some veteran journal keepers do not write every day. A journal can just be a log of your many activities and your responses to those activities, or it can be just a day timer where you keep appointments, addresses, and maybe even a phone log. It can be chiefly a confessional, a place to document your cares and concerns. Dannelle and Joanne have different styles of journal keeping. The models serve each of them well. We and other veteran journal keepers have found some useful, though different, ways to keep a journal. Our focus in this chapter is how journal keeping is particularly suitable for our work.

When you go up for promotion and tenure, for example, you will have to produce selected evidence about your activities and how they fit into your overall "research agenda." You cannot share everything you have done. You will have to pick and choose. Sometimes it is hard to recall all the things you have done and what they might mean in your career. Dannelle will share a method that documents activities, participants, reflections, and notes that became invaluable in consistently tracking, clearly identifying, and deeply reflecting on her work. Joanne will describe both her professional and personal journals where she, for example, reflects on meetings and networking at conferences, sorts out dilemmas and challenges in her department and even at times chats with her wiser self. Both authors have found journal keeping essential in sorting out the complexity of competing demands, unclear expectations, and head-throbbing stressors in their academic life.

The chapter is divided into four sections that answer the following questions: Why keep a journal? How can it become a habit? What are some models of journal keeping? What are some useful journal techniques? Our goal is to expand your notion of journal keeping and to show you some specific ways to use it to promote your successful bid for tenure.

## WHY KEEP A JOURNAL?

The reasons to keep a journal are legion. Dannelle finds that her journal helps her manage the day-to-day bustle in the academy. Because she records so many of her daily activities in her journal, her journal has become a "book" of her professional/personal life. Since all of her entries are recorded within one cover, it has become a metaphor for the wholeness she seeks, a way to bring the many of the parts of her life together in one place. As Tristine Rainer (1978, p. 18) writes, "It is a sanctuary where all the disparate elements of a life—feelings, thoughts, dreams, hopes, fears, fantasies, practicalities, worries, facts and intuitions—can merge to give you a sense of wholeness and coherence." Dannelle uses her journal in many concrete ways as well: to track discussion and decision-making in meetings, to make "to do" lists, to note important ideas developed with teaching and research partners, to list books read, and to write down favorite quotations. That is not enough though. Her journal is also the place where she reflects on her personal and professional, life as well as the intersection of those lives.

Joanne likes to say that it keeps her "rudder in the water." In other words, it serves as time to reflect or meditate on the day, the hour, the events in your life. It can have a real calming effect, as well as help her to sort out what's going on around her. When you are a new faculty member, you are bombarded with events and comments that you may not easily be able to decipher. Writing in a journal is a time to synthesize random pieces of information that help you to reflect on the norms and values of your new organization.

Gannett (1992) has asserted (citing Pamela J. Annas and Jonah R. Churgin) that keeping a journal or diary may be particularly suited to women because of its tradition as a place for private or personal discourse. Interestingly, she also uses the metaphor chosen for the title of this text, "I suggest that while the presence of women in the groves of academe, both as scholars and as teachers, continues to dilute or to change the male discourse forms of the university somewhat, the traditional academic forms are still strong drink for many women" (p. 199). Journal keeping, then, may be a practice that allows women and other marginalized faculty a private place to formulate complex thought before it appears in the harsh light of public academic discourse.

Privacy issues are important and should be carefully considered as you start the journal-keeping process. Where will you keep your journal? Will it stay at home or go to work with you? How will you ensure that you feel safe about its contents? Tristine Rainer's (1978) classic text, *The New Diary*, refers to what we are calling a journal, as a diary. She explores the topic of privacy in this way,

> There is no rule that a diary has to be kept secret, though there are many good reasons for wanting to keep it private. . . . You may tentatively consider ideas that you eventually reject, and that would be misunderstood if read by another. You might write delicate material that could hurt another. . . . You may simply want the freedom to write sloppily, ungrammatically, profanely somewhere in your life, or you may want the freedom to explore your lesser selves without making explanations to others. Therefore, you may wish to keep the diary in a locked, safe place to protect others from misunderstanding, misinterpreting or judging your writing. (p. 45)

One journal keeper kept her old journals in a safe deposit box at the bank. One woman had destroyed many of her earlier journals. She explained, "I used to worry about someone reading them and being hurt, [so] I destroyed all my old notebooks. I just have the two most recent ones. When I finally decided they were just for me, then I began to write more and feel OK about it" (Cooper & Dunlap, 1991, p. 76).

We are not alone in finding value in journal keeping in our professional lives. A study of veteran journal keepers indicates that they find the activity helpful in three major ways (Cooper & Dunlap, 1991). First, it helps them sort through the chaos and clutter of their lives. One woman stated that keeping a journal was "almost a way . . . of . . . making order out of chaos." For this woman, the process of putting words to experience had the effect of "putting things in perspective, giving them some distance, making them seem manageable because they can be named. I think it's a way that I kind of take charge of my experience" (Cooper & Dunlap, 1991, p. 72).

Second, it helps educators generate possible solutions to problems (Cooper & Dunlap, 1991). Once they have identified exactly what the problem is, journal keepers are able to brainstorm solutions and test their possible consequences. Veteran journal keepers report that they often use their journals to identify and evaluate possible goals, decide on a set of actions to solve a problem, and begin to systematically carry out these steps, checking periodically to see whether their decision still feels good or they need to modify their plan in some way. One woman used her journal as a way to track what went wrong during her workday. She states, "If I'm in the middle of the day at work and . . . I get upset about something . . . I write down notes to my self about things that I want to do better and feelings that I'm having and ways I think I can correct them" (Cooper & Dunlap, 1991, p. 75). It sometimes helps you realize when things are not going to change. One journal keeper explained that the process "forces me to be introspective and to deal with thoughts and feelings that I have inside me that I otherwise probably would not deal with. And I find that to be very therapeutic, a very freeing kind of experience. . . . Sometimes if you get to the bottom . . . you wish it were different, you know it can't be different, and so you accept it and go on" (p. 75). She says that she gains insights into solutions to problems as she is writing about them, or she comes to the realization that "that's the way it has to be (or it's going to be) and you know there isn't any solution or resolution to this one" (p. 75).

A third function that veteran journal keepers report is the ability to reread and rethink earlier experiences. "It's nice to know what you've learned," states one journal keeper (Cooper & Dunlap, 1991, p. 76). Another woman reported that rereading her old journals helped her when she felt stuck. Here the journal functions like a mentor. One woman commented, "It's . . . nice when you get stuck again to go, 'OK, um, I've been stuck before' . . . and there's something real reassuring to me . . . in knowing that I can work my way out of things . . . and if I need to go back and look, I can check that out" (p. 76). One woman read and reread about a disastrous decision she had made, commenting that every time she was tempted to do the same thing, she would go back and reread her journal, reminding herself over and over not to make the same mistake again.

The private nature of the journal process may help untenured faculty deal with situations that they feel they cannot discuss with their colleagues. If you are under a lot of scrutiny on the job, it is helpful to have a place to consider how to balance your life, the personal and the professional, the demands of the job to teach, conduct research, publish, and render service to the university and the community. Faculty need a place to struggle with setting their own set of priorities, even though those priorities might be different than the university's. A journal offers the privacy for both personal and professional decisions. One woman, a veteran journal keeper who was pregnant with a Down syndrome child, used her journal as a safe place to sort through her feelings as she appraised her options and rehearsed possible solutions. Louise DeSalvo, in *Writing as a Way of Healing* (1999), reports that many famous authors, such as Alice Walker, James Baldwin, and Virginia Woolf, report that they have consciously used the writing of their artistic works to help them heal from the thorny experiences of their lives, especially from dislocation, violence, racism, homophobia, anti-Semitism, rape, political persecution, incest, loss, illness (p. 4). To Louise, writing functions as a "fixer" (p. 6).

> As in photography, writing acts as a kind of fixer, like the chemical— the fixer—you use to stabilize the image. "Fixing things," I sometimes call it. And it acts as another kind of "fixer," with all its healing implications. I use my writing as a way of fixing things, of making them better, of healing myself. As a compass-like way of taking a "fix" on my life—to see where I am, where I've been, and where I'm going. (p. 7)

Journal keeping is a practice that these busy professionals sustain, despite competing demands, because they know it provides them with a rich contextual background and a steady retreat for the kind of reflection needed when sorting through the problems they face. These journal keepers are able to name and frame their problems, to brainstorm possible solutions, and to support themselves through a documentation of the past. Cooper and Dunlap (1991, p. 78) report that the journal, with its chronology, its layers of entries, may provide educators with the information they need to struggle with the complex world of higher education. Writing in a journal is in some ways a mysterious process. As one veteran journal keeper reported, "The writing process brings up stuff. I don't understand it. I don't need to understand it, but something happens when you begin to write. You get in touch with some other level and to this day, if I'm just real frustrated, then writing will be helpful" (Cooper & Dunlap, 1991, p. 79).

Beyond these personal uses, research has found solid evidence about the ways in which journal keeping can improve both physical and mental health. Writing about your problems can increase the level of disease-fighting lymphocytes circulating in your bloodstream and improve your blood pressure (Pennebaker & Beall, 1986; Pennebaker, 1997). It can improve lung function if you are asthmatic or improve your symptoms if you have rheumatoid arthritis. Louise DeSalvo, an English professor at Hunter College in New York and author of *Writing as a Way of Healing* (1999) says that intensive writing about her asthma (both its symptoms and how debilitating it made her feel) vastly improved her health. Given that new faculty women and minorities need to be in tip-top condition to launch their careers, staying healthy is a high priority. The work of being a new faculty member is hard, but taking the time to write about your problems is time well spent and could help to lighten the workload by reducing interference from physical worries.

## HOW DOES JOURNAL KEEPING BECOME A HABIT?

One thing we know for sure is that keeping a journal can become a habit, a pleasant habit. But, how do you get to that place? The paths that Dannelle and Joanne took to developing a habit of journal keeping were quite different. Yet for both over the years, journal keeping has become integrated and valued in their professional and personal lives.

Tristine Rainer speaks of the 1950s when diaries were a popular gift for young girls. "There was widespread merchandising of the one-year diaries with toy locks and keys designed for young girls. These parodied the long tradition of women's secret diaries. They also represented the tail end of the Puritan tradition of diary keeping as a self-watching, daily discipline" (p. 21). Growing up in the 1950s, Dannelle and her sister received one of these diaries for Christmas several years in a row. Even though the key was generic (similar to an old suitcase lock), she felt that the idea was that whatever she wrote in there was private. Dannelle enjoyed having a place to write about her life and kept a diary for five years. Then at age thirteen, her life changed. She started to waiver from the normal high-achieving path her parents had designed for her. Because of their great concern over her future, her parents decided to go to the one place where she kept her private thoughts, her diary. They confronted her with her borderline activities, detailed in her diary. She decided that she could be "the good girl" they wanted, but that killed the diarist in Dannelle for a long time.

During the 1960s and 1970s Dannelle made repeated attempts to start keeping a diary, a journal again. There are at least 10 blank books in her house now with only the first 5 to 10 pages filled. She would write in them only when disasters befell her life, and she wanted a place to sort things out. She waffled between using beautifully bound blank books and sterile laboratory notebooks. She realized that the beautiful volumes scared her because she felt she had to say beautiful and polished things in them. Too much of her writing was just unfinished and raw. The lab notebooks were not necessarily a good solution, because she could not seem to keep up with daily entries. She just did not have the idea of how a journal could benefit her. Yet she flirted with it for many years. Finally in the last ten years, she has found a way to keep a journal that adds to her life. It is not a burden to make entries, and it has become invaluable documenting not only her academic life but also her personal reflections. Using a journal has given her more quality time to reflect on her work. Using a journal has helped her make connections between the many, varied complex demands in her professional life.

Journal keeping has allowed her to become more comfortable with herself as a writer. In fact, she has become a student of writing and journal keeping. She asks questions about the process, monitors her own development as a writer, and seeks the experience of others as they have developed as writers. For example, one of her favorite writers, Peter Elbow (1973), observed his own writing process in the development of his book *Writing without Teachers* and speaks eloquently about how he studied the process of his struggle to find his own voice. Similarly, Dannelle has become fascinated with her own writing process. She asks, "How can I have ideas so clearly conceived in my head only to find them slip away from the tip of the pen?" She watches herself write and waits for the time when the muse will tap her on the shoulder with a surprise, a fresh idea, as she puts words on the page. She has added journal keeping to her university class requirements and often starts a class session with a freewrite (Elbow, 1978) in which she, too, participates. She describes freewriting as a time to dust out the cobwebs of the mind or cleanse the palate before being present in the class.

Joanne has been keeping a journal for 25 years, since she was given a blank book for Christmas in 1975. She not only kept both a personal journal and a dissertation journal while she was a doctoral student, but she studied journal keepers, as well. The dissertation journal became the depository for musings on her research findings, sketches of each participant, freewrites about the research process, responses to articles she was reading on the subject, to do lists, and rough drafts of particular chapters or sections as they unfolded.

For years she did not write every day, only when the spirit moved her. She used to write wherever and whenever she felt like it, morning, midday, or evening. Evening writings tend to sum up the day, musing on what has happened and what it means. Morning writings can do this also but have a tendency to look ahead, to the day or the week. Gradually, Joanne moved to writing daily, as a kind of meditative practice, and writing in the mornings when her head was clearer and she was ready to start the day. Here she was influenced by the work of Julia Cameron (1992), who advocates writing morning pages, at least three per day, as a way to enhance creativity. Joanne now views journal keeping as a positive addiction, one that is self-reinforcing enough that if she doesn't write for several days, she misses it. Not writing regularly makes her feel restless, as if she had an itch she had neglected to scratch, leaving her unfinished and distracted.

## WHAT ARE SOME MODELS OF JOURNALS THAT YOU MIGHT TRY?

### Dannelle's Professional/Personal Journal

There are a variety of ways to keep a journal. The journal that Dannelle described above is the one that she carries with her all the time—it "lives" in an eight by eleven inch graph-paper laboratory notebook with a hard cover. Yet, she also keeps another journal, a journal generated on the computer. Both have the one consistent characteristic of all journals and diaries—the date of the entry. That is where the similarity between these journals ends. Each serves its own purpose. Let us start with the journal that originates on the computer.

Some writers don't recommend keeping a journal on the computer (Cameron, 1992). The pen has a better connection to the brain. Yet Dannelle finds that one type of journal can be created on the computer, spontaneous writing (SW), as recommended by Robert Boice (1990). She saves and dates these writings and keeps a set of weekly entries in one computer file. Even though these writings are often ramblings about current events or observations, she prints them and puts them in a binder. She finds this computer-generated freewrite, spontaneous writing—even five minutes before more serious academic writing—cleanses the writing palate and makes her more present to the task at hand.

Dannelle's model for her other journal, the professional/personal handwritten journal, actually started years ago when she took college lecture notes. She used tablets with extra wide left-hand margins, where, after the lecture, she could summarize the key points of the lecture. This column became useful in other ways: she could ask additional questions, add notes from her readings, and define terms. This practice of using two columns is similar to what an anthropologist does when she gathers field notes. One column answers the questions: What is happening? What am I observing? The second column answers the questions: What do I infer about what I see? What questions does this observation bring up in my mind? Her professional/personal journal is first of all a log (see table 13.1 for a full description of each of the columns) with two columns.

Opening up the definition of what counts as appropriate content in a journal has allowed Dannelle to use it more often and with more direct benefit in her work. The content of her journal is not limited to narrative text, nor is it only drawings or meeting notes (See table 13.1). The processes by which she develops her thinking and reflection in the journal vary from questions generated in discussions with others, to prescribed exercises to concept maps that summarize all of the topics she has invested time on. She has no rules about what goes into the journal and what doesn't. During a meeting, she may even put her grocery list in the journal just to get it off her mind.

This professional journal goes with her to every meeting on campus, off campus, and at conferences. There are two sides to this journal. The more "public" side is divided into two columns—one about an inch or inch and a half wide, and the other larger column, which is about four

TABLE 13.1

A Model of a Professional/Personal Journal: Aspects and Page Format

| Overall Aspects | Column One: Journal Format | Column Two: Journal Format |
|---|---|---|
| Two columns<br>Pages numbered<br>Entries dated<br>Table of contents | Layout: Make two columns on the page by drawing a line down one side:<br><br>Column One: 3–4 times wider than Column Two<br><br>Contents of Column One:<br>Notes from meetings attended<br>Agendas of meetings<br>Diagrams that summarize thinking<br>Direct quotations from meetings<br>Notes from conference sessions | Layout:<br>Narrower than Column One<br>Contents of Column Two:<br>Date of entry<br>Attendees at meeting<br>Title of group<br>"To do" list from meeting<br>Note big ideas that link to other activities<br>Record nonmeeting-related ideas like grocery list<br>Doodles |

(continued on next page)

TABLE 13.1 (continued)

| Overall Aspects | Column One: Journal Format | Column Two: Journal Format |
|---|---|---|
| Benefits | Benefits | Benefits |
| Overall; | Actual record of meeting, agendas, notes Record of activities: For junior faculty, a way to record and remember the numerous committees, community activities, and events that need to be documented for promotion and tenure. | Column Two: quick way to see who attended meeting and its key themes. |
| Log Evidence Documentation | Usually projects continue over time; way to keep all ideas for that project as it develops; find notes from last meeting in earlier part of your journal. | Reflections in this column can help make connections to other work and become seed for articles and presentations. |
| Reflection Actions Linked to Projects | Quotations of participants allow for later reflection and developing an understanding of another person's or group's perspective. All activities and meetings in one place; do not have to dig through files for notes. | "To do" list next to meeting notes links activities with the context from which they were derived. "To do" list in this column like grocery list allows you to get that information down so you can be more present at the meeting. |
| Continuity Linkages across Work | Used to reflect on and develop ideas over time. Opportunity to link activities and ideas across various audiences. Facilitates spanning institutional boundaries, i.e., community agencies and the university. | Confusions can be noted here to be followed up on later. |

to six inches wide. In the larger column, she will write what she hears and sees at the meeting, which could include the agenda, brief minutes, visual diagrams of ideas presented, even quotations of meeting participants. In the smaller column, she locates the event in her life with the date, the names of the people present, and the location and the type of meeting (university, school, department, consulting, student advising, etc.). This smaller column might also contain questions for later reflection, ideas for connecting this project to other work she does, a "to do" list derived from the project, a comment on the content of the meeting, and even doodles. In the event the meeting is boring, or if something else is occupying her mind, she might include a totally unrelated topic in the smaller column like a shopping list for a dinner party. Dannelle finds that putting some of these random ideas down in the smaller column allows her to place them somewhere and go back to concentrating on the moment.

The second part of the journal is a more personal, narrative section. This section is her life story beyond the daily-ness of the events described in the other part of her journal. The problem was how and where to do this in a single journal. Did she want to intersperse it with the other pages? That might expose it to public scrutiny if someone read over her shoulder. It needed its own section. Yet if she wrote it like the regular journal forward through the book, she would have to estimate the number of pages she would need. Since she released herself from the constraint (guilt) that she had to write in it every day, it would be next to impossible to judge how many pages she would need. The solution was to flip the journal over and start writing from the back of the journal. When the two sections meet, the professional log and the personal reflections coming from the other direction, then Dannelle starts a new journal. She may write her personal reflections in the morning before work, on a plane going to a conference, or before a meeting begins. These reflections look different. They are less listlike and more narrativelike. They have two columns, but the smaller second column is usually only filled in with the date and the place where she is writing the entry.

## Joanne's Personal/Professional Journal

Joanne's journal has been a place to synthesize the personal and the professional, a place to spend some quiet time reading what is uppermost on her mind, and a place to dump the garbage that collects in the brain, filling it with needless worries and information. She has found that the writing process helps her to clarify what is really going on in her life and to dig deeper into an understanding of her own needs, motivations, and insights. An added side effect is that she has learned how to write freely and easily. It may come out a mess, never tightly organized and perfectly articulated, but at least she is able to get words on paper whenever she begins to write a professional paper. She states, "It makes sense if you think about it; you are bound to get better at anything you practice almost daily for over twenty years. If you played tennis every day for years, you are bound to get better at it." But that is not why she writes. She says she writes "to keep my rudder in the water." The writing process, for Joanne, is a meditative one. It helps to ground her in the present, just as meditation does. She often wakes up in the morning with her mind racing, thinking of the millions of things that must be done that day: bills to pay, phone calls to return, students to see, committee work that must be done, drafts of papers that must be written, and so on. She writes every morning now, and often these early morning writings contain to do lists, as well as assurances that yes, it will all get done somehow.

She also writes after professional meetings, sitting in the airplane summing up what she's learned and making a list of people she would like to follow up with, papers she's promised to send, and papers for which she would like to send. These writings have been enormously helpful in brainstorming future research. Ideas seem to come rapidly after an intense week listening to the work of others and connecting with those who have similar interests. Collaborative research projects are often born in these conferences, and it is helpful to document the follow up that needs to be done to continue the work.

All of this is dumped into her personal journal. There is a kind of synthesis that takes place when the personal and the professional are combined. To Joanne, it feels more whole than keeping these concerns in separate places. We are, indeed, both personal and professional creatures, and juggling these disparate parts can be one of life's central tasks (see chapter 10 for more discussion on balancing the personal and the professional). Other journal keepers report that they used to keep two journals, one professional and one personal but that it became too difficult to keep the two separate journals. They kept merging into one another (Cooper & Dunlap, 1991). Joanne does keep a journal at school, similar to the one Dannelle keeps, but it contains only records of meetings and notes on actions needed in the professional realm. For her, any musings on these events are kept in her personal journal at home. Part of this is a concern over privacy issues. Keeping her personal thoughts in her journal at home feels safer and more private to her. Privacy issues are an important component of journal keeping. If the diarist feels she cannot be open about her feelings and thoughts, it diminishes the positive effects of the journal process.

Often Joanne's journal entries take on the form of advice from her wiser self. Here for instance is a musing on a story one of her students told:

One of my nursing students talked about her friend who was a nurse in the check-out tent in Vietnam: intensive care, everyone in a coma. When the bombs hit, all the men would fall out of their bunks, pulling out all their tubes and spilling themselves onto the floor. This nurse had to hold them in their bunks, standing between the beds, waiting for the bombs to stop. Later, she married five times; never trusting that the one she loved wouldn't leave her. She probably *never* thought, when she started out just wanting to be a nurse to help the sick, that her life would unfold in this particular way.

What I've learned here is that we have no choice, life unfolds, relentlessly, whether we let it or not. Joys come, unexpected love, sorrow, little deaths, big ones, eventually our own . . . but in the meantime, it is *life* that unfolds, so we might as well let it, enjoy it, because it is going to happen, this living thing, until it ends, unfolding like a kaleidoscope in unexpected ways. Let it, Joanne. You really have no choice.

These writings serve as a kind of reminder of how to live. They help Joanne to stay balanced and focused on what is most important. Life in the academy can be demanding 24 hours a day. It is easy to get sucked into its relentless pace and to forget why you wanted to become a faculty member in the first place. The journal is a place to remember what it is you value and how you want to go about the business of living. Here is where the rudder image comes in. These writings can be a kind of rudder, helping you to keep in mind the reasons you wanted to do this work in the first place and the values you still hold about how to go about the work that needs to be done. The academy pulls you in many directions, not all of them healthy. You must decide, on a daily basis, what the work means for you and what is important to do, as well as what can fall away, and those answers are not the same for everyone.

During a panel discussion about getting tenure at a national conference, one woman said, you need to "not shoot yourself in the foot." She said that if someone wants to help you, to be your ally, you should let them, even if you don't agree with all their politics or their values. This is excellent advice. It is easy to get on your high horse and refuse to let someone help you because you don't agree with their politics. Only when you know clearly what your values are can you decide what you agree with, what you disagree with, and where you need to draw the line between what you are willing to accept and what you are not. This is where the journal comes in. It serves as a mirror, holding up an image of who you are, against all that others might want you to be and as a reflection of all you can be.

On some days life is so discouraging that Joanne simply uses her journal as a place to bolster the failing self. Here is a passage she wrote on the relentless nature of the work in the academy. She is thinking about how she spent her weekend: "I feel like I didn't do enough yesterday, but that's only because I didn't work all day. . . . I fixed the lock on my car and got a new driver's license. . . . I swam forty laps . . . I should have graded papers, but I didn't. It is *so hard* to do it *all*. Learn to forgive yourself, Joanne." For Joanne, these journal entries are a way of staying whole, of integrating the personal and the professional. Often academic life can leave you feeling cut off from your feelings, living perpetually in your head, a slave to the relentless demands of the job. The journal is a protection against this for Joanne, a place of synthesis or wholeness. Jane Tompkins echoes this need in her reflections on life in the academy (*A Life in School*, 1996). She speaks of an inchoate yearning for integration (p. 212) and states, "I wish that the college I bound my identity over to had introduced me to my heart" (p. 220). Keeping a journal is one way to stay in touch with your heart as well as your head and to come to some sense of wholeness and identity in what can be very confusing and stressful times for new faculty.

## WHAT ARE SOME USEFUL TECHNIQUES TO EXPLORE YOUR THINKING IN THE JOURNAL?

Sometimes it is helpful to stretch your thinking in your journal. You can do this by intentionally employing some exercises that allow you to think in different ways. In this section we will share with you some of those exercises that we have found particularly helpful.

### Freewriting

Freewriting (Elbow, 1973), spontaneous writing (Boice, 1990), and even its older cousin, automatic writing, used by the surrealists at the turn of the century (Rainer, 1978), all carry with them the challenge of putting the pen to the page and not stopping to edit, change, modify, clarify, or redo anything that you have written. There are several advantages to freewriting. First, it is time limited (usually 10 to 30 minutes). Second, it pushes you to write and write and write, every day. Third, sometimes the authors use freewriting to get to the heart of what they are thinking. Freewriting helps you push past the surface concerns and let interesting ideas bubble up. Often, we get surprised during a freewrite and find ourselves saying, Oh, I didn't know I believed that. Hum? Do I really think that way? Or, that is an interesting idea. I wonder if I can develop that further and explore it.

Peter Elbow's video on writing ends with a call to invite perplexity into your life through your writing. In response to that phrase and during a freewrite in class, Dannelle wrote:

> Perplexity . . . Peter Elbow says "writing invites perplexity and writing is a way to deal with perplexity." Perplexity. Writing causes or rather invites perplexity to join it at the picnic table. The feast is set. The words, the ideas, the connections—the past events, the social forces, the individual talents and capacities, the family, the friends, the education—all set out on the table, the picnic table. It is a joyous and yet, overwhelmingly complex situation. The sun is filtering through the willows. It is not a harsh heat and there is a lot, a lot on the table. The day when perplexity and writing sit down to engage in the feast. The table is set, the sun is bright; the guests are present. The feast should begin with perplexity. Perplexity. Owning complexity. Complexity compounded with wrinkled brows and squinting eyes. Complexity with feelings. Perplexity embraces complexity. Difficult to focus. Difficult to see. The day perplexity sat down with writing for a picnic.

A freewrite is just that: "*free* writing": very simple, no grammar rules, no spelling rules, no sense-making rules, just let the words tumble out of your consciousness and see where they lead, if anywhere, for at least 10 minutes. Elbow suggests that you might want to do it for 20 minutes to get the ideas that are on the top of your head cleared away to find the fresher ones below. The writing may seem to lead nowhere on the surface. Elbow (1978) believes freewriting is the heart, the energy, and the soul of good writing. It has an underground effect on the writer's confidence and fluency with words.

A corollary of freewriting is what Boice (1990) calls "generative writing," where the writer focuses her freewrite on an academic topic. By writing the topic at the top of the page, the writer explores that topic for a specified time, asking what she already knows about the topic, what questions she has, and on what aspects she needs to gather more data. It serves as a foundation for a potential paper. In later stages of generative writing, Boice affirms the power of pushing yourself to just get words on a page about a topic and not editing—yet. In fact this echoes a favorite phrase of one of my colleagues, Margaret Sands, "Don't get it right; get it written."

*Lists*

Actually, in our daily lives, we often make lists. We make grocery lists, to do lists, party planning lists, or vacation check lists. According to Rainer (1978, pp. 72–73) a list "can enumerate feelings, sense impressions, intuitions or thoughts without using complete sentences. Lists are time-savers and time-condensers." Lists are easy to make, since we make them all the time in our daily lives. They can summarize a period of time or a scholarly paper. They help you to anchor unresolved issues that may be floating in your head. They can help you to identify what it is that makes you happy or miserable on the job. Lists are a simple, but powerful tool that should not be overlooked.

Marilyn, a student in one of our classes, created this list.

I love it when . . .

- one of my kids tells me that he loves me for no reason
- old friends come out of the blue
- one of my sons holds the door open for an elderly person
- love is returned
- I pay bills and have $ left over
- the house is clean
- I put on old jeans and they fit
- the sheets are fresh and clean
- I go to put wash in the dryer and the dryer is empty
- I buy the perfect gift.

To use the idea of a list as a journal-entry activity, start with a short phrase or a sentence completion or a series of words that are related in some way. For example, "I feel successful when . . . ," "Faculty meetings are . . . ," "My writing is . . . ," "Promotion and tenure are. . . ." "What concerns me most right now is. . . ." The list might take on a new form such as a list of significant events in your years at this university or a list of all the places you have lived in your life. Then just let the ideas flow and write whatever comes to mind. You can set a time limit for yourself or just stop when the energy runs out of the activity. The advantages of lists are that they are fast, structured, and not threatening. A list is a quick way to check in on the range of feelings you have about something (Cooper, 1991). Finally, lists can also become compost for your academic writing. Joanne, for example, made a spontaneous list of findings for her dissertation in her journal that served as an outline for her concluding summary.

## Dialogue

When you write out a dialogue in a journal, you are creating a fictitious conversation with yourself and another part of your life. From this dialogue you gain insight into a person, event, or subject you wish to understand. To write a dialogue, you address the subject, whatever it may be, and simply allow it to speak to you in response (Rainer, 1978; Cooper,

1994). With whom or with what could you converse? Actually, when you let your imagination explore this idea of conversation, the list of potential partners is endless. Let's list some possible examples: aspects of your personality, people you know, historical figures, dream figures or objects, your pets, images, parts of your body, your health, your car, or even the chair in front of your computer. Dialogue affirms the potentiality of growing and changing through the process of interaction. Often you don't know quite where the conversation will lead, but you may find yourself surprised by the result.

Here is an example of a dialogue Susan, one of our twenty-something students, had with doubt.

ME. Why do you keep bothering me?

DOUBT. How am I bothering you?

ME. You constantly enter my thoughts. You make me scared.

DOUBT. What are you afraid of?

ME. Making a mistake. Settling. Not being able to hear my intuition.

DOUBT. Do you think you are making a mistake?

ME. No, I don't believe in mistakes, just experiences.

DOUBT. Do you want to go through this experience?

ME. I think so.

DOUBT. That's weak. What do you want?

ME. I want to know. I want to be 100% sure.

DOUBT. 100% is very rare. Will you settle for 65%?

ME. No. I'm unsettled.

DOUBT. I can tell.

ME. Why are you here?

DOUBT. To make you think.

ME. I think too much. I just want to be.

DOUBT. Then be.

ME. Nice, guilt trip.

DOUBT. Who said anything about guilt?

ME. I guess it is a reflex reaction. My parents use guilt.

DOUBT. Is this about your parents again?

ME. I didn't think so. Sometimes I feel so cloudy. I can't differentiate between my own thoughts and my parents'.

In working on this book, Dannelle had a dialogue with Sacred Grove.

DANNELLE. Hello, Sacred Grove, How are you today? You look so bright and beautiful. Can I come in?

SACRED GROVE. Well, maybe. What do you care about me anyway?

DANNELLE. I wonder who you are and what you are doing in my life. What makes you so sacred?

SACRED GROVE. The holiness, the purity, I am the light at the end of the tunnel, the tall trees, the open areas, the soft grasses. I am sacred, untouchable by mere men and mortals. I am above you. You—the raw, the real, the gritty, the grotty and the profane.

DANNELLE. Now, now, don't get on your high horse—to use a mixed metaphor!

SACRED GROVE. Well, come in and you shall see. It is delightful to be here—protected, away from the real world.

DANNELLE. I think that being sacred is too elite for me. I want you to be accessible to all. You have to open up.

SACRED GROVE. Have you no standards, woman!

DANNELLE. Sure, I have standards, just not your standards!

SACRED GROVE. I am beautiful but not better. Shoot, I am better. I am keeper of the sacred text, the pure knowledge that must be passed on.

DANNELLE. But, Mr. Sacred Grove, that is the knowledge of the privileged.

Even though the Grove was an inanimate object, Dannelle found that it could "converse" with her and provide her with fresh insights. During the dialogue she was disturbed by the purity, inaccessibility, and elitism of the Sacred Grove. She also realized from her inadvertent use of "Mr. Sacred Grove" that for her, the academy is still essentially male.

## Concept Mapping

Especially for those of you who are visual learners, one activity that is particularly useful is concept mapping (Deshler, 1990). A concept map depicts key ideas with their parts and visually depicts the relationships between these ideas. There is usually a centerpiece in the map. To construct a concept map, first of all select a topic, such as the projects in which you are currently involved. Then make a list of all the different aspects of these projects. For example, say you selected the topic "aspects of my academic work." Then list the types of committees you are on and any products developed, the classes you are teaching, the articles you are working on, the publications you have from the past, and so on. After you have made that list, remember you can always go back and add to it. Then look at the list and reflect on whether or not there are any themes or common processes that tie these disparate pieces of your life together like learning community, motivation, leadership, collaboration, teaching adults, etc. Put that in the middle of the map and begin placing the activities around the map indicating how they could be examples of this larger theme. You are beginning to conceptualize how the disparate pieces of your work actually might relate to one another.

Last year, for example, a colleague came to talk to Dannelle about clarifying her research agenda. Mindy wanted some help conceptualizing her work as a coherent whole. She was teaching a variety of classes in secondary level teacher education, working on a universitywide mentoring project, volunteering at a local high school to help teachers work with diverse students, and advising Latin American students in the teacher education program. What was the centerpiece of this work? After they listed all of her various activities from teaching, and committee work to writing and presenting at conferences, Mindy talked about her values. To Mindy it was important that she mentor her students, foster collaboration among colleagues, and build a diverse community. As they talked further, Dannelle realized that potentially there was a relationship between all of the parts of her work. Together they sketched the concept map shown in figure 13.1.

At the center of Mindy's work is the concept of "collaboration." All the aspects of her work can be viewed as ways to think about how to develop and foster collaboration among colleagues, students, and teachers she works with in the schools.

## CONCLUSION

In the final analysis, you as a journal keeper must find your own way. You will need to experiment with what method works for you. You may find that keeping a log and a "to do" list is enough and will provide you with the documentation you need when promotion and tenure time comes around. We have provided you with compelling reasons to take the time to keep a journal that is more narrative in form: it may relieve stress, improve your health, and give you insights and connections to your own intuitive knowledge. Veteran journal keepers report that it helps them sort through the chaos in their own lives, provides a place to brainstorm possible solutions to problems, and allows for reflection on earlier experiences, as a way to support the self. We have shared with you some of our most effective journal-keeping techniques that include freewriting, listmaking, dialoguing, and concept mapping.

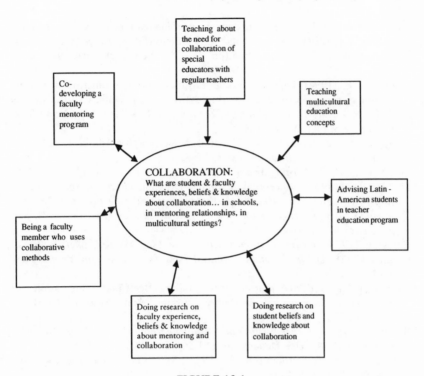

FIGURE 13.1

For you readers who are women and minorities, in particular, who have to negotiate the tenure process and traverse unknown pathways with little guidance, a professional/personal journal can become your own "wiser-self," helping you to document and organize what you do to balance your life. Whether it is a professional journal for work, a personal journal at home, or a computer-generated journal, whether you write daily, weekly, or sporadically, the point is to write, to get your thoughts down on paper in order to clarify what it is you are thinking and feeling. The more clear-headed you are, the more you will be able to do the fine work of which you are capable. The more you reflect on what is going on around you, the more resources you will find within yourself and the more likely you will be able to carve out a successful academic life.

## REFERENCES

Boice, R. (1990). *Professors as writers*. Stillwater, OK: New Forums Press.
Cameron, J. (1992). *The artist's way: A spiritual path to higher creativity*. New York: Jeramy P. Tarcher/Putnam.

Cooper, J. E. (1991). Telling our own stories: The reading and writing of journals or diaries. In C. Witherall and N. Noddings (Eds.), *Stories lives tell: Narrative and dialogue in education* (pp. 96–112). New York: Teachers College Press.

Cooper, J. E. (1994). Digging, daring and discovery: The function of journal writing in professional education. In C. Brody and J. Wallace (Eds.), *Ethical and social issues in professional education* (pp. 103–116). New York: State University of New York Press.

Cooper, J. E., & Dunlap. D. (1991). Journal Keeping for Administrators. *The Review of Higher Education*, 15(1), 65–82.

DeSalvo, L. (1999). *Writing as a way of healing*. San Francisco: Harper.

Deshler, D. (1990). Conceptual mapping: Drawing charts of the mind. In Mezirow, J. and Associates (Eds.), *Fostering critical reflection in adulthood: A guide to transformative and emancipatory learning* (pp. 336–353). San Francisco: Jossey-Bass.

Elbow, P. (1973). *Writing without teachers*. London: Oxford University Press.

Gannett, C. (1992). *Gender and the journal*. New York: State University of New York Press.

Holt, S. (1994). Reflective journal writing and its effects on teaching adults. In *The Year in Review*, vol. 3. Dayton: Virginia Adult Research Network. (ED375 302).

Kerka, S. (1996). *Journal Writing and Adult Learning: ERIC Digest No. 174*. Washington, DC: U.S. Department of Education. (ED 399 413)

Osterman, K. F., & Kottkamp, R. B. (1993). *Reflective practice for educators*. Newbury Park, CA: Corwin.

Pennebaker, J. W. (1997). Writing about emotional experiences as a therapeutic process. *Psychological Science* 8(3), 162–166.

Pennebaker, J. W., & Beall, S. K. (1986). Confronting a traumatic event: Toward an understanding of inhibition and disease. *Journal of Abnormal Psychology* 95(3), 274–281.

Rainer, T. (1978). *The new diary: How to use a journal for self-guidance and expanded creativity*. Los Angeles: Tarcher/Putnam.

Schneider, P. (1994). *The writer as artist*. Los Angeles: Lowell House.

Tompkins, J. (1996). *A life in school: What the teacher learned*. New York: Addison-Wesley.

# CHAPTER 14

# Conclusion:
# Composing an Academic Life

## Joanne E. Cooper
## and Dannelle D. Stevens

In her text *Composing a Life* (1989), Mary Catherine Bateson makes a case for "life as an improvisatory art," a way of combining "familiar and unfamiliar components in response to new situations," which follow "an underlying grammar and an evolving aesthetic." She speaks of improvisation as the constant effort to "make something coherent from conflicting elements to fit rapidly changing settings" (p. 3). It seems that women and minority faculty are often struggling in precisely this way, to fashion a way into the sacred grove by making a coherent professional life from the conflicting demands of teaching, research, and service. They often work in a setting that rapidly changes given the kaleidoscope of students, colleagues, department chairs, and deans that revolves around academic life today. Bateson asserts that a good life "has a certain balance and diversity, a certain coherence and fit" (p. 3). It is this balance and fit that we, the authors of this text, hope for in the lives of our readers.

The academy can offer individuals a wealth of exciting new ideas. Sadly, however, as the experiences of new faculty indicate, much of what new faculty learn is not about freedom and respect, but about bigotry and oppression. Like Janice Koch (chapter 7), they learn to doubt themselves, to the point of not recognizing their own excellence, even when their institutions do. Like Barbara Curry (chapter 8) or Pat McDonough (chapter 9), they learn to sense danger and disapproval, if they are different in any way. Yet, all these authors have been able to break through those fears and barriers and find acceptance.

All can be seen grappling with their sense of themselves as adults learners, the context in which they work, the process of learning, and the configuration of these three elements. Each of our chapters, then, contributes to a convergence of the learner, the context, and the process of adult learning. As we, the editors, read across these chapters, we see a set of key themes that capture a meaningful message to you, as new faculty.

## UNDERSTAND THE NATURE OF YOUR
## INSTITUTION AND ITS TENURE PROCESS

All campuses have their similarities and their differences. First of all, new faculty must be aware of the type of institution they are entering. Is it predominantly a teaching institution? or a research institution? While with any job, a new hire must adjust to the prevailing expectations or environment, Braxton and Berger (1999) found that faculty who are more interested in a teaching-oriented institution will adjust better to such a campus than will faculty at the same institution who are more interested in research. Thus it is imperative for you to clearly understand the nature of the institution you are entering and to know your own preferences.

As Foster-Fishman and Stevens in chapter 12 and Bronstein and Ramaley in chapter 3 urge, you must read closely and carefully all materials given to you about the tenure process. These materials constitute your basic guide. Listen, document, and clarify in writing all statements made by your chair, your dean, and promotion and tenure committees about the process and expectations for you in particular. As Koch underscores in chapter 7, "Being an agent of one's own future is part of feeling entitled."

If you are going to use an alternative route to tenure, the matter of institutional fit becomes even more imperative. First, you must clearly ascertain whether your institution is open to alternatives. Then you must become a student of the process, clarifying your department's expectations and your own work in the scholarship of teaching or the scholarship of outreach. Read about these alternative routes and their rationale. Then, as Foster-Fishman and Stevens so eloquently demonstrate, weave this rationale throughout your own argument for tenure.

Finally, as Bronstein and Ramaley (chapter 3) and McDonough (chapter 9) have urged, listen carefully for any indication of trouble or for any concerns that seem to be presented. Closely scrutinize all letters of evaluation. Look not only for what is said but also for what is not said. If you are confused about the meaning of what was written, ask for clarification.

## ACKNOWLEDGE THAT THE PERSONAL, PROFESSIONAL,
## AND POLITICAL ARE INTERWOVEN IN THE ACADEMY

First of all, recognize and accept that you have strong feelings about the process and that this is an appropriate response. Using a journal, as

Stevens and Cooper discuss in chapter 13, will help you to identify those feelings. Journal keeping can also serve a cathartic function, helping you to surface and then "dump" feelings that may be unproductive. Many veteran journal keepers report that writing helped to bolster them when they began to doubt themselves (Cooper & Dunlap, 1991). As Koch has demonstrated in chapter 7, these feelings can cloud your perceptions of what is going on at work. So it can be imperative that you recognize and deal with your strong emotional responses to life in the sacred grove.

Second, use the intersection of the personal, the professional, and the political to your advantage by strategizing when it is best to present all you are to an institution, as McDonough so clearly described in chapter 9. Timing can be crucial. Cooper and Scherr also discuss this in relation to age issues in chapter 5.

## BE PROACTIVE IN PURSUIT OF YOUR GOALS

Find your allies in the institution. Reach out to those in your department, those across campus and those across the nation. As Benham and Ortiz urge in chapter 5, search for your mentors or "womantors" and do not be afraid to call on their expertise. Likewise Bronstein and Ramaley in chapter 3 and Collay in chapter 6 underscore the importance of both seeking out allies and being an ally to others. Allies or mentors can be found within as well as outside the institution's walls, as both Hollingsworth in chapter 10 and Cooper and Nojima in chapter 11 point out. Search for those who have expertise in whatever areas you may need help, whether it be in the writing/publishing, the teaching, or the research process. As Hollingsworth (chapter 10) suggests, you might even find journal editors who may serve as mentors.

Many of our chapter authors urge you to know your department chair and to make sure she or he knows you and your work. The wise advice of a department chair can be heard in this text (McDonough, chapter 9). In addition, Bronstein (chapter 3) and Hollingsworth (chapter 10) urge you to discuss your work with others freely, letting them know of your activities and your success. Even though this seems like "bragging," it is really an important way of letting others know of your work. They may never know about your work if you don't share it with them. Moreover, they may be able to make connections for you with others who share your interests. Discussing your work is a marvelous way of exploring with colleagues the intersections of their work and yours, creating fertile ground for possible collaborations. Attend department meetings and participate on committees. Be a visible and active member of the academic community. You may be tempted to hide at home, but try to resist that temptation. There is always the danger of being judged as someone who is not a team player.

Strategies for establishing collegiality can be found in Hollingsworth's advice to reach out to colleagues and editors (chapter 10), in McDonough's advice for working with your department chair (chapter 9), in Curry's discussion of the role of advocacy (chapter 8), and throughout the case studies of the experiences of others (Cooper & Temple, chapter 2).

## CLARIFY EXPECTATIONS AND MANAGE YOUR TIME

In addition to establishing collegiality, Menges and associates (1999) have described two additional issues new faculty face: clarifying expectations and managing time. Within the pages of this book is a wealth of advice from veteran academics to help you effectively meet these challenges.

Strategies for clarifying expectations can be found in Cooper and Nojima's advice on teaching (chapter 11), in Foster-Fishman and Stevens' work on the scholarship of outreach (chapter 12), as well as throughout Bronstein & Ramaley's discussion of the "pitfalls and possibilities" of the tenure process (chapter 3). Stevens and Cooper in chapter 13 also offer sound advice for new faculty to keep a professional/personal journal in order to clarify their own understanding of what is said and not said to them regarding their work.

Advice for managing time can also be found throughout this book. Cooper and Nojima (chapter 11) discuss the common temptation for new faculty to spend all their time on teaching, neglecting to establish a strong research agenda. One of the greatest challenges for new faculty is balancing work and family demands. Collay in chapter 6 brings us the voices of many new faculty in a variety of family situations who have coped with this dilemma.

As a final note in this section, we list the above four strategies that our authors have identified. We know this list is not exhaustive. Yet we also know it is the wisdom of our authors who have learned how to survive in the academy.

- Understand the nature of your institution and its tenure process.
- Acknowledge that the personal, professional, and political are interwoven in the academy.
- Be proactive in pursuit of your goals.
- Clarify expectations and manage your time

The short-term and immediate benefits of using these strategies are that you will place yourself in a position of being in more control of your professional life and the promotion and tenure process. You will be armed with a repertoire of strategies designed to help you become a valued insider not an undervalued outsider in the sacred grove. The long-term benefits accrue as you continually activate these strategies summarized above and described in greater detail by our chapter authors. Yet there are deeper implications for your personal and professional development. Brookfield (1995) and Bateson (1994)'s work on adult development helps us understand the deeper impacts of being proactive as well as reflective about our growth. Let us now consider the longer-range benefits not only to you personally but also to the institutions that you inhabit.

## MAINTAINING IDENTITY AND INTEGRITY

Much is at stake for new faculty who aspire to tenure, and the path upon which they tread can be treacherous. Being a new faculty member is a risky business. Essentially, you have put yourself and your career into the hands of your senior colleagues, the reviewers of the manuscripts you hope to publish, and the institution in which you work. The risks, as you have read in this book's chapters, are typical of adult learners (Brookfield, 1995): the feelings of fraudulence Janice Koch discusses (what Brookfield calls "the imposter syndrome"), the loss of innocence as your previous assumptions about academic life come crashing down around you, and the disappointment you feel if your trust is betrayed.

Lieberman and Miller (1991) describe the imposter syndrome as "a general lack of confidence, a pervasive feeling of vulnerability, a fear of being found out" (p. 103). Such feelings are made worse because of the privacy ethic. There is often no safe place to air your uncertainties. We would urge you, as new faculty, to find or create a safe place to talk about your experiences and your doubts about your own abilities. One colleague we know started a cross-disciplinary, cross-campus group known as WIT (Women for Integrity and Tenure). Essentially, it served as a support group, a place to find out what was happening across the campus, and a peer editing group, a place to have your writing critiqued in a safe and respectful atmosphere. Integrity is an essential element in this formula. We would hope that as new faculty members who reach the tenure goal, you arrive feeling you have maintained a sense of identity and wholeness. Brookfield (1995) encourages the use of critical reflection as a tool for new faculty in maintaining their sense of integrity and identity. Throughout this book, chapter authors have urged you, as new faculty, to reflect on the culture of the academy and your particular place in it (Bronstein & Ramaley, chapter 3), to reflect on how to keep a balance between your personal and professional life (Collay, chapter 6), and to use a journal regularly as a safe place to document all your reflections (Stevens & Cooper, chapter 13). Your efforts to maintain balance in your personal and professional lives, as well as finding a place where you fit into the existing culture, will serve you well as you work toward a sense of integrity.

We would urge you as new faculty to seek out the company of those who are willing to reflect honestly and openly with you on your work in all its triumphs and disappointments. By finding a community of supportive peers, new faculty can create a forum "where private stories of critical process can be aired and compared." Such a community can provide "a safe haven, an emotional buffer against the lowest moments" (Brookfield, 1995, p. 245), combating feelings of fraudulence as well as providing a sense of common experience. These communities can be created locally or nationally. One such community for us is the Research on Women and Education Special Interest Group (SIG) of the American Educational Research Association. Others, such as the Gay and Lesbian SIG, or the Research on Asian and Pacific American SIG may serve similar functions for you, our readers. In other fields, such as the sciences, there are organizations such as Women in Science or the Society for Women Engineers that may provide such a haven.

It is important that you find a place of trust, openness, and safety as you move through the sacred grove on your tenure journey. Communities that build trust slowly and encourage open reflection on experience may be the single most important support you can find. As Brookfield has stated, "the capacity for trust anchors us morally and spiritually. On a personal level, it nurtures loving relationships. On a social level, it makes collective effort possible. On a political level, it undergirds the creation and maintenance of democracy" (p. 267). We believe that the creation of more democratic institutions of higher education is a key step to making academic life more welcoming to women and minorities. Small steps, such as the creation of pockets of trust and openness in the communities we have described above, bring us closer to our vision of the academic world we wish to create. Each step is a "message of possibility" (Bateson, 1990, p. 241) for the future.

## WOMEN AND MINORITIES
## IN THE ACADEMY: A FINAL WORD

This text is meant to support those who desire entry into the community of scholars and to encourage those who welcome them. Granted, this journey is an uncertain one, but as Mary Catherine Bateson (1994, p. 235) asserts, "The self is constructed from continuing uncertainty, but it can include or reflect community . . . can be both fluid and stable, can be fulfilled in learning rather than control." Our hope is that we have provided some tools for dealing with that uncertainty, ways of tracking events that are both fluid and stable, the means for learning about the self and the academy as you move through it, contributing your energy, your hopes, and your lives to higher education.

Our ultimate goal in this endeavor is the fostering of learning and growth in our students, the next generation of scholars and citizens. Learning and growth are partly dependent on strong role models, those who provide women and minorities with a sense of possibility, which is based first and foremost on what Goodlad (1979) calls "the philosophy of self-transcendence." Goodlad argues that "strong feelings of self-worth are prerequisite to and perhaps instrumental in acquiring close identification with the other" (p. xv). If we are to build communities of difference within higher education, we must begin, one faculty member at a time, to strengthen the self-worth that is required for that society to exist. One of the most powerful tools at our disposal is the ability to create a community within the academy that welcomes the other, affirming the value of diversity in strengthening the communities we are at once building and proclaiming (McCall, 1999).

Granted, such a community is difficult to create or sustain. However, this text is witness to both the ability to create such community on individual campuses and the national community out of which this book arose. We trust this text offers hope for the future and fuel for our dreams. We dream of a community of difference, one that is enriched by its constituents in all of their diversity, that comes together in conversation around the issues that could tear higher education apart. But that conversation must not be closed to half of society's citizens, or it becomes a dead conversation, an endless round of empty questions, or worse yet, no conversation at all. If we give in to the "petty and vicious capacities" (Readings, 1996, p. 191) of communities in academe, if we forget how to laugh together and work together, embracing each other's differences, then this will be the twilight of the university's critical and social function.

We conclude with a note of hope, that this text will add to the rich diversity of university faculties, enlivening the conversation with the views of the other, those who for too long have been shut out of the conversation, the outsiders in the sacred grove. The university may not always like what it hears from these others, but it is imperative that it listen. As university president Annette Kolodny's (1998, p. 256) grandmother used to tell her, "A good conversation was one in which everybody talked. But a

great conversation was one in which some participants also listened."
Here then is the charge for academe, the call to create conversations in
which everyone talks, and we are all listening.

## REFERENCES

Bateson, M. C. (1989). *Composing a life*. New York: Atlantic Monthly.

Bateson, M. C. (1994). *Peripheral visions: Learning along the way*. New York:
HarperCollins.

Braxton, J. M., & Berger, J. B. ( 1999). How disciplinary consensus affects faculty. In R. J. Menges and Associates (Eds.), *Faculty in new jobs: A guide to
settling in, becoming established, and building institutional support* (pp.
243–268). San Francisco: Jossey-Bass.

Brookfield, S. D. (1995). *Becoming a critically reflective teacher*. San Francisco:
Jossey-Bass.

Cooper, J., & Dunlap, D. (1991). Journal keeping for administrators. *The
Review of Higher Education* 15(1), 65–82.

Goodlad, J. I. (1979). Foreword in J.M. Becker (Ed.), *Schooling for a global age*.
New York: McGraw-Hill.

Kolodny, A. (1998). *Failing the future: A dean looks at higher education in the
twenty-first century*. Durham, NC: Duke University Press.

Lieberman, A., and Miller, L. (1991). Revisiting the social realities of teaching.
In A. Lieberman and L. Miller (Eds.), *Staff development for education in the
1990's: New demands, new realities, new perspectives* (pp. 92–112). New
York: Teachers College Press.

McCall, A. L. (1999). Can feminist voices survive and transform the academy?
In L. K. Christian-Smith & K. S. Kellor (Eds), *Everyday knowledge and
uncommon truths: Life writings and women's experiences in and outside of
the academy* (pp. 83–108). Boulder, CO: Westview.

Menges, R. J., & Associates. (1999). *Faculty in new jobs: A guide to settling in,
becoming established, and building institutional support*. San Francisco:
Jossey-Bass.

Readings, B. (1996). *The university in ruins*. Cambridge, MA: Harvard University Press.

# APPENDIX

# *Tattered Covers: An Annotated Bibliography*

Aisenberg, N., and Harrington, M. (1988). *Women of academe: Outsiders in the sacred grove.* Amherst: University of Massachusetts Press.

> This work has become a classic for women entering the academy. They interviewed over 60 women to find out what university life was like following the period of retrenchment in the early 1980s, where many women lost their jobs. The themes that they identify "depict an experience of professional marginality and of exclusion from the centers of professional authority" (p. xii). Women found themselves in a two-tiered system, where their opinion was not valued, and they were relegated to women's traditional roles. Over ten years later, I have found that their descriptions of academic life ring true. They remind me to be ever vigilant about the subtle and not so subtle ways that the academy systematically disadvantages women.

Bateson, M. C. (1989) *Composing a life.* New York: Penguin.

> This compelling piece of nonfiction has been required reading for academic women for a decade and is as powerful today as when it was published. Bateson weaves her story and those of four colleagues/friends into a colorful tapestry depicting women's lives, families, scholarship, and activism. She challenges all of us to resist being enculturated into unhealthy, dichotomized lives and to choose meaningful lives that heal.

Boice, R. (1992). *The New Faculty Member.* San Francisco: Jossey Bass.

> This is a very detailed, useful, and thoroughly researched book on faculty socialization and productivity. Boice is very pragmatic about settling in, getting connected, securing resources and telling what to expect and what has been useful for other faculty.

Boice, R. (1990). *Professors as writers: A self-help guide to productive writing*. Stillwater, OK: New Forums Press.

> The subtitle of this book sums up its theme. Based on numerous research studies over two years, Boice offers a "brief, programmatic framework" for colleagues who want to "write more productively, painlessly and successfully" (p. vii). The strength of the book is that it is based on research studies conducted with faculty at different stages in their careers. His advice is relevant and tailored to a variety of faculty concerns. I have returned to this book time and time again to recall some strategy or techniques to increase my productivity. I have often given this book to new faculty members and received very positive reviews.

Caplan, P. J. (1993). *Lifting a ton of feathers: A woman's guide to surviving in the academic world*. Toronto, Canada: University of Toronto Press.

> Caplan guides women through the halls of the academy from graduate student to full professor. This book includes real life stories with timely advice. For anyone contemplating entering the academy, it is a useful handbook to orient the professional at any stage about the ins and outs of committees, teaching, and research.

Elbow, P. (1981). *Writing with power: Techniques for mastering the writing process*. New York: Oxford University Press.

> When I was struggling with writing my dissertation, an accomplished scholar suggested that I purchase this book. Without putting it down, I read it from cover to cover. From that point on I was propelled into finishing my dissertation and continuing to write and publish. Elbow is a lively cheerleader for powerful writing that expresses what you want to say. He offers advice at not only the creative phase but also at the revising and editing phase.

Grumet, M. (1988) *Bitter milk: Women and teaching*. Amherst: University of Massachusetts Press.

> Grumet challenges educators to look more carefully at the unexamined content and context of curriculum in schools, especially through the lens of gender. She draws from philosophy, psychology, sociology, the fine arts, and other fields to paint a complex picture of schooling. It's a challenging text to read but offers the tenacious a deeper understanding of what traditional education has wrought.

Lamott, A. (1994). *Bird by bird: Some instructions on writing and life.* New York: Doubleday, Anchor.

> Anne Lamott is required reading for all those seeking a publication record who feel blocked by the demands of daily life in the academy and stymied by their workload, family pressures, or their own feelings of fraudulence. In this delightfully authentic narrative about her own struggle with the writing process, Ms. Lamott offers helpful hints about how to keep going by writing even in the face of adversity. "Bird by bird" refers to her own writer/father's advice to her younger brother when he allowed his report on birds that he had three months to write to wait until the night before it was due. "Just take it bird by bird, buddy," her dad said to her brother.

McIntosh, P. (1985). *Feeling like a fraud.* Wellesley, MA:Wellesley College, The Stone Center, paper No. 18.

> In this first of two papers on feeling like a fraud, McIntosh describes in detail the significance of those feelings for the way we frame our own realities in the academy and our own goals as we participate in the academic hierarchy. For all tenure candidates who suffer from feelings of fraudulence, this paper helps to expose the "true" frauds, namely, those who have never had these feelings.

McIntosh, P. (1989). *Feeling like a fraud. Part two.* Wellesley, MA:Wellesley College, The Stone Center, paper No. 37.

> This second paper, a sequel to the first, helps the reader to explore the ways in which a personal sense of authenticity can give rise to an awareness of dissonance between what one feels and how one is expected to perform in the public sphere. McIntosh encourages us to seek new ways of bringing the authenticity of our private selves into the arena of public work and performance.

Rowntree, D. (1981). *Statistics without tears: A primer for non-mathematicians.* New York: Scribners.

> Rowntree tackles our fundamental discomfort, even fear, of statistics. He begins with writing about gnomes coming out of the forest and asks whether one can predict the characteristics of the rest of the gnomes based on that one observation. From that point on, he gently takes the reader through sampling, descriptive statistics and inferential statistics. I used this book in graduate school to make sense of my statistics classes and still refer to it today to help me get back into that frame of analysis.

Thyer, B. A. (1994). *Successful publishing in scholarly journals.* Thousand Oaks, CA: Sage.

> Only 125 pages long and in the Sage series *Survival Skills for Scholars,* this book is designed to be a quick read with lots of helpful advice. The book is about "maximizing the chances that your work will eventually be accepted in a respectable journal" (p. vii). I found some of the strategies affirming and insightful.

Tierney, W. G., and E. M. Bensimon. (1996). *Promotion and tenure: Community and socialization in academe.* Albany: SUNY Press.

> This book contains accurate and familiar stories. It is essential because it is replete with lessons learned, strategies, and visions of how the tenure process can be made better.

Toth, E. (1997) *Ms. Mentor's impeccable advice for women in academia.* Philadelphia: University of Pennsylvania Press.

> Feminists are often accused of lacking a sense of humor about the dilemmas in their everyday lives. While this accusation is tainted by the privilege of those making the accusations, no one can cast Ms. Mentor as too dry. It is articulate, pointed, informative, and compelling. It is a handbook for any junior faculty member and should be on the table of every tenure review committee meeting.

Turner, C. S. V., and S. L. Myers Jr. (2000). *Faculty of color in academe: Bittersweet success.* Allyn and Bacon.

> This book depicts the journeys of many minority faculty members, describing the complex entanglement of feelings that life in the academy has elicited, as well as strategies for increasing minority faculty in the academy today.

Whicker, M. L., J. J. Kronenfeld, and R. A. Strickland. 1993. *Getting Tenure.* Newbury Park: Sage.

> This book is very specific and pragmatic and contains many ideas and details that most of us tend to not think about or forget about in daily life.

In addition, we've included two websites you might find useful:

http://www.aaup.org/

> American Association of University Professors home page. This Web site lists a series of Web-accessible reports on women and minorities in higher education.

http://www.ala.org/acrl/ressept00.html

The Association of College and Research Libraries produced this article entitled "Diversity Web Sources in Higher Education." The article cites no less than 55 Web sources that include "institutional vision on diversity issues, recruitment of minority faculty, and library organizations working to achieve diversity and related issues." For those looking for a starting point in exploring diversity in higher education, and for resources related to the history, development, and current status of minorities in the United States, this is the place.

# AUTHOR BIOGRAPHIES

**Maenette K. P. Benham** in an associate professor of educational administration at Michigan State University. Her inquiry and service work are linked to (1) the use of narrative to reveal issues and practices of ethnic minority school leaders; (2) the study of the intersection of educational policy and native/indigenous peoples; and (3) the examination, development, implementation, and assessment of school-family-community collaborations that build healthy and culturally appropriate learning environments for children and youth.

**Phyllis Bronstein** is a professor of psychology at the University of Vermont, where she teaches family and group therapy in the clinical doctoral program. Her research interests include the long-term effects of parenting and family relationships on child and adolescent development and the professional advancement of feminist and ethnic minority faculty. She is currently completing a revised edition of her co-edited book *Teaching a Psychology of People: Resources for Gender and Sociocultural Awareness* to be published next year by the American Psychological Association.

**Michelle Collay** has been assistant professor and director of secondary student teacher placement, associate professor and director of graduate education programs and is currently visiting associate professor at Pacific Lutheran University in Tacoma, Washington. Collay's research interests are teacher socialization and school-university partnership with a particular focus on how women experience entry into and professional development within schools and universities.

**Joanne E. Cooper** is an associate professor in the Department of Educational Administration and coordinator of the Higher Education Program at the University of Hawaii at Manoa. Her research focuses on the study of women and minorities in education, the study of organizational and curricular change, and the study of narrative as both phenomenon and method. Her latest books include *Let My Spirit Soar: Narratives of Diverse Women in School Leadership,* and *Indigenous Educational Models for Contemporary Practice: In Our Mother's Voice* (with Maenette Benham). She is the 1994 recipient of the University of Hawaii's Regents Medal for Excellence in Teaching.

239

**Barbara K. Curry** is an associate professor at the University of Delaware in the Department of Human Resources, Education, and Public Policy. Her research has focused on higher education or adult and postsecondary education and professional development, including the treatment of gender, race, and ethnicity. It has also focused on the adult learner and adult identity development and clinical or psychosocial aspects of organizations, including those related to structural, functional, and human relations issues. In addition to this, she is a clinical social worker.

**Pennie G. Foster-Fishman** is an assistant professor in the Department of Psychology at Michigan State University. She received her Ph.D. in organizational/community psychology from the University of Illinois at Chicago. Her research interests primarily emphasize human service delivery reform, particularly the processes and outcomes of current ideological and structural changes within human services delivery systems. She also investigates multiple stakeholder collaboration, coalition development, program evaluation, and empowerment. She has consulted with a variety of human service delivery and nonprofit organizations, as well as with a variety of community-based coalitions, aiming to improve their collaborative processes and outcomes.

**Sandra (Sam) Hollingsworth** is the director of reading and language arts at the Developmental Studies Center, a nonprofit agency in Oakland, California. A former published historian and K–12 classroom teacher, she has an academic background from the University of California, Berkeley; Michigan State University; and San José State University. In those locations, she studied teachers' developmental understanding of literacy instruction. Her latest books are entitled *Teacher Research and Urban Literacy Education* and *Personal, Community and School Literacies: Challenging a Single Standard*. Her passion for social justice issues in her personal life and her work earned her the 1999 research award on behalf of women and minorities from the American Educational Research Association.

**Janice Koch** is an associate professor of science education in the Department of Curriculum and Teaching at Hofstra University. Her research explores broadening the participation of women in science and technology. She is co-author of *Gender Equity Right from the Start: Resources and Activities for Teacher Education in Mathematics, Science and Technology* (1997) and author of *Science Stories: Teachers and Children as Science Learners* (1999). She is the 1995 recipient of Hofstra Univerisity's Distinguished Teacher of the Year award.

**Patricia M. McDonough** is an associate professor and chair of the Department of Education at the Graduate School of Education and Information Studies at the University of California at Los Angeles. Her areas of research include cultural studies; social class stratification, especially within education; organizational analysis; college access; and lesbian, gay, and bisexual issues at the postsecondary level.

**Sheryl E. Nojima** is the assistant dean of the College of Engineering at the University of Hawaii at Manoa. She is responsible for student academic affairs functions, including admissions, academic advising, maintenance of student records, course scheduling, student grievances, and undergraduate program accreditation requirements. She has served in her current position for five years but also worked as a professional engineer for ten years before entering the world of academia. Her research interests include adult learning, curriculum planning, and faculty socialization.

**Anna M. Ortiz** is an assistant professor of higher adult and lifelong education at Michigan State University. Her research work is focused on multicultural issues in higher education, specifically studying ethnic identity development in college students and multicultural education strategies in postsecondary education settings. Other research interests include professional issues in student affairs administration, such as the collaboration between academic and student affairs.

**Judith A. Ramaley** is president of the University of Vermont. Her academic interests focus on higher education reform, and she has played a significant role in designing regional alliances to promote educational cooperation. She contributes nationally to the exploration of the changing nature of work and the workforce and to the role of higher education in the school-to-work agenda. She is deeply interested in the relationship between civic responsibility and higher education in promoting good citizenship among students and has written extensively in this area.

**Mary Woods Scherr** is an associate professor. She teaches adult development and qualitative research methods at the University of San Diego. For three years she directed both the master's and the doctoral programs in leadership studies. Her research interests include women in leadership and the spiritual journeys of educational leaders.

**Dannelle D. Stevens** is an associate professor at Portland State University in the Graduate School of Education. She is interim chair of the Department of Curriculum and Instruction and project director of the

Bilingual Teacher Pathway Program. With a degree in educational psychology, she is interested in strategies that foster faculty development (mentoring, action/classroom research) and that build community-university partnerships.

Jacqueline B. Temple is an assistant professor at Portland State University in the Graduate School of Education. She is also a teacher educator in a combined special education–elementary education licensing program. Her focus is to prepare educators in curriculum content and instructional methods that are inclusive and multicultural. In addition, she has participated in creating a universitywide mentoring program for new faculty, especially designed for women and faculty of color.

William G. Tierney is the Wilbur Kieffer Professor of Higher Education and the director of the Center for Higher Education Policy Analysis at the University of Southern California. He has recently completed a book on the organizational redesign in higher education and a second work on rethinking faculty roles and rewards in schools of education. He writes frequently on issues of access and equity.

# INDEX

Academic freedom: affirmative action and, 57–67; as core value in education, 59; economic security and, 59; individual rights and, 59; protection of free speech and, 59; as root of tenure system, 2, 5, 57–67; Supreme Court and, 59–60

the Academy: acceptance in, 120; adaptations in, 120; characterized as the Sacred Grove, 4; culture of, 31, 32–37; difference and, 121; discrimination against women in, 6; faculty preparation in, 18; finding a home in, 71–87; as idealized community of scholars, 118–120; joint/split appointment in, 6, 27; judgments of value in, 121; male norms in, 93; myths of, 91, 119, 166; oppression in, 225; outsiders in, 120; peer governing structure of, 121; pretenure departure of women and minorities from, 6, 8; racism in, 9, 11; sexism in, 9, 11; socialization as "other" in, 91–96, 113; structural organization of, 18; survival in, 119; views of teaching in, 164–167; as welcome ground, 71, 72

Activism: political, 44

Adult learner, 10–12, 69, 145, 223

Advocacy: in the academy, 49, 121; groups, 123; pretenure presence of, 128; as public matter, 121; self, 120–122, 121

Affirmative action, 7; academic freedom and, 57–67; in challenges to negative tenure decision, 52–53;

as phase in multiculturalism attainment, 32–37

Ageism: confronting, 71–87; implications within departments, 46

Aisenberg, N., 3, 4, 5, 97, 103, 111

American Association of Higher Education, 104

American Association of University Professors, 59, 63

Annas, P.J., 205

Antonio, A.L., 3, 6, 8, 9, 183, 196

Anzaldua, Gloria, 150

Appeals: constructing tenure, 46, 49–53

Applebaum, D., 6

Association of American Colleges and Universities, 33

Astin, H., 6

Austin, A.E., 165

Authenticity, 108

Banks, W.M., 6

Bartunek, J.M., 194

Bateson, Mary Catherine, 12, 89, 91, 99, 151, 225, 231

Behavior: acceptable, 32; organizational, 94; political, 32, 33; social, 32, 33

Bell-Scott, Patricia, 151

Bender, E., 174

Benham, Maenette, 69, 71–87, 227

Bennett, J.B., 72

Bensimon, E.M., 5, 64, 127, 128, 165, 166, 167, 168, 179

Berger, Arthur, 154

Berger, J.B., 226

Bisexual issues: tenure and, 128

Blackwell, J.E., 6, 64
Boice, R., 27, 164, 166, 168, 169, 170, 179, 211, 217, 218
Bowen, H., 60
Boyer, E.L., 164, 173, 174, 182
Braxton, J.M., 226
Bromberg, H., 58, 59
Bronstein, Phyllis, 2, 37–53, 226, 227, 228
Brookfield, S.D., 163, 164, 170, 172, 175, 230
Brown, M., 127, 128

Caffarella, R.S., 11, 12, 145
Cameron, J., 211
Caplan, P., 6, 91
Carse, J., 170, 175
Carter, K., 70
Case studies, 17–28; application timing, 23; gay issues, 25–26; perseverance, 20–22; personal knowledge and, 18; priority-setting, 19–20; racism, 24–25; reality of professional life and, 18; self-doubt, 23–24; split appointments, 24–25; time management, 19; value of, 17
Caspar, G., 174
Chait, R., 60
Chavez, R.C., 3
Chickering, A.W., 167
Churgin, J.R., 205
Clark, S.M., 64
Class: learning and, 11; social, 3; working, 93
Coaptation, 119
Colbeck, C., 72
Coleman-Boatwright, P., 33
Coley, Soraya, 154
Collaboration, 24, 40, 53–54; networking and, 45
Collay, Michelle, 69, 89–105, 227, 230
Collegiality, 38, 44, 45; establishing, 10, 228; expectations of, 169; lack of, 72; teaching and, 169; tenure process and, 139–141

Collins, Patricia Hill, 152
Committees: involvement in, 43, 54; as networking source, 43; time for, 43
Compatability: with institution, 122–126; peer judgment and, 123; signals of, 123
Concept map: development for reflection, 216–217
Conference presentations: based on publications, 39, 160; importance of, 20; time for, 39; of written material, 160
Cooper, Joanne, 1, 3–12, 17–28, 69, 71–87, 163–176, 203–223, 225–232
Corcoran, M., 64
Creswell, J.W., 127, 128
Culture: of the academy, 31, 32–37, 103; campus, 17; changing, 35; curriculum requirement for, 36; denial of, 31; departmental, 31; dominant norms of, 34; expectations of, 108; heterosexual, 129; indigenous, 94; institutional, 31, 32–37, 165; majority, 34, 35; modification of, 104; organizational elements of, 18, 164; of silence, 129; unacknowledged existence of, 31
Curry, Barbara, 69, 117–126, 225

Department chairs, 19–20; beginning of impact on faculty, 127–128; family leave and, 92; mentoring role, 136, 140; nurturing role, 127, 134–137; proactivity by, 134–137; professional development obligations, 136; relationships with pretenure faculty, 27, 127, 140; role in promotion process, 44–46, 127; structuring of work opportunities by, 128; unfair treatment by, 20, 21
Departments: boundaries in, 32; culture of, 31; customs of, 32;

issues in, 18, 19–20, 44–46,
127–142; political issues in, 18,
19–20, 127–142; support from,
44–46, 139–140; views on
importance of teaching, 20
DeSalvo, L., 207, 208
Deshler, D., 221
Des Jarlais, C.A., 6
Diamond, R.M., 165
Difference: assessment of suitability
for tenure and, 138; as exception,
119; exclusion and, 122;
marginalization of, 129;
qualifications for professional
contributions and, 120–121; role
of advocacy and, 117–126; as
threat, 4
Dillard, Anne, 156
Discrimination: acceptability of, 134;
against gay and lesbian faculty,
128–129, 131; in tenure process,
50
Diversity. *See also* Multiculturalism;
commitment to, 31; cultural, 43;
as economic necessity, 34;
exposure to, 36; institutional
definition of, 33; lesbian, gay and
bisexual issues, 128–132;
promotion of, 36; seeking, 37; as
social justice, 34
Driscoll, A., 180, 186, 189, 191, 192,
193, 194
Dunlap, D., 206, 207, 208, 215

Edgerton, R., 184
Education, higher: academic
freedom as core value in, 59;
collegiality in, 72; current values
in, 18; knowledge of diversity in,
9–10; opening to
underrepresented groups, 34;
presence of women and
minorities in, 9; reform of, 72
Egan, K., 70
Elbow, P., 156, 209, 217, 218
Elliott, O., 58
Empowerment: fostering, 129

Entitlement: denial of, 112; feelings
of, 108–109; internalization of,
110, 112; personal, 110; struggle
for, 112–114
Environments: cooperative, 128; gay-
affirming, 129; hostile, 128;
multicultural, 33, 34; nurturing, 35;
sociocultural, 12; welcoming, 72
Estefan, Gloria, 151
Ethnicity: learning and, 11;
politization of, 118
Evaluations: keeping copies of, 50;
on-going, 66; of outreach
scholarship, 187 *tab;* pretenure,
46; for promotion, 37; publication
and, 40; for raises in salary, 37;
reappointment, 46; of scholarly
accomplishments, 198–199 *tab;*
self, 107; student, 48–49, 165;
teaching, 165, 166; for tenure, 37
Evans, S., 109
Exum, W.H., 6

Faculty: allies, 19; collegiality, 10, 38,
44, 45, 72; diversity and, 9;
facilitation of learning process by,
174; fragmentation, 72; as gate
keepers, 122; gender-based
expectations of, 104; isolation, 72;
race and, 7–8; redefining roles of,
182; "revolving door
phenomenon," 8; socialization of,
165; "team players," 22, 38, 44;
union, 21
Faculty, gay, lesbian, and bisexual,
127–142; coming out, 131, 132;
common injustices and, 134;
concerns about treatment from
colleagues, 128–129;
discrimination and, 128–129, 131;
homophobia and, 8, 72, 132, 133;
institutional norms and, 129;
issues for, 128–129;
marginalization of, 129; safety for,
129; silence of, 128; special needs
of, 127; students and, 133; tenure
experiences, 25–26

Faculty, pretenure: as adult learners, 10–12; alliances for, 20; assignments of lesser value for, 119; "at-risk," 34; balance between research and teaching for, 19, 165, 179; clarification of expectations by, 10; committee work and, 43–44; establishment of collegiality by, 10; evaluation reports, 28; expectations of, 10, 37; initiation of interactions by, 169; institutional culture and, 31, 32–37; isolation and, 169; juggling responsibilities, 27; life priorities and, 44; loneliness and, 169; mentoring for, 65; messages on importance of teaching to, 165; networks and, 27; occupational satisfaction levels, 12; political activism and, 44; political issues and, 18; priority-setting, 26–27; problems encountered by, 17–28; relationships with students, 42; relations with department chairs, 21, 27, 127; responses to department culture, 31; retention of values, 34; seeking trustworthy colleagues, 27; stress levels among, 12; support for as factor in attrition, 65; support systems for, 27–28, 44–46; teaching challenges for, 167–170; teaching responsibilities, 163; time management, 10, 228–229; training for teaching, 167

Faculty, White male: academy designed for, 91–92; access to Sacred Grove, 4; family committment and, 94–96; full-time, 6; positions of power and, 109; salaries of, 7; tenure rate, 6; threats to by women and minorities, 4

Faculty, women and minority: balancing work and family responsibilities, 89–105; career goal interpretation, 3; community support for, 97; composing lives, 103–105; devaluation of qualifications, 8; discrimination and, 6, 50; expectations for, 35; family committment and, 94–96; feeling fraudulent, 107–114; feelings of entitlement for, 108–109; field clustering, 7; full professorships and, 7; full-time, 6; influence on institutions, 98–99; intellect seen as inadequate, 118; intellectual integrity and, 96–98, 229–230; isolation of, 6; legitimization as intellectuals, 104; as less valued, 119; marginalized status of, 26, 103, 119; as mothers, 89; multiple roles for, 90; need for balance for, 102–103; need to imitate mainstream male faculty, 93; need to prove earning of position is deserved, 6; as "outsiders," 4, 6, 91, 113; as "parent," 94; recruitment of, 34; research methods of, 3; salary inequities, 7; sensitivity to communities, 97; socialization of graduate students and, 64; stereotyping of, 119; teaching anxieties of, 169; teaching possibilities for, 172; tenure rate, 6; understanding departmental culture, 31; visibility of, 6; work style preferences, 3

Fairweather, J.S., 11, 61

Family: balancing with work, 89–105, 98; defining, 91; engaging in problem solving, 100–101; expectations, 108; extended, 100; influence on work, 99; institution's efforts to shape sense of, 101; issues surrounding, 44; measured against work, 96; as priority, 100; reconceptualization of place in intellectual development, 98–99; responsibilities, 89–105; as study sources, 99; support for, 100; viewed as unprofessional, 94

Family and Medical Leave Act, 92
Farnsworth, L., 50
Ford, A., 60
Foster-Fishman, Pennie, 179–201, 226, 228
Fraudulence, 107–114; coping with feelings of, 108, 229–230; critiques of the hierarchy and, 112; as imposter syndrome, 223; positions of power and, 109; as self-doubt, 107–114; up side of, 112
Freire, P., 153
Frierson, H., 8
Froh, R.C., 184

Gannett, C., 205
Garza, H., 8
Gaskell, Jane, 152
Gender: balance, 43; educational inequities and, 107; issues, 26, 35; learning and, 11; politics of, 137; roles, 104; role socialization, 40
Glassick, C.E., 182, 183, 191, 192, 194
Glazer-Raymo, J., 6, 7, 183
Gmelch, G.H., 127
Goldberg, Natalie, 148–150, 151
Goodlad, J.I., 231
Goulston, W., 148
Grappa, J.M., 91, 104
Gray, D., 174
Gray, P.J., 184
Greene, Maxine, 152
Gregory, S.T., 94
Gupton, S.L., 100

Halcon, J.J., 6, 8
Hall, R., 71
Hameresh, D., 6
Harleston, B.W., 37
Harrington, M., 3, 4, 5, 97, 103, 111
Harris, M., 71, 72
Harvey, W., 8, 65
Hierarchies: acceptance in, 111; belonging to, 108; breaking down, 114; classroom, 114; critiques of, 111; entitlement and, 111; non-

perpetuation of, 111; of power, 108; working outside, 108
Hilbrun, Carolyn, 151
Hillesum, Etty, 72
Hollingsworth, Sandra, 147–161, 227, 228
Holt, S., 204
Home, academy as, 71–72
Homophobia, 8, 72, 132, 133
hooks, bell, 150, 170, 172
Huber, M.T., 182, 183, 191, 192, 194
Huff, Anne, 157, 158, 159
Hutchings, P., 174, 184

Identity: career issues and, 118; coaptation and, 119; compatibility of, 120–122; construction of, 119; cultural, 73–80; defining value and, 118; development, 119, 125; individual, 118; institutionalization of, 118; loss of, 119; maintaining, 229–230; multiracial/multiethnic, 119, 120; national, 119; private, 103; problematization of, 117; professional, 18; public, 103
Institutions: change in, 9; changing culture of, 35; compatability with, 122–126; diversity in, 31; efforts to shape one's sense of family by, 101; expectations of, 10; missions of, 32, 164, 182; multicultural transformation in, 36; norms for demonstrating competence, 32; societal obligations of, 181; support from, 44; transitional phases of, 31; type of scholarly work valued in, 32, 33; understanding nature of, 226
Integrity: professional, 18, 96–98, 229–230

Jackson, K.W., 8
Jalongo, M.R., 70
Jarvis, P., 11
Johnson, R.N., 181, 183

Johnsrud, L.K., 6, 7
Jordan, David Starr, 58
Journals, 11, 227; appropriate
    content in, 211; automatic writing
    in, 217; cognitive activity
    stimulation and, 204; computers
    and, 211; concept mapping in,
    221–222; defining, 204; dialogue
    in, 219–221; format, 212–213 *tab;*
    freewriting in, 217–218; as habit,
    209–210; health aspects, 208;
    impact of, 204; lists and, 218–219;
    models of, 210–217; personal,
    203–223; privacy issues, 206, 207;
    problem solving in, 206;
    professional, 203–223; reasons for
    keeping, 205–208; rethinking
    experiences through, 207; sorting
    function, 206; spontaneous writing
    and, 211, 217; techniques for,
    217–222; in tenure process, 204;
    use by women, 205–206; value of,
    203

Knowledge: advancement of, 164;
    application of, 39; construction,
    181; conveyance of, 164; disputing
    what counts as, 4; experiential, 18;
    generation of, 181; integration of,
    39; narrative, 69; personal, 18;
    reasoned, 69; self, 138–139, 170,
    172
Knowles, M.F., 37
Koch, Janice, 69, 107–114, 225
Kottkamp, R.B., 204
Kronenfeld, J.J., 137, 138
Kugel, P., 167, 170

Ladson-Billings, G., 97
Lambert, L.M., 184
Lamott, Anne, 156, 160
Lattuca, L.R., 167
Learning: adult, 10–12, 69, 145, 223;
    application in, 174; discovery and,
    174; forms of inquiry in, 174; how
    to write, 148–152; integration in,
    12, 174; interactive context in, 11;

issues in, 11; as knowledge
    building, 181; life informing, 98;
    misrepresentation of, 181;
    personality and, 12; process, 11,
    12; remedial, 168; structural
    context in, 11; student, 20; task
    complexity, 12; teaching as, 174;
    to teach literacy, 153
Lesbian issues and tenure, 128–132
Lieberman, A., 229
Lightfoot, Sara Lawrence, 150
Locke, Lawrence, 154
Louis, M.R., 194
Lynton, E., 180, 186, 188, 191, 192,
    193, 194

McBath, J., 64
McCall, A.L., 10, 231
MacDermid, S.M., 91, 104
McDonald, Barbara, 86
McDonough, Patricia, 69, 127–142,
    225, 228
Macedo, D., 153
McEvans, A.E., 6
McEwan, H., 70
McIntosh, P., 107, 108, 110, 111,
    112, 113
McNaron, T.A.H., 8, 128, 131, 134
Maeroff, G.I., 182, 183, 191, 192,
    194
Manning, K., 33
Martinez-Aleman, A., 71
Massy, W.F., 72
Maternity: leave, 44; scheduling, 92
Maynard, Mary, 156
Menges, R.J., 6, 10, 228
Mentors, 24, 45, 128; department
    chairs as, 136; finding a match,
    124–125; formalization of process
    for, 65; lack of, 8; multiple, 125;
    relating to, 125; seeking, 27–28,
    34; social, 34; special academic,
    34; vulnerability and, 125; for
    women and minorities, 6
Meritocracy, 120, 121
Merriam, S.B., 11, 12, 17, 18, 145
Mickelson, M.L., 8

Middleton, S., 103, 104
Miller, L., 229
Minorities. *See* Faculty, women and minority
Mintz, B., 128, 131, 134
Miskin, V.D., 127
Multiculturalism: added to curriculum, 36; attainment process, 33; attempts at acculturation phase, 34–35; competence in, 36; defining, 33; good intentions phase, 34; improving climate phase, 35; phases of, 33–37; transformation phase, 36–37; "White male" frame of reference in, 37
Myers, S., 3, 6, 8, 183

Nakanishi, D.T., 6
Narrative: of ageism, 81–86; of cultural identity, 73–80; as documentation of outreach scholarship, 189–195; of family responsibilities, 89–105; of gender, 73–80; race/ethnicity, 73–80
Networks, 27; across departments, 27; committees as source for, 43; creating, 101–102; importance of, 22; influence on process, 45; judgment in selection of, 101; national, 27; as opportunity for collaborations, 45; for support, 101–102
Neumann, A., 98
Noffke, Susan, 152
Nojima, Sheryl, 163–176, 227
Nyquist, J., 18, 72

Oliver, M.L., 8
Olsen, D., 64, 166
Ortiz, Anna, 69, 71–87, 227
Osterman, K.F., 204
Outreach, 179–201; benefits of, 193; context of, 187 *tab,* 190; criteria for scholarship in, 198–199 *tab;* critical reflection on, 194–195; defining, 201*n*2; difficulties with

documentation process, 196, 197, 200; documenting scholarship of, 184 *tab,* 195–196; impact of, 187 *tab,* 193–194; link to institutional mission, 191; link to job description, 191; narrative document, 189–195; outcomes of, 192–194; portfolio elements, 184 *tab,* 185, 186, 188–200; process documentation, 191–192; project description, 191; resources for, 191; setting, 190; significance of, 187 *tab,* 191; structuring scholarship of, 184 *tab;* as work of scholars, 182

Padilla, R.V., 3
Pagano, J., 70
Palmer, P.J., 163, 164, 170, 172, 175
Pankhurst, Emmeline, 86
Park, S.M., 3, 8, 9, 181, 183, 196
Pascarella, E.T., 166
Patitu, C., 8
Perrow, C., 128
Peterson, P., 98, 99
Piercy, Marge, 151
Polkinghorne, D., 69
Publishing, 38; dissertation, 38, 40; early submission, 38; editor contact and, 39, 159–160; importance of, 20; journal, 38; necessity for, 165, 179; ongoing, 38; persistence in, 39; requirements for publication, 159; tenure process and, 147–161
Purvis, June, 156

Quinlan, K., 184

Race: learning and, 11; politization of, 118, 137
Racism, 72; affirmative action programs and, 7; as barrier to tenure, 8; confronting, 71–87; historical, 58; institutional, 6–7, 8, 9, 11
Rainer, T., 205, 206, 209, 217, 218–219, 219

Ramaley, Judith, 2, 32–37, 226, 227, 228
Rausch, D., 65
Reinharz, Shulamit, 156
Reisser, L., 167
Research: applied, 36, 37; balanced with teaching, 19, 165, 179; challenge to traditional agendas, 98; community-based, 37; criteria for scholarship, 198–199 *tab;* developing line of, 37–40, 152–155; on ethnic minority populations, 8; expectations about, 11; interests of women and minorities in, 3, 4; labeling as nonacademic, 6; masculine values and, 8; as "men's work," 8; by minority faculty, 8; necessity for, 40; as priority, 164; quantitative, 6; on social change, 6; stories and, 113; value of individual and, 121
Reyes, M., 6, 8
Rhoads, R.A., 128
Riessman, Catherine Kohler, 156
Roosevelt, Eleanor, 26
Ross, Edward, 58, 59
Rothblum, E., 128, 131, 134

Sacred Grove: changing landscape of, 9–12; defining, 1–2; entrance for women and minorities, 3; gender and, 3; limited access to, 4
Sadao, K.C., 6, 7
Sandler, B., 71
Sands, M., 218
Sartre, Jean-Paul, 152
Scherr, Mary Woods, 69, 71–87
Schneider, P., 204
Scholarship: of application, 182; content of, 39; criteria for, 198–199 *tab;* of discovery, 39, 182; as generation of knowledge, 181; inclusive definition, 180–183; of integration, 182; level of productivity required, 38; multiple forms of, 182; outreach as, 180,

182, 183–200; as process of learning, 181; produced from research, 179; restricted notions of, 181; reward structures for, 181; of teaching, 173–175, 182; tenure process and, 38–40; towards tenure, 179; undergraduate instruction and, 166
Schon, D.A., 183
Schuster, J., 60
Self: advocacy, 120–122, 121; awareness, 204; concept, 12; disintegration of, 119; doubt, 107–114, 163, 175; exploration, 145; knowledge, 138–139, 170, 172; private, 120; public, 120
Service: consideration of family and, 94; departmental, 43; expectations about, 11; institutional, 43; masculine values and, 8; as professional service, 197; regional/national, 43; as scholarship of application, 197; tenure process and, 43–44; time for, 43; types of, 43; value of individual and, 121; as "women's work," 8–9
Sewell, Marilyn, 151
Sexism, 40; as barrier to tenure, 8; institutional, 8, 11; pervasive, 8; women of color and, 9
Sexual orientation. *See also* Faculty, gay, lesbian, and bisexual; discrimination and, 128–129; learning and, 11; politics of, 137
Shakeshaft, C., 109
Shulman, L.S., 174
Silin, J., 133
Silvervan, Stephen, 154
Slick, G.A., 100
Smith, M., 12
Social: behavior, 32, 33; boundaries, 33; capital, 108; change, 6, 40; entitlement, 107; functions, 45; justice, 26, 34, 36; pathology, 119; relations, 45; skills, 20

Socialization: academic, 94; bidirectional scheme of, 9; of faculty, 165; gender role, 40; graduate student, 64; learning about oneself in, 10; as "other" into the academy, 91–96, 113; of outsiders, 103; for positions of power, 109; process, 10

Solmon, L.C., 8

Sorsinelli, M., 166

Spirduso, Waneen Wyrick, 154

Stanford, Mrs. Leland, 58–59

Stanley, Liz, 156

Stark, J.S., 167

Stein, W., 6

Stevens, Dannelle, 1, 3–12, 179–201, 203–223, 225–232

Stories: of ageism, 81–86; children's, 99; of cultural identity, 73–80; of family responsibilities, 89–105; of gender, 73–80; lesbian journey to tenure, 129–134; of race/ethnicity, 73–80; science, 113, 114

Strickland, R.A., 137, 138

Support: within department, 44–46

Swcheinberg, Cynthia, 154

Tack, M.W., 8

Teaching: anxiety over, 168; aspects of, 40–41; balanced with research, 19, 165, 179; challenges of, 167–170; children's experiences and, 99; classroom confidence and, 170; collegiality and, 169; commitment to, 20, 166; criteria for scholarship, 198–199 *tab;* as critically reflective practice, 172–173; as dynamic endeavor, 173; as equivalent of whitewater rafting, 163–176; evaluations, 166; excitement of, 171; expectations about, 11; fear of failure in, 171; feedback, 27, 168; isolation and, 169; lack of prestige in, 166; as learning, 174; masculine values and, 8; methods of inquiry in, 174; mixed messages on importance of,

165; negativism toward, 165; portfolio elements, 184; pretenure faculty responsibilities for, 163; as priority, 164; problems with students, 42–43; professional boundaries in, 42; recognition for, 166; relations with students, 41–42; remedial, 168; scholarship of, 173–175, 182; self-doubt and, 163, 175; skills, 40; stories and, 113, 114; student-centered, 4; student expectations, 42; styles, 113; suggestions for, 170–173; tenure process and, 40–43; time for, 41, 165, 166, 168; training for, 167; unrealistic expectations and, 167–168; valuation of, 61; value of individual and, 121; views in the academy, 164–167; as "women's work," 8–9

Temple, Jacqueline, 1, 17–28

Tenure: academic freedom and, 2, 5, 57–67; accountability and, 60; alternative criteria for, 65–66; attacks on, 57; barriers to, 6, 8, 20, 21, 49; bisexual issues and, 128; "clock," 11, 44; compromising values for, 31; criteria, 20; criticisms of, 60–61; deferment of, 124; difference and, 117–126; family as barrier to, 94; as fiscal problem, 60; gender and, 1; graduate student socialization and, 64; guidelines, 27; guidelines for evaluation of scholarship for, 198–199 *tab;* health and, 102–103; historical parameters, 58–60; job security and, 2; journey toward, 3–12; mentoring and, 65; politics, 26, 127–142; preparing case for, 46–53; privileging of research by, 61; protection of untenured and, 61; race and, 1; revision of calendar for family issues, 93; risk-aversion and, 60–61; roots of, 2; solutions to problems with, 61–62; tacit

Tenure *(continued)*
knowledge of, 1; unproductivity and, 60; valuation of teaching and, 61

Tenure applications: guidance needed in, 23; impartiality in review, 21; knowledge of system, 22; networking and, 22; preparation for, 21

Tenure process, 26; anxiety and, 111; beginning, 37; building tenurable record in, 139; career building, 37–46; collegiality and, 139–141; compatability and, 122–126; constructing appeals, 46, 49–53; contemplation of, 110; department guidelines for, 123–124; destabilization of, 126; difference and, 122; discrimination in, 50; dissenting opinions and, 138; documentation of scholarship, 50, 51, 183 *tab*, 184; dossier presentation in, 124; external reviewers in, 48; file preparation, 109–111; getting support for, 47; impact of review committee on, 137–138; information gathering in, 47; insecurity with, 110; journals in, 204; letter solicitation for, 48–49; loneliness and, 110, 125; making a persuasive case in, 31–55; material gathering, 47–49; moving ahead, 37; negative decision in, 51–53; objectivity and, 125; organizational flexibility and, 139; performance contracts in, 66–67; personal issues, 54; political, 137; positive outlook on, 53–55; preparation for, 46–53; pretenure evaluations, 46; principles for success in, 138–142; proactivity in, 227–228; problems in, 49–53; procedural irregularities, 52; public nature of, 121; publishing and, 147–161; reflecting range of faculty roles in, 182; scholarship and, 38–40; self-doubt in, 107–114; self-knowledge and, 138–139; service and, 43–44; social, 137; staying on track, 37–53; strategies, 26–28; stress and, 46–47, 123, 125; student evaluations and, 48–49; understanding, 226; use of collaboration in, 40; withdrawal from, 124; writing and, 147–161

Terenzini, P.T., 166

Thompson, J., 64

Tierney, William, 2, 4, 5, 8, 9, 57–67, 86, 127, 128, 129, 131, 132, 134, 165, 166, 167, 168, 179

Tompkins, J., 163, 167, 168, 169, 217

Toth, E., 93, 94

Trautvetter, L.C., 6

Trust, 19

Turner, C.S.V., 3, 6, 8, 64, 183

Volunteerism, 43

Wamser, C.C., 181, 183

Washington, V., 8, 65

Welty, Eudora, 151

West, M.S., 6

Whicker, M.L., 137, 138

Whitt, E.J., 10, 12, 167, 168, 169

Wilger, A.K., 72

Wilson, R., 92

Wingard, T.L., 8

Women. *See* Faculty, women and minority

Women and minorities. *See also* Faculty, women and minority; absence in the Academy, 6–9; challenges to traditional teaching, 4; interests in new kinds of research, 4; mentors and, 6; as mothers, 89; as "outsiders," 3, 4, 6, 113; as threat to White males, 4; undervaluation of, 6–9; visibility of, 6

Women for Integrity and Tenure, 229

Woolf, Virginia, 103, 151, 208

Writing: automatic, 217; "below thought," 149, 150; children's experiences and, 99; confidence in, 148; data analysis and, 155–156; data collection and, 155–156; developing a line of research for, 152–155; developing resources for, 154; editing, 158; finding topics, 152–155; free, 217–218; grants for, 154; groups, 101; as habit, 148–150; journal, 203–223; learning how, 148–152; music and, 151; in one's own voice, 156–158; practice, 148–150; presentation of at conferences, 160; promotion and tenure advantages, 200; publication requirements, 159; reading other women's works and, 150–152; as reflection, 200; rewriting, 160; scheduling time for, 154; spontaneous, 148–149, 211, 217; steps to publication, 155–159; taking risks with, 156–158; technical, 154; tenure application and, 23–24; tenure process and, 147–161; timed exercise in, 148–150

Zinsser, William, 156